# With Thanks
# To My
# Guardian Angel

*An Autobiography*

Bruce McIntosh

Diadem Books

Diadem Books
Newcastle-upon-Tyne
www.diadembooks.org.uk

ISBN: 9798697241608

# DEDICATION

Thanks to Col. Ashok Choudry for giving me the motivation to start writing my life story.

Thanks to Christine Docherty and Bethany Docherty for their clerical and technical advice and support.

Thanks to Ian Turner for his professional help in publishing.

And not forgetting, of course, that Guardian Angel of mine.

# CONTENTS

*'For he will command his angels concerning you to guard you in all your ways.'*

Psalm 91.11

# CHAPTER 1

## EARLY YEARS IN YORK

I was born on the 27th April 1926 in Heworth Village, which is a suburb of York. My full name is Bruce Cattanach Scott McIntosh, a unique name in a world of 7.5 billion souls. My father was George Mitchell McIntosh and my mother Margaret Miller McIntosh (nee Johnston). My sister Isobel Margaret McIntosh was born in Cullen, Banffshire on 9 the April 1925. I suppose then that I am a Yorkshireman, fully qualified by birth to play cricket for the county. But I am also a Scotsman because all my forebears were from the northeast of Scotland and all my genes are pure Scottish.

My father and mother, with Isobel, had moved down from Aberdeen to York just a day or so before I was born, so I was so nearly born in Aberdeen. My father was employed by the Post Office and he accepted a promotion, which took us south into England. He had started as a Messenger Boy delivering telegrams at a very young age. He was outposted to Crathie well up the Dee valley near the Balmoral Estate where the Royal Family stayed. He used to deliver to all the members of the Royal Family and did this until he joined the Army at the start of WWl. He served with distinction reaching the rank of Sergeant in the Royal Artillery and was injured and gassed for his troubles. On demobilisation he moved to an office job in Aberdeen and then onwards to promotion to York. He was a keen golfer and was very good at it with a nil handicap and many cups to prove his prowess. He continued playing well into his 90's and for many years his score for a round was below his age.

My Mother was part of a large family and had a quiet upbringing in Cullen working as a shop assistant until she was married.

My eldest son Robert has researched some way back into family history and reached my Great, Great, Great, Great Grandfather called George McIntosh born in 1755. Thereafter there was a John, two Williams and another George. Geographically the places associated with them are Cullen, Rothemay, Golspi, Rhynie and Aberdeen. On the Mcintosh side the names Reiach, Morrison, and Wood appear. On the Johnston side the names are Forbes, Sutherland, Brock and Donaldson. All are good Scottish names and I can truly claim to be a Scotsman first and a Yorkshireman second. In my younger days I could claim to be eligible to play football and rugby for Scotland and cricket for Yorkshire and England. Sweet dreams!

My memory only goes back to Grandparents on the McIntosh side. George McIntosh was born 1826 and died 1944. He was a granite stone worker who lived in Aberdeen all his life. Margaret McIntosh (nee Reiach) was born in Inverkeithny Banff and died in 1946 in Aberdeen. I never knew my Grandparents from my mother's side of the family. James Johnston born 1846, died 1925, was a shepherd who lived in Cullen. There is a wonderful photograph of him with his sheep taken in Cullen in the early 1900's and my youngest son Andrew has it on the wall in his house. My Grandmother Isabella Johnston (nee Forbes) 1854-1926 was born, lived in and died in Cullen. I still remember my grandparents on my Father's side having spent many happy holidays in Aberdeen in my early years.

My stay in Heworth Village was short lived as the family got the tenancy of a newly built council house at 71 Sixth Avenue, in Tang Hall York, where I lived for many a long year. Happy, happy days as I remember. I suppose I lived a very sheltered life in my very early days. Both my parents spoke in Doric, the language of the north east of Scotland, and I am sure my first instincts were to speak Doric rather than the Yorkshire dialect, which bears no resemblance to it. I can remember my early years quite well, spending my time mostly in the gardens of the house. We had a garden back and front and I remember the layout of the lawns, bushes and plants. There was a brick shed in the back garden which I used as my den. There was also a brick wall between us and the next house which was used for bouncing and catching a ball. I spent endless hours throwing and catching all types of balls and the experience stood me in good stead later in life in all types of sporting activities.

At weekends I wore a kilt and I remember long walks to the nearby parks on a Sunday, which in those days was strictly observed as a day of rest.

York was a beautiful city to grow up in. It had a population of around 100,000. The Romans first lived there from about 100BC and much of the old Roman infrastructure still stands. The City Walls are the pride and joy and still enjoyed by walkers to the present day. Many of the old battlement gates are also intact. In the late 1920's the four main industries in the city were the railways, chocolate factories, the military and agriculture.

The city was an important stop on the east-coast line from London to Scotland. It was about equidistant between London and Aberdeen and an essential refuelling stop. It also had a large engineering depot and a train carriage building facility.

Both Rowntree's and Terry's had large chocolate factories which provided jobs for many thousands of people. Hugely successful concerns swallowed up by even larger firms (Nestles) 60 years later. There was also a sweet factory called Craven's who suffered the same fate.

York was the HQ for Northern Command so there were always plenty of soldiers around the many barracks in town and also airmen from numerous airfields around the city There were many farms both arable and livestock around York and farmers did their business in York. There was a good market with much local produce on sale and a huge cattle market

It was also well known for the large number of Churches in the City and even more Pubs and Taverns. Even in my early days it was a magnet for day-trippers from all over the world. It also had plenty of entertainment with the magnificent Theatre Royal and the Empire Theatre. It had numerous Cinemas. I can remember visiting all of them in my younger days, but few now remain. I wonder what happened to the Regal, Odeon, Picture House, St.George's, Tower, Rialto, Clifton, Regent, Grand, Electric - or was it the Scala?

For sporting activities there were professional Football and Rugby teams a good cricket team, plenty of rowing on the river and a top-class racecourse. York was easy to get around. From where I lived in Sixth Avenue it took about 20 minutes to walk to the centre. There was also a good bus service running along

Fifth Avenue which got you there in 5 minutes. Most people had bicycles to help them as well with their travel. The centre piece of the City is York Minster an ancient but majestic cathedral. It has two rivers, the main one being the Ouse used both for pleasure and commerce and the Foss and each of them regularly flooded parts of the City after heavy rainfall.

The estate I lived at Tang Hall was newly built after WW1 as part of the homes for heroes' campaign. Our family fully deserved one as my father had served in France as a Sergeant in the Royal Artillery and had been both wounded and gassed fighting the Germans. It was a brand new house and as I remember had 3 bedrooms, a bathroom, a separate toilet, a kitchen, a sitting room, a pantry and a coalhouse. It had a big garden at the back and a small one at the front. Running water and both a gas and electricity supply. The bedrooms and toilet were upstairs. There was a fireplace in the sitting room as our source of hot water and heating in the wintertime. I had my own bedroom at the back of the house. I thought it was heaven, but realise now that the rooms were quite small, and it was most difficult to keep the house warm in the depth of winter when ice formed on the inside of the windows. I must have been tough in those days.

Sixth Avenue was traffic free, more or less, with lots of trees and a good place for playing. There was a brand new school about 200 yards up the road. It was in the form of a capital H with the 4 legs being different schools (Avenue, Glen, Third Juniors and Senior School). At he middle of the H were the communal office and hall accommodation. I was allocated Avenue school. A further 200/300 yards along there was beautiful Glen Park, nice gardens, 2 bowling greens and 4 tennis courts. I remember it had a park attendant called Mr Smith who guarded it with his life and had a voice like a foghorn which he used to warn off any misbehaving boys who dared step out of line. There was also another beautiful and much bigger park about half a mile away with a stream running through it with ducks in a pond. There were some local shops round the corner in Fourth Avenue just a short distance from home. Most of our shopping was done there and I well remember The Thrift Store for our groceries and Allots the hairdresser along with Fawberts,

Mercers and Grieves for sweets, papers and so on. I could earn a half penny for running messages for some elderly neighbours on my lucky days.

Many other families moved in around us at the same time. Luckily there were boys of my same age and we soon got together to form our little gang. Directly across the road there was Wilfred Mellor who was a year older than me. His father worked for Terry's and was able to purchase cheap mis-shapen chocolates so that was a bonus for us. Next door there was Donald Simms who was a year younger and his brother Douglas, two and a half years older, who considered himself too old to mix with our younger group. Just at the corner of Fifth and Sixth Avenue there were two brothers, Terry and Peter O' Hara. They had moved from Ireland. Terry was my age and Peter a year younger. Then close by in Fifth Avenue were Dennis Johnston, just over a year older and Laurie Barker and Edgar Masheda both about the same age as me. We soon made friends and we were a nice little gang who played together and had adventures for many years. I was more fortunate than my sister Isobel who only found one friend in Kathy Wright, who lived round the corner in Fifth Avenue.

I started School at the age of 5. Along with 49 others, roughly even between boys and girls, I joined the reception class at the Avenue School in 1931. We sat 2 to a desk in 5 rows of 5 desks. It was a real shock to me. I had been looking forward to starting school but was taken by surprise by what happened. There were two or three things against me. Firstly I had ginger hair and freckles. This was like a red rag to a bull with the numerous yobs in the class, chanting "ginger, you're barmy, you will have to join the army!"

Secondly, and of much more importance, was that they all spoke a foreign language. They spoke with a broad Yorkshire accent and I mostly spoke Doric in line with my parents' upbringing. I was looked upon as an alien. To compound it, at weekends, my parents used to take me and my sister for an afternoon walk to the Park. I usually wore a kilt and if seen by yobbie schoolmates got the extra insults for being dressed like a girl. There was one thing to my advantage however. I was a tall and reasonably well-built lad standing a couple of inches taller than the next biggest. They soon got the message in my foreign language that any rough stuff would end up with them being the losers. The name calling lasted many a long year but I was above all that and it never really got to me.

The more significant thing was that my education did not start for a long time as I was unable to understand what the teacher was on about. I got the reputation of being a bit of a "Thicky" and for a couple of years sat with the dunces group. I remember my reading was awful and I had the same book for months on end. It was about 20 pages long. There was a picture and one word on each page, for example: 'A cat with CAT under it. A pig with PIG. A dog with DOG.' I was no better at my sums so it was a bad start for me.

My salvation I think came from our little gang at home. They educated me in broad Yorkshire lingo and something clicked. I gradually moved up the class. The staff were really very good, headed by Mr Scaife, and my teachers were Miss Mercer, Miss Shaw, Mrs Calvert, Miss Masterman and Mr Vasey. I had them each for a year as I progressed up the school.

Over the years we were always given a small bottle of milk every morning at play time and I have vivid memories of thawing it out on the radiators in the middle of winter when it was frozen solid. I started getting adventure books from the local library which I read avidly and I also took a keen interest in maths. My father had a rather good book called I think '50 ways of working out difficult problems.'

I remember very clearly a most significant day in my life. By this time I was about 10 and getting close to the exam which would decide my future education. A school inspector was coming. We were warned to be on our best behaviour and no nonsense. He came into our class and started questioning: 'What is a noun, a verb, an adjective? Who wrote this or that book? How do you spell this or that word?' I found it easy stuff and my hand was always up.

Then he gave us a sum to do. It was a trick one really which I had seen before in my father's book. What is seven and a half pence multiplied by 239 in pounds shillings and pence? Groans came from the class. 'Impossible,' they complained. My hand was up in a split second.

'Seven pounds, nine shillings and four pence halfpenny, sir.'

Ironic laughter from the yobs. The teacher blushing in embarrassment.

A short delay then the inspector said, "That is correct."

No laughter now but gasps of awe. The inspector, just to check, asked me another one. 'Four pence and three farthings multiplied by 241?'

Straightaway, "Four pounds fifteen shillings and four pence and three farthings Sir."

"Right again. Well done," and with that he left.

I had gone up in the world as I was now some kind of master mind. I even had ten minutes with the Headmaster who patted me on the head for demonstrating how clever his pupils were. But it was easy. The short cut to the answer lay in there being 240 pence to the pound. Work it out for 240 times four pence and three farthings and it is the same as saying work out one pound multiplied by four and three quarters. Easy: four pound fifteen shillings, and then add the balance of an extra four pence and three farthings and 'Bobs your Uncle' that is the answer.

A short time later I sat the examination and depending on the result I would go to the councils Local Grammar School (top 5%), the Higher Grade School (next 50%) or a Senior School (bottom 45%). I was awarded a Scholarship to a fee paying top private Grammar School in York; one of two scholarships on offer. The transformation was complete from the dunce to the top lad. Was this luck or the first stirrings of my Guardian Angel? More of that later.

I still think I got the nod from the school inspector who I don't think had ever received a correct answer to his problem

One thing that I never managed to learn was how to swim. When I was in Mrs Calvert's class we were taken to St Georges' Baths to learn how to swim. I must only have been about 7 years old and this was a totally new experience for me. It was a big noisy place and I stood at the side of the pool at the deep end. Some idiot pushed me in and I landed up out of my depth spluttering and coughing and just flaying about. Luckily a lifeguard got to me and pulled me out. Not a pleasant experience and one that has clouded my view of swimming all my life. It wasn't until I joined the army later in life that I overcame the dread of water and it is still not much to my liking.

I have already told you of the very select little gang I was in. Over our younger years, the friendships grew and we spent hours together practically every day. We were all keen on sport and so it was natural to play mainly football in the winter months, and cricket during the summer. A little bit of rugby came in as well, usually with the ball manufactured out of old newspaper tied up with string. None of our families were wealthy, and there was a good deal of make-do-and-mend. Goal posts, of course, were made from our jumpers being piled up, and for cricket a tree trunk was as good as stumps.

Later when we reached our teens, cycling became a favourite. You had to have a cycle in York - everybody did. We mainly had old cycles renovated, as new ones were far too expensive. When we got to 16 years old, Wilf Mellor and myself even owned a tandem, which was a real experience! The cycling stood me in good stead later on in my life when I was in the army, but that is a tale for later.

Behind the rows of houses where Dennis Johnston lived in Fifth Avenue there was a stream called Tang Hall Beck. If you crossed it, you came to a railway line on an embankment, run by the Derwent Valley Light Railway. It was just a branch line, which ran for about 5 miles out of York to transport cattle and various other goods to the outlying rural community. There were only four or five trains a day. Crossing the line, you came to a clay quarry, quite deep, which had lots of little trollies on railway lines to transport the clay. All very dangerous really, and strictly out of bounds to the gang. The stream used to vary in width depending on the rainfall, and was frequently too wide to jump over; a few well-placed stepping-stones did the trick though. Boys will be boys I suppose, and we were attracted to the adventure of making many trips into forbidden territory. We never suffered any mishaps, but at times the clay on our clothes and wet socks and shoes must have given the game away.

Sixth Avenue was a good street to play in; little traffic, with a car using it at most a couple of times a day. Tradesmen used to come out with their horses and carts. The milkman came once a day, and people came out with jugs to be filled.

The ice cream man was a regular and popular visitor. He was an Italian called Capaldi, who did a roaring trade. The coalman was another regular, and they looked big, tough chaps who put sacks on their backs to deliver, and whose hands and faces were always as black as coal. The odd policeman came around, but we saw them coming and we were as good as gold!

From a very early age, my Father took me to a football match every Saturday afternoon. York City had just formed a team and played in a minor league. I remember going to a game played at their ground at Fulfordgate. It was the other side of the city, and we had a tram ride to get there and back. The team moved from Fulfordgate to a new ground at Bootham Crescent when they were accepted into the Football League. That was in April 1932, so my first memories were back to the age of 5. The new ground was about couple of miles away, but we always walked there and back, about a 40 minute walk each way. On the way there, my Father always gave me a halfpenny to buy 6 tangerine drops, which lasted me the whole match.

York were only a small club, but I became an avid supporter, and still am in my nineties! They are the first result I look for, and the score still evokes joy or misery. Over the years, they have been up and down, but have had some astounding results such as reaching the semi final of the FA cup in 1955, and some years later beating the mighty Manchester United at Old Trafford 3-0.

Along with our sporting activities, our little gang always kept abreast of world affairs. We knew what was happening in the world, and had our views on it. I was always looking at the morning paper (in our house The Daily Herald). We also had a radio, and I followed the BBC news. I can remember our first radio, which was run off an accumulator battery. The battery had to be taken to the shop to be recharged every other week.

It was early days in broadcasting, nothing like the wall-to-wall coverage of the present day. We could forecast a war coming with Germany and Italy by the mid 30's. We were all so confident that we were far stronger than them, and in any case, France was on our side. How naive we were.

I must write a little about the holidays I went on in my early years. They were magical, and remain so to this day. From a very early age, I was taken up to Aberdeen for my summer holidays; the thrill of getting a train at York Station, and the long journey to Aberdeen. Luckily, we were on the main east coast line from London to Aberdeen, and it was a through journey with no changes. The scenery along the east coast consists of fabulous panoramic views of the sea and sandy beaches along the whole route. From Alnmouth to Berwick, onto Dunbar and Edinburgh, over the Forth Rail Bridge, up through Fife to St Andrews and Dundee, then the last stage up through Arbroath, Montrose, Stonehaven, Cove Bay then, finally, Aberdeen. Aberdeen was double the size of York, and a beautiful city. Buildings made from Aberdeen granite always looked clean and sparkled in the sun, which always seemed to shine. The trams running round the city were modern and streamlined, much superior to the rickety old ones in York.

I stayed at my Grandparents' house in Powis Terrace to the north of the city. My Uncle Bob and Auntie Helen also lived there along with my Auntie Meg. Helen and Meg were my Dad's sisters. Helen was married to Bob, who ran a plumbing firm in Aberdeen. He was a successful businessman, and had a car - a rarity in those days. Aberdeen has a long sandy beach backed by grassy dunes where links golf was played. There is also a large harbour, so there was always plenty of shipping to be seen. Aberdeen has many wonderful parks and gardens, all maintained to the highest standards, and it has been dubbed many times as the floral capital of the UK.

It is also a big sporting town, with its football, cricket, golf and ice-skating. It was a joy for me as a young lad, to go to Pittodrie, the home of Aberdeen Football Club, and be in a crowd of 40,000 odd supporters and see them play Rangers or Celtic. My Uncle Bob used to take us out at the weekend for trips in his car. We went along the Dee valley towards Aboyne, Balloter, Braemar and Balmoral, where the royal family has their home.

The scenery was magnificent, with trees and hills, and a general air of history and wealth.

One year, I remember the journey was different. We took the train to Newcastle, and went down to the Tyne Quayside, and boarded a small cargo boat the 'SS Highlander,' which plied its trade between the Tyne and Aberdeen. It was a great adventure getting on in the early afternoon, and arriving in Aberdeen at breakfast time. The Highlander was sadly sunk in WW2 by a German bomber. Prior to that, it had been attacked several times, and had shot down 2 Heinkels with its deck gun. I had fond memories of it.

For part of the holiday, I was always taken to Cullen where my Mother came from. My sister Isobel was born there also. My Auntie Molly still lived in the gatehouse of the massive Seafield Estate, where the Earl and Countess of Seafield lived in Cullen House. Cullen is only small, with a population of about 2000. It is a small fishing port, and has a magnificent beach backed by sand dunes and a golf course. The gatehouse was situated about 50 yards from the beach. What could be better? I had full access to the tens of thousand acres of land around Cullen House, and the sand just a minute walk away. Bliss!

The gardens of the gatehouse rose steeply on the side of the hill, and there was plenty of livestock there in the way of hens, chickens, ducks, sheep etc. A large railway viaduct overlooked the gatehouse, where the highland railway trains operated. At the top of the garden, you were level with the track, and we had endless fun waving at passengers on the trains arriving or leaving Cullen station - just like a scene out of the famous film 'The Railway Children.' The locomotives on the highland lines, big powerful engines with massive wheels to cope with the steep slopes, bellowed masses of steam, and were a sight to behold.

We also sometimes went for a week's holiday to Yorkshire's east coast, mainly at Scarborough. It was always a magical place, and still is in my mind. Memories abound of its two expansive bays with miles of golden sands. A hill with a big ancient castle between the two bays was full of interest, and overlooked a working fishing and pleasure boat harbour.

The place is very hilly, and has acres of wonderful flower gardens, and wonderful views for miles around. Peasholme Park was a boy's dream, with its boating lake and amusements. I also remember day visits to Bridlington, Filey and Whitby.

The autumn of 1937 found me starting a new life at Archbishop Holgate Grammar School in Lord Mayors Walk, York. This was a new experience for me. It was a very prestigious school, which had been founded by the Archbishop of York in 1545. One of the top schools in York, it now had about 550 pupils. Half of them were boarders who came from all over the north of England, sons of rich Industrialists, Farmers and Land Owners. The rest were local lads, sons of the upper class in York who had sufficient money to pay for the school fees. I was but a lowly lad from a council estate, who had a free scholarship.

Gone were my early school days when the only subjects were English and arithmetic, and we sat in the same classroom all day. Now it was English Language, English Grammar, Latin, French and German. Add onto that Algebra, Geometry and Trigonometry, followed by Biology, Chemistry and Physics. Also History, Geography, Religious Studies, Woodwork, Gymnastics and Sport. Each subject had its own set of textbooks, with a different teacher and classroom. No wonder my head was in a swirl! I also had homework in three or four subjects a night, which was new to me.

I soon adapted to the changes, and easily held my own. We had an assembly every morning led by the headmaster, with prayers and hymns, which were mostly unchanged since the school was started.

We were divided into five houses for competition purposes, each with a different colour. The biggest house was Boarders (white), followed by Dean (red), Holgate (green), Johnston (yellow), and my house Ebor (blue). All the masters were university graduates, and wore gowns with their university colours on them. All of them carried canes and made frequent use of them.

They were certainly impressive, and I remember their names and most nicknames still. "Fungus" Carrington (Latin), "Doggy" Duchene (French), "Blossom" Ward (German), Harry Watts and Truscott (English), "Bony" Thompson (History), Max Ebbage (Gym), Galloway (Biology), Foster (Physics), Nick Holderness

(Chemistry), "Shoddy" Johnson (Geography). Others were Wright, Frith and Adams. The headmaster was A.B. Hodgson. They were pretty good at their jobs, good teachers, and I give thanks for them. I was a dead loss at woodwork. It took me two years to make a simple wooden stool, and after all that time, the four legs were all different lengths. There were lots of after-school clubs to choose from. I opted for chess club, and enjoyed it when I managed to beat the older boys in competitions. The school was also very good for sport, with football and rugby union in the winter terms, and cricket, tennis and athletics in the summer. I was best at football, specializing in goalkeeping. Against stiff competition, I was picked for the junior school football team. My main rival was a lad called Peter Pickering, who later in life became a very good all-round sportsman. He played goalkeeper for York City AFC, and was transferred for a record fee to Chelsea in about 1950. He also played first class cricket for Northants.

I was a regular attender at school, having very little time off. I did, however, dodge school on the last day of the summer term in 1938. My Aunt and Uncle (Helen and Bob) were visiting York from Aberdeen on their holidays. Uncle Bob loved cricket, and booked to see England play Australia on the first day of the fixture at Headingly, Leeds. There was a great debate to see if I could skip school a day to go to Leeds. I must have pleaded well, as I was allowed to go. This was a dream come true to see all my cricketing favourites in action. I remember the teams well; Edrich, Barnett, Joe Hardstaff, Wally Hammond, Eddie Paynter, Price the wicketkeeper, Hedley Verity, Dougie Wright, Bill Bowes and Ken Farnes for England. Fingleton, Brown, Barnett, Don Brad man, McCabe, Badcock, Hassett, Waite, O'Reilly, McCormack and Fleetwood Smith for Australia. The day was sunny, the ground was full, but the cricket was pretty slow. I sat there all day and England were 223 all out, but still a great thrill! England lost in the end by 5 wickets.

Our school day was from 9.00am till 12.30pm, then 14.00pm up to 16.00pm. We had a half-day off on Wednesday (usually spent on school sporting activities), and also spent Saturday morning at school, the only school in York that had to attend on Saturday morning. It was about a two-mile walk to school, and I

13

had to go home for lunch, so there were four journeys a day totalling 8 miles. I used to walk it come sun or snow. Part of the way, I used the city walls that were built in Roman times.

Walking briskly, I could cover the distance in 30 minutes. If I was slightly late, I could cut it to twenty minutes, which happened frequently. It was good going, as I usually had a school bag full of books to carry. It certainly kept me fit, and has stood me in good stead for many years.

*Grandfather James Johnston in Cullen*

*Dad with me and Isobel in Tang Hall Park*

15

*Mother with me and Isobel in Aberdeen*

*Back seat driver*

*Early days in York with Isobel*

*Early days in York with Isobel*

*I look good in a kilt*

# CHAPTER 2

## WORLD WAR 2

It became increasingly clear at the start of 1939 that trouble was brewing. Germany became very aggressive, and our country was very softly spoken, and continued to appease them (no doubt because we were woefully unprepared for war). Things became serious when, in the middle of the year, everyone was issued with gas masks. They were awful things to wear, and how we would have survived if we needed to wear them is hard to see. Also, each house had had a dozen corrugated iron panels delivered (the kit for making an Anderson air-raid shelter). It involved digging a big hole in the garden, and then bolting the iron panels together, and putting it in the hole. All the soil dug from the hole was then put on top of the shelter, to protect you from bombs and metal fragments in the case of the raid. It gave pretty good protection, apart from a direct hit, which was most unlikely.

The big problem was that the hole got flooded after heavy rain, so we had to continually bail out the water to make it habitable. We later fitted some wooden flooring above the water line, which was of some help. Nevertheless, all the effort paid off as it was much used in the following few years. And so the fateful day came on Sunday 3rd September 1939, when war was declared. I recall sitting at home with the rest of the family at 11.00am, and hearing Neville Chamberlain intoning the words "and so we are now at war with Germany." Gosh! What were we going to make of all that? Surely we must be all right, as France was on our side, we had a good navy and, we beat them the last time.

The start of the war saw a lot of changes. A state of emergency was declared, with lots of restrictions and rules to follow. Cinemas and theatres could not open, and all sports events, where crowds were expected, were cancelled. Ration books were issued to make sure everyone got a small but fair amount of essential food that was likely to become scarce. Some imported food such as bananas and fruit would not be seen again for many years. Petrol was rationed, and car journeys, with the exception of Government business, were restricted. All premises had to be blacked out at night to avoid any light escaping. Air raid wardens would patrol around at night, and any breeches of the rules were frowned upon. Gas masks had to be carried at all times. But, the start of the war turned out to be a great anti-climax. Nothing dangerous really happened. No bombing from enemy aircraft at home, and little action along the frontiers with Germany. So, as the end of 1939 drew near, many of the petty restrictions were lifted, and life continued as normal.

It was around this time that I joined the Boy Scouts, who had just formed a troop at our local Presbyterian church. I was appointed the patrol leader of the Eagle patrol, which consisted of 8 boys. I think I was picked as leader because I went to the posh Grammar school, and the others didn't! We had lots of fun each week, and during the warmer weather, we used to go to the countryside around York for camping expeditions. I also joined a youth group run by the local Parish church, which was very close by. It had about 200 members, so lots of new friends were made.

It was about this time that I got my first bicycle - not a new one as they were too expensive, but one to put together from parts from other bikes in the local garage. Not much to look at, but it was the pride of my life, and made travel much easier. Alas, it was forbidden to use it for school. I soon became an expert cyclist, and could mend punctures, adjust brakes, and do all manner of repairs with my eyes shut. It stood me in good stead for later in life, as you will read later.

School was much the same at this time, although we had practice drills to get to the air raid shelters at regular intervals. A gradual change of teachers also occurred, with some being called up to the armed forces, and being replaced by stand in teachers, including some women. Shock and horror when we first heard of this, but it soon became accepted as the norm!

The first signs of a real war came early in 1940, when the Germans invaded Norway and Denmark. We helped to put up a little resistance helping to defend Norway, but to no avail, as the Germans triumphed. There was still no inkling that we might be getting into real danger. It all started to go down hill on May 10th 1940. I can remember the day well.

It was a beautiful sunny day, and my Dad and I had gone out for a bike ride - about a 20 mile round trip - and we had a lovely time. When we got home, the radio news was telling us that the Germans had invaded Holland and Belgium, and the war was really starting. The next few weeks were depressing, as the German forces swept everything before them.

Our army was defeated, but made a miracle escape from the beaches at Dunkirk, with the help of lots of little boats, but, worse still, the French surrendered, and the Germans were celebrating in Paris. It was a shock to find out we were not as good as we thought we were. Funnily, not for one moment did I think we could do anything but win the war! The country then suffered endless bombardment from the Luftwaffe, and imminent invasion was expected. Life was starting to get grim.

It was about this time that the first bombs were dropped on York. I can remember clearly my Mother waking me up in the middle of the night, telling me to get to our shelter as quick as I could. There was the sound of a German plane overhead, and it was dropping flares, which lit up the whole place. I got out of the back door, making for the shelter, when there was the sound of a whoosh and whistle, and then number of explosions as the bombs hit the ground. I certainly broke the speed record from the back door to the shelter! Luckily, the bomb missed us by half a mile or so. The headline in the local paper the next day read "German bombs hit the dead centre of York." They had landed in the local cemetery. That was the first of many raids.

Night after night, the air-raid sirens sounded late in the evening, and the all clear was not sounded until 5.00 or 6.00am in the morning. It became routine, to sleep all night as best you could in the shelter, though not to be recommended when it was a cold night. No allowance was made for missing school, and where ever and for how long I slept, I still had to be at school for 9.00am.

It was at this time that I was also on a rota at school to act as a firewatcher. Our school buildings were old, and fire would have quickly destroyed them. The danger of incendiary bombs starting fires was real, and 20 or so boys were on guard every night. We had been given training to deal with the incendiaries. They were only small things, and if you got to them quickly, were not much of a problem. We also got paid sixpence a night for our efforts. Riches indeed!

Thankfully, the RAF saw off the threat posed by the Luftwaffe. The navy was still good enough to discourage Hitler from mounting an invasion. So, the year ended much better than could have been hoped. In fact, we could celebrate some success in North Africa against the Italians, who foolishly thought we were a walkover.

The war was now beginning to bite. It began to dawn on me that we were woefully weak, and the Axis powers held by all the aces militarily. Our cities were being bombed at will, with many casualties. Our limited resources were stretched with food, clothing and fuel being in short supply. U boats were sinking our ships in large numbers, but all that didn't break the resolve we had to come out of it victorious. York continued to get its share of air raids throughout the year; not on a massive scale, but sufficient to keep us on our toes, and on the alert.

Hull, a port some 40 miles east of York, saw more action than we did. The German raiders came in from the North Sea, and dropped their loads on Hull, but by the time they had finished their bombing runs, they were near enough York for air raid warnings to be constantly in force, with consequent disruption to life.

I remember on many occasions looking out of my bedroom window in the direction of Hull, and seeing a red glow in the sky. We got used to it all, and became a bit blasé. My pal Wilf Mellor, from younger days, used to go to York Theatre Royal with me one evening each week. We got the cheapest seats in the Gods (Gallery) way up at the top (3 pence each), and were richly entertained with murder mysteries, comedies, dramas and also dear old Shakespeare. I remember walking home one cold winter night at around 9.30pm, the sky was cloudless and the moon was full. We just reached the top of Sixth Avenue, very near home, when we heard the noise of an aircraft. No air raid siren had sounded, but we knew by the engine tone that it was German. We tried to spot it in the moonlit sky, but we couldn't see it. A moment later, we heard it go into a dive, followed by the whistle of bombs, then several explosions about a mile away at the Gas Works. A bomb hit the Retort House, but missed the more vital gas tank. These incidents in no way deterred us from usual routine of going out to meet friends at Scouts or Youth groups.

One other thing sticks in my mind - I had cycled to a Scout camp being held at Brandsby, a small village about 10 miles east of York. There must have been about 10 tents at the site in a Farmer's field. We were still in danger of an invasion, and early one morning, we heard the sound of a low flying aircraft. We spotted a German plane that looked remarkably like the ones used by their parachutists. It passed over us at a distance and went away. We searched all day to see if anyone had parachuted down, but never found a thing. A false alarm in the end, but you could never be sure. It was probably a rookie pilot who had lost his bearings.

At school, things continued much as usual. I was now playing Rugby Union rather than soccer. I found it rough and tough, but not as good as being a goalkeeper in a soccer team. We were told it built character, but I am not so sure about that! Thugs could get away with anything. During this period, you couldn't look forward to your usual nice summer holidays as some coastal places were strictly out of bounds. Bonfire Night on 5th November was, of course, cancelled during the war. Birthdays and Christmas were also austere, but not enough to dampen our usual joyful spirit.

The war continued to go badly for us. After some success in North Africa, Rommel and his Africa Corps arrived on the scene, and we were brought back to square one again. Hitler's armies swept through the Balkans, and the Greek Islands with little opposition. In June, Germany invaded Russia and, by the end of the year, were at the gates of Moscow and Leningrad, with huge Russian losses. In December, Japan attacked the USA at Pearl Harbour - just the start of a series of setbacks. Again, the outlook was bleak. There were crumbs of comfort for us. Our spirits were raised when the Navy sank the battleship Bismarck in the Atlantic. Because of other commitments, German planes made fewer raids on us.

The threat of invasion seemed to pass, and at last we had two more allies, with a lot of potential power to draw on. We all pulled together to do our bit. My Father still worked at the Post Office, but he was also their Chief Air Raid Precautions Instructor, which kept him busy. My Mother was in the Women's Voluntary Service, which offered aid to all people in need. By this time, my sister had finished her schooling, and had gone on to a year at a Secretarial College to train as a Shorthand Typist, but she was also a trained First Aider.

I did my bit in the summer holidays when farmers asked for help in gathering the harvest. There must have been fifty or more of us school lads, who cycled ten miles or so each day to outlying farms to give assistance from 8.00am to 18.00pm. A lot of the time we helped to harvest the flax crop. It was cut by machine, and we bound and stacked it. I remember the machine was always having breakdowns, during which time we sat under the hedge enjoying a nice break in the sunshine. We even got paid a shilling a day for our troubles. Riches indeed for me! Really life could have been much worse. Roll on 1942, and better news perhaps.

1942 was a very significant year. The war was going very badly, and by the middle of the year, the German army had reached Stalingrad and the Caucasus, where all the big oil wells were situated. Rommel was at the doors of Cairo and the Japanese had swept all before them and were on the Indian borders, threatening Australia in the south, and seeming unstoppable. It had been a cold winter with food, clothing and fuel shortages, and never any good news.

It was also the year that I would leave school and get my first real job. The year ended better than it started, with the Allies gaining strength, and the enemy being pushed back all over the world. The Germans were beaten at El Alamein, and the Allies invaded Algeria and Morocco with some success. The Germans were trounced at Stalingrad, and the Japanese suffered their first defeats of the war. At long last, something to celebrate! It wasn't without blood and tears however.

On 29th April the Luftwaffe attacked the City of York, in some force. I remember it well - it had been a very nice sunny day, and I had spent the evening on the stray near where I lived, playing Puddox with friends from the Youth club. Puddox was a local game from the area, a kind of mixture of cricket and rounders. I went to bed as usual, feeling sleepy after all the fresh air, but was woken at about 01.45am by the siren, and quickly made it to the shelter. The raid started at 02.00, and the all clear was sounded just after 04.00 - two hours of constant bombardment.

About 1000 HE bombs were dropped, along with 10,000 incendiaries. There were around 30,000 houses and premises in York, so it worked out at 1 HE bomb for every 30 premises, and an incendiary bomb for every three houses. Over a hundred people were killed, and some thousand individuals injured. The City was undefended, with no AA guns in the area, but ultimately there were some RAF night fighters around, and several planes were gunned down. There were lots of fires burning. The railway station suffered, and the Guildhall was destroyed, but amazingly the magnificent Minster was unscathed. It took a day or two to get some semblance of order in the City, but we took it on the chin and were soon working together to clean the mess - I even got a day off school! Mind you we were expecting the raid. Some weeks earlier the RAF had raided Lubeck because they had been diverted from their main target. Lubeck was a similar City to York in so far as it had a lot of ancient buildings, and wasn't really a very legitimate target. This had infuriated old Hitler, who vowed revenge. He resorted to all the old cities mentioned in the Baedeker Travel Book, which had been popular with German tourists before the war. The main cities of Canterbury, Exeter, Bath and Norwich had already been bombed, so it didn't take a genius to work out that we were next in line.

This was now about the time when end of school exams were being held to obtain a School Certificate, which was a valuable document representing the depth and quality of your knowledge. It took a couple of months for the results to be published, a nerve wracking time, but I shouldn't really have worried, as I got very reasonable results. Not top of the class, but far enough up to make me happy.

My youth group split from the Church it was attached to, and began life on its own. Our leader was a fine gentleman by the name of Stanley Victor Oglesby. He was a local businessman, who was the owner of a firm called Scrutons -who manufactured a baby medicine called Nurse Harvey's Mixture, which was a best seller nationwide. He purchased premises in St Savioursgate, York, which we used as our new meeting place. One of our activities was a music group, which met to listen to and discuss classical music records. It was at this stage I developed a real love of serious music, which would last all my life. I liked most kinds of music, with all kinds of instruments. I tried many times to play music, but I was hopeless as it - much to my shame.

The summertime arrived, and I left school for the last time. I searched around for a job to occupy my time, and to earn a little money. I applied for, and got a job in an Architect's office (J.W. Pentney) in Coney Street, York. I had a good result in Art in my School Certificate, which probably helped me. He was a leading architect, and had in fact designed the first school I attended. Business was fairly slack however, because the war had stopped all new building, and emphasis was on repairing damaged buildings. He had the responsibility of looking after the repair and maintenance of all Church buildings, including Ministers' housing in the Diocese of York.

Life was pretty boring, and not really what I wanted. Luck was on my side. My Father played golf with a Bank Manager, and that somehow resulted in me being offered a job as a Bank Clerk at The Westminster Bank in Pocklington, a small township around 15 miles east of York, on the road to Hull. This I accepted with great joy, as working for a Bank was very prestigious at that time. Double the pay as well, up £1 a week. It required a bus trip out to Pocklington and back each day, about an hour each way, which was a bit of a bind. It meant an early start for a 30-minute walk to the bus terminus, and late back in the evening.

I loved the job, it was just what I wanted as I was always good at figures. It was a 3-man branch, with a Manager, Chief Cashier and myself as the junior dogs body. It was great meeting people, dealing with cash, and generally dealing with all the ledgers and balancing the books of account. The bus passed the RAF Bomber Base a mile outside Pocklington, where squadrons of Halifax Heavy bombers were based in full view of the main road, so it was always an interesting journey to and fro. There were British,

25

Canadian and Free French crews who used the same bus as me, which was a great experience.

There was a big RAF presence in Yorkshire. Heslington Hall, which was only a couple of miles away from where I lived, became the HQ for No 4 Group of Bomber Command. There were about 20 Bomber Stations within a 15-mile radius of York, who were able to put 500 planes in the air for the night bombing campaigns against Germany. I can remember summer evenings hearing the roar of engines, as the bombers got ready to take off. I would stand in the garden watching Squadrons circling York to gain height before setting course for their targets. I got very clever at guessing what the target would be as they set out on their flight paths. A slightly earlier take off with an eastern course meant Berlin was the target. Southeast it was an attack on the Ruhr, and a southerly track was probably the U Boat pens on the Atlantic coast of France. I was always asleep when they returned at 4 or 5 o'clock in the morning, but I know my Mother was always awake to hear them come back.

So, life continued with danger and shortages. There were signs of a brighter future war wise. The Japanese were soundly beaten at the battles of the Coral Sea and Midway, and in North Africa, our old adversary Rommel was beaten at El Alamein. Put out the flags, we are on our way!

In April, I had my 17th birthday. This meant I could join the Home Guard. This was an organisation set up in 1940 as really the last defence of the country. It was mostly made up from men too old to join the regular forces, and lads of 17 waiting to join the forces. Since the big air raid on York, an Anti Aircraft Battery had been established on York racecourse (The Knavesmire). A few regulars manned it, but the bulk of the manpower was provided by the Home Guard. This was just what I wanted to be - a Gunner in the Royal Artillery. It involved two parades a week, one on a Sunday morning for 3 hours, and the other an all-night effort from 7.00pm to 7.00am the next morning. I had to get special permission to be late into work on those mornings. So, No 1 Sub Battery of York 108 AA "Z" Battery had a new recruit.

The "Z" Battery comprised 64 twin rocket launchers, a square of 8 lines each with 8 launchers. A full salvo would send off 128 rockets, if you were lucky. They were cheap and shoddy, and prone to misfiring. They were not particularly accurate, as the elevation and direction markers were to the nearest 5 degrees. Nevertheless, this was part of their beauty. When a full salvo was fired, the rockets certainly spread themselves out and produced a large box of explosions, very unlucky for an enemy aircraft if it was within the area of the box. The rockets were about 6 feet in length, and quite slim, but heavy enough to make a 17 year old puff when they were being loaded! The armourers who set the fuses on the tip of the rockets were regular troops, but the Home Guard then took over for the loading and firing.

I soon got the drill to perfection, and was able to be operational in next to no time. We used to practice live firing at Hornsea on the Yorkshire coast. I got the shock of my life at the first live firing, as the noise when the rockets left the launcher was beyond belief. I think my poor hearing later in life was in some part due to this.

After about 3 months of active service, I was promoted to Lance Bombardier in charge of 4 launchers. My main duty was to clear any misfires, which was a perilous occupation, as there were many stories of mishaps of rockets exploding as soon as they were touched. There were no air raids on York whilst I was on duty, so I never saw any real action there. I can remember one night whilst I was still a Gunner. I was allocated duty as an observer from 11.00pm to 1.00am - a stint of two hours. It was a bitterly cold night with no one about. My relief didn't turn up at 1.00am or at 3.00am, and it wasn't until 5.00am that the Orderly Officer discovered a half frozen observer still keeping watch. Disgraceful really, but I suppose it was just the older people taking unfair advantage of the young ones. I resolved that if ever I were in a place of authority, such a thing would not happen on my watch. And it never has.

During December, small Luftwaffe raids were attacking London, and this had been putting a strain on the defenders. A call was sent out for Volunteers to spend 2 nights in London to relieve the situation. I volunteered for this, and for a couple of nights, I manned a "Z" Battery based at Forestgate, Dulwich, London. We were in action for about half an hour each night, firing off half a dozen salvos. No misfires, and I don't have any idea if we got anywhere near hitting anything. All I can remember is that I was practically deaf for a few days - a salvo of 128 rockets is fearsome!

Apart from all this, my time was spent cycling, theatre going, watching York City play football, and attending night school to try to pass the preliminary examinations for The Institute of Bankers. On the cycling front, I can remember two things in particular. Wilf Mellor, my friend from childhood, had received his calling up papers from the Army. We decided to celebrate by borrowing a tandem to go to Scarborough for the day. Wilf steered at the front, whilst I pedalled from the back. It was a strange feeling at first, but we managed fine, and easily covered 100 miles in the day. Scarborough in the middle of the war was not the same as I had remembered from earlier years. There was lots of barbed wire, and no access to the sands.

Another incident happened one Saturday afternoon, when a group of us from our youth Club were cycling about 20 miles out of York. We heard the sound of low flying aircraft, and then machine gun fire. At very low level, a Beaufighter was pursuing a Heinkel bomber. The Heinkel dropped six bombs which landed in a field about 200 yards away, and then soared away into the clouds, still being fired at by the Beaufighter. It was all part of life in those days, and didn't get a mention in the paper. I think the Germans got lucky and made it home.

My sister Isobel was a qualified shorthand typist by this time. She got a job as the personal secretary to Mr Oglesby, the inspiration of our Youth Club. The winter was cold, and lots of snow fell on York. I remember the cold winter mornings, when I left the house at 6.30am in the dark, to walk to the bus terminus to catch the bus to Pocklington. I still thoroughly enjoyed working at the Bank, and soon got au fait with all the routines one had to follow.

One of the perks of the job was that a lot of farmers banked at our branch. They used to call in about once a week to do their transactions, and often brought in a little gift of a few eggs or some bacon. With food rationing so meagre, this was like manna from heaven, and my Mother used to be joyful on the days I brought in some extra food. I still remember the packed lunches I took to Pocklington, which were invariably marmite sandwiches followed by a biscuit. The funny thing was, we remained fit and healthy on so little, and there were very few obese people around.

The year drew to an end, and the outlook was much brighter. The Axis powers were being pushed back all over the world. The Russians had the great victory at Stalingrad, the first of many. Hitler had been cleared out of North Africa. We had landed in Italy, and they were out of the war, and the Americans were island hopping in the Pacific. The only minus point was that the Japanese were still on the borders of India. The omens seemed much better altogether for the Allies. I always said, jokingly, that it all happened since I put on my uniform for the Home Guard. The enemy must have got a real shock.

*Sister Isobel, 1942*

*Dearest mother, 1942*

# CHAPTER 3

## WORLD WAR 2
## ON ACTIVE SERVICE

1944 started off as a copy of 1943, catching the early bus to Pocklington. Trudging in the dark through snow and ice in the bitter cold. The bus was always full with airmen going back to their stations. Many were often left standing in the cold because the bus was full. I was lucky, as I had a pass, which gave me priority to get on board. Life at the Bank had its perks and was most enjoyable.

All was about to change however. I was 18 on 27<sup>th</sup> April, and on that day, a letter arrived from the War Office - I was being called up to join the army, and had to report on 18<sup>th</sup> May at the Green Howards Regimental Centre, at Richmond in North Yorkshire. So, it was a sad farewell to my job at the Bank, and a chance to have a holiday for a week before I departed. It was going to be a big change, but I was looking forward to it. Sunny Thursday arrived, and I had to say my farewells to my family and friends. My Mother and sister shed a tear or two as I left. As I had been in the Home Guard, I was obliged to travel in my uniform, but had been instructed to remove all badges of rank (my Bombardier's stripes), and my Royal Artillery identification of cap badge and shoulder flashes. The uniform was worn and decrepit, and wasn't improved by the outline of the stripe being clearly visible.

I arrived at Richmond Station just after midday, along with just over a hundred other lads. They were a motley bunch, mainly from the cities of Leeds and Bradford in West Yorkshire. They were all in civilian clothes, and I was the only one in uniform. I was very relieved to join the army, as 5% of conscripts were picked by ballot to work in the coalmines, which were hard pressed for manpower. I would have been useless as a miner, so breathed a sigh of relief. A Sgt Smith met us with a few other

NCOs, who soon had us loaded into 3-ton trucks and taken to the Barracks.

The first few days seemed to be taken up by medical examinations, injections and intelligence tests. Everyone apart from me was issued with 2 new uniforms. I only got one as I was already in uniform. We also got a greatcoat, boots, socks, shirts and a gym kit. We were split into 3 Platoons each of about 35 recruits, and each Platoon was allocated a Nissen Hut for accommodation. It was a shock when we had to fill empty palliasses with straw to sleep on. Lights out at 10.30pm, with reveille at 6.30am, signalled by a trumpet call. All the lads talked with a very strong dialect from West Yorkshire, so it was like starting school again trying to understand what people were talking about.

There was a Lance Corporal assigned to each hut, and in my case, it was the son of a Baronet, who had a big estate in Yorkshire. He had a Public School education, and was very posh. He had the same difficulty in understanding the dialect, and he insisted that I slept in the bed next to him. His sister married into Royalty a few years after the war ended. He himself was later commissioned, and served in one of the Guards Regiments.

The next couple of weeks were a whirl of activity, as Sgt Smith and his team tried to instill a modicum of military discipline and order to the rabble he had been given charge of. It was a job and a half for him as most of them were clueless. I found life easy. The 6.30am reveille was a long lie in for me. The job was on the doorstep, so no more long walks to the bus and tedious journeys. Food was made for you, no hard studying in the evening, and there seemed to be so much free time. Although they ran us about, I am sure it didn't reach the daily mileage of walking and running that I used to do.

It soon became clear that the majority of the Platoon were educationally backward, and physically unfit. Trying to teach them marching drill on the square was just hard work. Half of them didn't know their left from their right, and some marched with their same arm and leg going in the same direction. Sgt Smith used to explode! He had a fine command of the English language, and a range of swear words that he used to emphasis his points. I wasn't used to swearing, being brought up in a strong

Presbyterian ethos, and never encountering it in my sheltered occupation in a Bank. I found it quite hilarious at times, although my fellow soldiers on the receiving end of it would not agree. All my fellow soldiers seemed to think it was obligatory to use at least one swear word per sentence. It just wasn't my style, but I got to like all my colleagues, and was very forgiving.

I remember having to help a lad who slept the other side of me. He was a big lad called John Darbyshire. When he stood to attention, he looked like a sack of potatoes. He didn't have any idea of making up his bed properly in the morning. We were instructed to do it in a standard fashion, with blankets folded in a certain way, and accurate to a fraction of an inch. Mess tins, webbing and boots also had to be displayed in the proper manner. John didn't have a clue, and every morning at inspection, the NCO just threw his equipment all over the floor, and made him do a lot of press-ups. He was just incapable of doing it right. In the end, I agreed to make his bed every day as he was really being picked on. He was useless at most things, but show him a piano and he became a different lad. He could sit at a piano and without music, play all the popular tunes of the time beautifully, and give us hours of entertainment. He would never make an infantry soldier, and what became of him I do not know. At least I tried to keep him out of trouble!

The length of our initial training was 6 weeks, a very short time given to turn us from rookies into some semblance of soldiers capable of following orders and fighting. After 3 weeks, we were issued with rifles - Lee Enfield 303s, and were told to treat them as our best friend, keep them clean, well oiled and ready for firing. It added another complication for the Drill Sergeant, as there was a lot more to practice and perfect.

Needless to say, there were lots of rifle inspections, and woe betide any one whose rifle was dirty. They even allowed us on the rifle range after another 2 weeks. That was the first time I had ever fired a rifle, nowhere near perfection, but not a bad shot. They had much more of a kick to them than I had anticipated. We were also introduced to the Bren Gun, 2" mortar, Sten Gun and various hand grenades. With a little bit of field craft and route marching, we were beginning to bind together like a proper army unit, although still far from perfect. We were let out of

Barracks for the first time at this point, and managed to have a look around the quite nice market town of Richmond.

Nearing the end of our 6 weeks, a Passing Out Parade was to be held. There were strict orders to be at our smartest, with our best uniform on. It was a Hobson's choice for me. The old, scruffy uniform from the Home Guard fitted the best, but looked its age. The new uniform that I had been issued with looked pristine, but was several sizes too small for me, and looked ridiculous. I chose my old uniform, of course. Our Platoon Commander, a 2/Lt Latimer by name, was most displeased with my appearance. I was sent off in disgrace to put my newer uniform on.

He didn't know what to say when I came back, as I looked so untidy! Off I was sent to change again. The next day, I was given a new battledress from the QM stores. It was fitted, and much better material than anyone else had. I used it for best for a long time.

Our 6-week training was ending. During this time, D Day occurred, and the war was really hotting up. We all waited with bated breath as to what our futures were. The next stage was normally a 12-week advanced infantry course, and thereafter a posting to an operational infantry battalion. I could see myself in action in France before the end of the year. 50% of the Platoon were posted to the advanced course, mainly to The West Yorkshire Regiment or The Green Howard Regiment. Others were posted to other services, such as Royal Artillery, Royal Engineer, RASC etc. One person was held at Richmond to rerun the 6-week course.

The last posting to be given out was for myself. That was to 28th Training Battalion, based in Holywood, Co. Down, Northern Ireland. This was a special course for potential leaders. Happy days! I must have done something right. I had certainly enjoyed my first 6 weeks in the Army, and felt as if I was a soldier. The 6 weeks of activity had certainly improved me physically and mentally. I knew I was far in advance of the rest of the Platoon. They hadn't the advantage of a Grammar School education of course, but they didn't hold that against me.

The beginning of July 1944 saw me en route to Northern Ireland. This required a train trip up to Glasgow to catch the ferry to Belfast. The ferry was a 3 to 4 hour journey over open waters in the Irish Sea, with no escort of any sort - easy meat for any roving U Boat. I was picked up at the docks in Belfast, and taken to Princess Barracks in Holywood, a pleasant coastal town on Belfast Lough. It was a much larger and more modern Barracks than Richmond, with properly built huts for accommodation, much better than the old Nissen Huts. Security was much tighter there, as there had been a lot of anti British IRA activity before the war, and it still lingered on. All firearms had to be placed under lock and key every night. I was part of a company-sized number of newcomers, who were then allocated into 3 Platoons. My Platoon Sergeant, by the name of Jenkins, soon introduced himself, and let us know what he expected of us. He was an excellent teacher, who taught us a lot.

The landscape around Holywood was very hilly and wooded, with many streams coming down the hillsides. Sergeant Jenkins appeared to be very happy when his Platoon was wading in water, which was a daily occurrence. I suppose he was trying to simulate the conditions we might face in combat, so I didn't hold it against him. All the lads in the Platoon had their wits about them, so there were no passengers, and drills and inspections were of high quality.

For three lovely hot and summer months, we honed our knowledge of weapons, both German and our own. We learned everything there was to know on field craft, and Platoon attack and defence procedures. Physical activity was stepped up, and it required a 15-mile run first thing every morning. Long route marches carrying full equipment were routine, and the roads and fields between Holywood, Bangor and Newtonards became very familiar, as was the steep hillside at the back of the Barracks. We all took it in turns to act as senior and junior NCOs, and I loved the sense of authority this gave me. I still found it relatively easy, as I was super fit by this time, and had put on a bit of weight with the bigger Army rations. What I liked least was night exercises, and I never really found it comfortable operating in the dark.

One incident stands out in my memory. We were on a camouflage exercise which involved approaching a slightly elevated bunker over open ground, which had a few bushes for cover. We were each armed with a firecracker. The objective was to hit the bunker with the firecracker without being spotted - a near impossible task. There was no way it could succeed by going the shortest way with everybody being spotted, so I decided to go the long was around, which involved a half mile dash up a hill, through some woods, and approaching from the far side. From the edge of the wood to the bunker was around 100 yards, but there was a dip in the ground about 20 yards out of the wood, and my calculation was that if I could reach the dip unseen, I would be hidden from sight until I reached the bunker. I was also banking on the lookout at the back of the bunker being distracted when something interesting was happening on the other side.

My plan worked to perfection, and it only took just over 5 minutes to be under the wall of the bunker without being spotted. I then lit the firecracker, and dropped it over the bunker wall. Unfortunately, it fell into their stock of firecrackers, which went off with a big and sustained bang, leading them to evacuate the spot pretty sharply. The whole thing ended in chaos! I was expecting the worst for wrecking the day, but nobody complained. I was always an advocate for putting a little surprise in now and again.

We used to practice the same drills for attack and defence that had remained unchanged since the war started. My view was that the Germans must have known exactly what we would do, and would be well prepared for it. Nobody took a blind bit of notice of me! The other major thing was that we had to learn to swim. This was a great barrier for me, as the result of my experiences as a very young lad. Every week, we were taken to a public swimming pool in Belfast for practice. I overcame my fears of water, and managed to pass the swimming criteria. It was not, however, my favourite pastime.

Towards the end of September, I was told I had to report to a WOSBY (War Office Selection Board), to be tested for my capability of becoming a Commissioned Officer. This was to be held over 3 days at Dundrum, just a few miles south of Holywood. It was lovely little seaside town, looking out onto the Irish Sea. I reported there along with 11 others from various units. These included senior NCOs, but we were all given similar clothing so that no one could tell each other's ranks. What a difference I found! The beds had white sheets on them - a big difference to sleeping on a straw palliasse. The mess room had table clothes on the tables, napkins and a full set of cutlery. Best of all, the meals were served by ATS girls.

We were split into three teams of four for various tasks to be undertaken, and were asked to perform various team tasks (which usually involved oil drums, ropes and logs) which seemed on the face of it to be impossible. I took my time to think about the problems, whilst others jumped in with a quick decision to impress that they had leadership qualities. So often, they got into such a mess, and had to take advice from a better thought out plan. I think I won on that one.

There were so many face-to-face encounters, where my general knowledge and outlook on life was probed to some depth, which I didn't mind at all. The clincher was a period where all 12 of us had to give a thirty minute speech. Most of them were uncomfortable with this, and couldn't speak for more than 5 or 10 minutes. You could pick your own subject, which was a doddle. My chosen subject was Anti Aircraft Launchers, and experiences in a "Z" Battery. I was absolutely au fait with the subject, with no fear of contradiction, and they listened in astonishment to the things they knew nothing about themselves. Needless to say, a week later, I was informed that my next posting, in a couple of week's time, should be for Pre OCTU training at Wrotham in Kent. Great joy - I was on my way. I had thoroughly enjoyed my stay in Holywood. The Ulster people were most friendly, and tea and cakes were offered every weekend for free from the good townsfolk of Holywood.

I was now being posted to Wrotham in Kent to a Pre OCTU. Before going, I had been granted a 7-day leave pass. So, it was the return ferry to Glasgow, and then onto York. It was nice to be home with family and friends, even for such a short time. The family were glad to see me, and thought I was looking in good shape, and a little more self-assured than when I left. Being able to use an iron to press my uniform, and to do all kinds of things for myself seemed to surprise them. I think, on the whole, that they were rather proud that I had achieved so much in such a short time.

The nice time at home was over in a flash, and then I was on a train down to London en route to Wrotham. London looked a drab place, with nothing much other than buildings covered in sand bags for protection, and lots of bombed out derelict places. The capital was still under attack from Vl doodlebugs and V2 rockets. It was hard to bear after 5 years of war, and the campaign in Europe going so well.

Wrotham was just a small village some 30 miles south of London, situated in a wooded area at the top of a 200-foot escarpment, which ran for many miles across the Kent countryside. In peaceful times, it was just a pretty village with little happening there. Now, there was an Army Camp holding a couple of hundred troops. It was situated in doodlebug alley - so called because all the V1s fired from Northern France came over this spot, heading for London. Some hundred anti aircraft guns were deployed along the escarpment as the last defensive barrier. By the time I got there, the numbers reaching the skies above Wrotham were much decreased, as our armies in France had overrun a lot of launching sites.

The V2 rockets were coming regularly each day and night. It was a strange sensation as you could hear the echo of the explosions away north in London, and a few moments later the sound of the whoosh as it entered the airspace above us. There was no defence against it, other than overrunning the launch sites. We were retaliating, and it was the first time I had seen a 500 strong US Air Force bomber stream going overhead. It was absolutely frightening, and woe betides anyone caught under it when they reached their target.

The camp was in a rural setting, with Nissen huts spread out under the trees. Back to Nissen hut accommodation again, but these were a little superior to those in Richmond. The staff was made up mainly of Sergeants from the Guards Regiments. Their standards were very high, and if you fell below, they made it very clear that wasn't accepted. They did have to call us Sir, which was a big change, but they were the bosses. You had to toe the line even when being ridiculed, as they seemed to have the power of life and death over you. A word from them, and you could be off the course, never to return. My fellow Cadets were a good bunch of highly educated and motivated chaps, many from posh, public schools and affluent families. The staff tried to break us by pushing us over our physical limits, but we stuck together and never faltered.

The 200-foot escarpment was always a challenge, but after the hills at the back of the Holywood barracks, it was all very manageable. The biggest test was the assault course. It was a tough one, which took about 20 minutes to complete, and really tested you. Whenever we did it, which was usually daily, we were told we were not putting enough energy into it, and always had to go round a lung bursting second time. Also, I think I dug more slit trenches during my stay at Wrotham than the rest of my army career put together. There was also an awful lot more night work, which I never did like. The best part of the course for me was that we spent a week learning to drive trucks, and also a week on motorcycles. At the time, it was a cold snap with snow and ice, so motorcycling wasn't much fun!

It was towards the end of 1944 that we were told that we would be posted to India to complete our education at an Officers Training School (OTS) there. That was a shock, as we were all anticipating joining units in France for the last push to defeat Germany. So, the year drew to an end. The allied advance in France had been halted on the borders of Germany. If only they had got better intelligence on German forces before the Arnhem episode, the year would have ended better. The US forces in the Pacific were going great guns also, and the only sad thing was that the Japanese were still on the border with India. Is that where I would end up in due course?

After a couple more weeks at Wrotham, we were sent home on a seven day embarkation leave. Such a short time to say cheerio to family and friends! My Mother was very weepy at the thought of her only son going away overseas for such a long time, I am sure she had convinced herself that I would not return. The week was a strange period for me. I was now geared out as an Officer Cadet, wearing white flashes under my cap badge and shoulders, and I was authorised to wear a collar and tie. This totally confused the many service men stationed at York. They invariably saluted me as they passed by, and I saluted them back.

There was no need for it at all, as I was not yet a commissioned officer. The week passed too quickly, and I soon found myself heading back south on the train to London.

The Embarkation Centre was located at the Great Eastern Hotel in the middle of London. It was a very posh hotel before the war, before it was requisitioned for this purpose. It had a lot of its shine and glamour over the war years, but it proved excellent accommodation. We had a lot of spare time, and were allowed out and about, so it was a first class centre for us, being so near to all the attractions of Central London.

I was in a batch of around a hundred cadets who were introduced to our batch commander. He was called Lt.Col R.N.D.Frier, and had the insignia MAHAR on his shoulder flashes. Meeting him was a life changer. Luck, or that angel of mine? He was returning to join his Battalion in India after a period of leave. He was an affable, approachable officer, quite unlike any I had met before. He wore the ribbon of the MC, which he had been awarded for an action near Tobruk, in the North African campaign, whilst serving with a Punjabi battalion in the 4th Indian Division. I likened him to more of a benevolent headmaster of a school than a seasoned Army Officer. We were issued with tropical kit and dosed up with all kind of medicines. We also got issued with Roman Urdu text books, which we had to study.

Life still had its moments of excitement. I went to watch Tottenham Hotspurs football team play at White Hart Lane - their famous ground. It was a Saturday afternoon, with about 25,000 spectators in the ground watching the match. Thirty minutes in, the unmistakable sound of a Vl doodlebug was heard, and it was plainly visible flying at about 5000 feet, coming towards us. When it was directly overhead, the engine cut out, and it started its steep dive to earth. It exploded about 400 yards from t he football ground - rather too close for comfort. It was one of the last ones to make it to London, as launching pads were still being overrun and put out of use. The V2s continued to fall on us, but the chances of getting a direct hit were very low, so it didn't affect our lives that much.

The great day (February 14th) arrived, and we were on the train to Liverpool, where our ship awaited. It was called the

Durban Castle, a pre war, luxury liner, which plied the route to South Africa. There wasn't much luxury about it now in its job as a troopship. It held about 2000 service personnel, as well as its crew, and was overcrowded. Our draft was lucky to be berthed on a deck above the waterline, in a fairly large room. We were issued with hammocks, which we slung above the mess tables that filled the room. It was a brand new experience, but once you got used to getting in and out of them, sleeping in them was reasonably comfortable. It took just a minute or two to pack them away in the morning, and there we were at our mess tables, having breakfast. All portholes were blacked out, of course, so it was rather claustrophobic.

We had regular lifeboat drills, as we would be going well into the North Atlantic, where the modern U boats still had the capacity to sink a lot of ships. In the Irish Sea, we joined with many other ships to form a large convoy. There were several large liners as I remember, such as the Georgic, Strathavon, all of 20,000 to 30,000 tons, and in all must have been carrying about 20,000 service personnel. We had a fine escort of Destroyers, Corvettes and Frigates, together with a small Aircraft Carrier.

We spent about 5 days in the North Atlantic, giving the Bay of Biscay a big detour. We woke up one morning to see North Africa and Gibraltar on the horizon. Then, into the Mediterranean, where the convoy broke up, and we went our individual ways at our own speeds, along the North African coast towards Suez. There were reports of U boats still operating in these waters, but we made safe passage.

By this time, the weather was warming up, which was much more acceptable than the cold and wind of England and the Atlantic. Days on board passed reasonably quickly. There were always some lectures, keep fit periods, along with plenty of time to relax and play cards or board games such as Monopoly.

There were moments of high interest and excitement. Part of a detachment of airmen included a Flight Sergeant Physical Training Instructor named Freddy Mills. He was the current light heavyweight boxing champion of Great Britain, and also the Empire Champion. The Captain of the ship thought if Freddy would display his boxing prowess each day, it would raise the morale of all on board. Freddy agreed that each day, he would box 20 opponents, with a one minute round for each. A boxing ring was set up on deck, where most of the passengers could get a good view. Everyone got the chance to volunteer, and hundreds of names were put in the hat, with a lucky draw for 20 each day. I got lucky, and spent a minute in the ring with the Champion.

Freddy was a well-built lad, with muscles like Tarzan, and all his body was covered with a thick mat of hair. It was like boxing with a gorilla! Freddy wore big boxing gloves, so a blow would be dispersed and not hurt as much. We wore normal boxing gloves. Most fights, including my own, were just gentle sparring, with Freddy blocking any punches with his extra big gloves, and him not throwing any big punches. However, each day there were a number of smart alecks who thought they were tough enough to have a real go at Freddy. It always ended the same, with Freddy recognising them quickly, and him throwing a KO punch - to the vast cheers of the spectators. It was all good-natured fun, but it allows me to boast that I fought a draw with a boxing champion!

After the war, Freddy became World Champion. On retirement, he got involved with Soho gangsters, and was found dead one morning. The killer was never found, and it was a poor end to what had been a good boxer.

I found I also had plenty of time to talk to Lt.Col Frier. The regimental flash of MAHAR intrigued me. We had been told of all the Indian Regiments we could join, but the Mahars had never been mentioned. He told me about the history of the Mahars, and how in the present emergency they had been accepted again as a recognised Regiment. It was sufficient to whet my appetite, and I vowed that I would make the Mahars my first choice Indian Regiment. We were soon through the Suez Canal, a great experience, and then down the Red Sea, passed Aden, with the weather getting hotter. Then, after four weeks on board ship, there we were in Bombay - safe and sound, and somewhat wiser.

We disembarked the following day, and were soon on the impressive electric train to Kalyan, a transit camp some 30-miles north east of Bombay. This was were we would spend a short period of time getting our land legs back, and acclimatising to our new situation. Kalyan was a vast military camp, which you passed through both coming into and going out of India. What a strange but exciting feeling, being in a new country, and all that was in front of us for the rest of the year. We were housed in big open plan Barrack Huts, with about thirty people in each. Our charpoys (new to us) were in three rows of ten, each with mosquito netting. It was remarkably comfortable after a month of sleeping on hammocks. We used the Sergeants' mess facilities for eating and recreational purposes. I can remember a supply shop called Shamshuddins, which was like a modern supermarket, full of loads of desirable items and food that we hadn't seen for a very long time, so we made good use of it, and I'm sure Shamshuddin made a pretty good profit too.

The blazing sun was hard to cope with at the start, and there was little green vegetation, with the earth like dried mud and very dusty. They let us take life very leisurely. The war now was getting progressively better, with the collapse of the German army and the 14th Army starting to advance with prospects of victory in Burma. After a very good three weeks of relaxation, the orders came through for us to report to Bangalore OTS in a week's time. But then, my luck ran out. I began to suffer very bad bouts of nose bleeding. There was no stopping it, and the medical people thought it was getting too serious. I was shipped off to see a specialist doctor in Bombay, who kept me under observation for a couple of weeks.

He seemed to get control over it, and I was finally released back to Kalyan. Alas, my draft had already gone to Bangalore, and I was alone. After a short delay, I managed to make my way, alone, to Bangalore, to meet up with my old buddies. I was now a month behind them, and the inevitable happened as it was decided to put me back, to join the next draft, which was due shortly. It was not really what I wanted, but I just had to accept it with good grace.

Bangalore was a wonderful city. It was located on some higher ground, and had such a superb climate - more like a typical English summer than Kalyan could ever hope for. There was an abundance of greenery, with plenty of water from the monsoon rains, which came at regular and predictable intervals.

We were housed in individual rooms, with sheets on the beds, and plenty of assistance with cleaning and laundry etc. They issued us with bicycles to get around camp, as it was extensive. It was named Aundh Camp, and was situated on a plain some 2 or 3 miles from the centre of the city. It was a tough, but enjoyable course from which I learned a lot. I had a day off when VE Day was declared, with great celebrations. I was so pleased for my family in York, that their ordeal was now over, and life could start to get more normal, and better for them.

At the same time, I also got an increase in pay, as I managed to pass the Urdu examination - thanks being due to an excellent Munshi, who sweated blood trying to drill the language into us. We also began receiving Japanese Campaign Pay of 69 rupees a month - equivalent to just over £5 at the time. Strangely, this got paid right up to the day I left India, even though the war ended in 1945.

There were plenty of sporting activities at the OTS. The most memorable was when the football team was picked to play against a touring UK international 11. This was all part of trying to keep the troops happy. Many good footballers joined the Army, so it was easy for them to pick a touring party to play a number of matches. We had a good team, as they were all young lads. The touring team had many famous names, including Dennis Compton and his brother Leslie, who played both football and cricket for England. Another one was Andy Black - an inside forward, who played for Heart of Midlothian and Scotland. No mean opposition in that lot!

It was one goal each with around five minutes left, and the referee awarded them a penalty. Dennis Compton picked up the ball and put it on the spot. I was the goalkeeper, and was jumping up and down, ready to dive left or right, depending on his run up and the angle of his body. No such luck, as he gave nothing away with his demeanour. I stood stock still in the middle of the goal, and he shot the ball very fast at me. I put up my arms to save my face being hit, and the ball struck them and sailed safely over the bar. We drew, with 1-1 being the final score.

Afterwards, I was speaking to Dennis in the dressing room, and he said he was not sure which way I was going to dive, so he shot straight down the middle. I chalked that one up to me!

Dennis later went on to be more famous at cricket, being England's best batsman for a long period just after the war.

In August, the war in the Far East came to an abrupt end, with the use of the atom bomb. We were on some exercises in the jungle when we heard a bugle sounding a strange call. It turned out to mean "No parades today," and we got back to Bangalore to celebrate. I'm sure my family at home said a little prayer of thanks also, as my life expectancy had just shot up by many years. If there had been a bullet meant for me, I am sure it would have been shot at me in Operation Zipper, which was a plan to capture Singapore in 1946. So, thank you to the Americans, who had made the right decision. The bombs killed a lot of people, but not a fraction of the number who would have perished if we had fought at Singapore and also invaded Japan. Following that, we did see a number of POWs who were in a very poor state after their captivity. It did not endear the Japanese to us. The Course now seemed a bit of an anticlimax, with no more war to fight, but we kept our heads down to the final passing out parade.

I finally became a commissioned Lieutenant with the Argyll and Sutherland Highlanders, with the service number 364311. Mission achieved! I certainly was not the top cadet, but I think I was fairly well-up the pecking order. I had fairly firm principles that I worked to, and I think I stayed faithful to them. My psyche was more geared to love, joy, peace, kindness, faithfulness, self-control and gentleness, rather than war, killing, maiming, revenge and general nastiness.

I fired rockets at German planes over London as part of my duty. I only hope I did not kill or maim anyone. It was rather an impersonal way to fight, a bit different to killing someone at close quarters. I am pleased that I was never put to that test. I am sure I would not have been found wanting, but it would have left a big scar on my conscience.

We spent Christmas in Bangalore, and a group of us celebrated by going to a Chinese restaurant in Cavalry Road in the centre of the city. It had a Christmas meal of 15 courses! That was way over the top of course, but a lot of them were very small. It was an act of shear indulgence to celebrate after years of austerity. For a couple of weeks, we moved to a new campsite right in the main street of Bangalore. It was next to an Italian

POW camp, and they were very keen on playing football. We used to look over the wall and cheer them on. They were very good, and always played with a couple of thousand of them as spectators. We were waiting for our postings to our Indian Regiments. We had a choice from what appeared to be a comprehensive list of Units. The Mahar Regiment however, was omitted. I wrote their name in pen at the bottom of the list, and put my tick against it. My Guardian Angel must have been watching over me, as, with great joy, I was posted to Kamptee to join the Mahars. Mission accomplished!

Early in January, I set out for Kamptee, calling at Madras for a two-day visit on the way. I remember going to a horse race meeting for the first time in my life, and found it most confusing. My friends urged me to place a small bet on one race. My horse won, but when I went to collect my modest winnings, the bookmaker had vanished, so nothing was forthcoming. It really turned me off horse racing for the rest of my life.

I eventually arrived at Kamptee to be warmly greeted at the Regimental Centre. I stayed there for a couple of weeks, and there was little or no activity going on. I only remember the Officers' Mess and the Bungalow on the hill, which I shared with three others. I cannot remember any office buildings, parade ground or accommodation for any troops at all. I led a very sheltered and peaceful existence. I suppose the high tension that had been the norm during the war, had been overtaken by a more laid back approach. I didn't complain, and really enjoyed the break with little responsibility, in what were beautiful surroundings.

At the start of February, I was informed that I had been posted to join 3MAHAR, stationed at Fort Sandeman in North Baluchistan. My dream had come true, as Lt Col Frier, my draft commander on my way out to India, commanded 3MAHAR. Mike Cauldwell and Bill Griffin were also posted there at the same time. This posting meant a long rail journey to reach our destination. We packed all our worldly goods into our kit bags, and along with our bedding rolls, set off in good heart. We went northwards, and must have passed through Delhi during the night, because I have no recollection of seeing it. The train took us to Ludhiana, where we had two meals during a long wait. Then, it was a journey to Lahore, where there was another connection to be made. We had to spend two nights in a hotel in Lahore, and we spent our time sightseeing. It was a very beautiful and interesting city, with many fine buildings and public gardens.

The next leg of our journey was to Quetta. It was a long haul and it was interesting to see the change in countryside as we went west, with the lush green vegetation changing to a more arid landscape, and after crossing the Indus some spectacular hills and mountains. We eventually arrived in Quetta and again had to spend four nights in a hotel before starting on the last leg of our journey to Fort Sandeman. By this time we found it very cold, and there was still snow on the mountain peaks that encircled Quetta.

A huge earthquake had largely destroyed the place in 1935, when some 60,000 people perished. We found little evidence of the damage, as much rebuilding work had been done. There was certainly a change in appearance of the townsfolk. We were now clearly in Muslim territory, and it was very different to the Hindu way of life to which we had become accustomed. All part of the learning curve we were on.

Fort Sandeman was located just over 200 miles north of Quetta, and the last leg of the journey was by a narrow gauge light railway, which snaked its way up the Zhob Valley - about a twelve hour journey. We arrived weary, but full of anticipation, at Fort Sandeman, the end of the line on February 21st. Until the Zhob Valley expedition in 1884, the area was practically unknown to the Europeans, and in 1889, the Zhob Valley and Gomal Pass were taken under the control of the British Government. In December, the town of Zhob, then known as Apozai, was occupied by the British, and named Fort Sandeman after Sir Robert Sandeman, the First Governor of Zhob Province.

3MAHAR were part of the Zhob Brigade, which was the northern most regular military force in Baluchistan, just a few miles from the Afghan border, and at the southern end of the Frontier, which stretched northeast wards for some 400 miles. Fort Sandeman was also the headquarters of the Zhob Militia, part of the Frontier Corps. These British officered forces of tribal irregulars, who also included the Gilit Scouts, the Tochi Scouts, the Kurram Militia, the South Waziristan Scouts, and perhaps the best known, Khyber Rifles, kept the day to day peace.

The Zhob Militia traced its origins back to the 1870s, and was the oldest of these local levies. In the 19th century, the thinking was that the Zhob bordered South Waziristan and Afghanistan and, if secured, would make a very defensible border should the Russians attack through Afghanistan. All part of the 'Great Game' as it was known in those times. They manned small, often isolated forts and posts throughout the territory - the work being done by foot patrols of platoon strength, often covering 40 miles a day over harsh ground. They were incredibly tough, and discipline was very strict. Zhob Brigade was a regular garrison force, showing the flag and demonstrating that this was part of British India.

On occasion it would mount a column northwards to Sambaza, which was the HQ of the left wing of the Zhob Militia, to link up with units of the Wana Brigade coming south through Waziristan to the border post of Gul Kutch. Generally, Fort Sandeman was a quiet post in frontier terms, though that was a position maintained only by strict vigilance and observance of all frontier rules.

Fort Sandeman was built around several small rocky outcrops, on a plain at some 4,700 feet, ringed by distant mountains of around 11,000 feet. The cantonment was purely military, but there were a few locals, their houses and bazaar. The place was dominated by The Castle, which was the residence of the Political Agent, the effective civilian ruler of the area. He had the final say, and even the Brigade CO could not move without his say so. It was a dangerous job, as a Political Agent was murdered at Fort Sandeman in the 1920s. One of its advantages was that it was mosquito free, due to its high elevation. Its climate was extreme, with very cold snow and icy winters, and red-hot baking sun in the summers. To us young British officers, it seemed a place of mystery and potential danger, which we looked forward to enjoying.

We were warmly greeted by 3Mahar, and I was pleased that Lt.Col Frier recognised me. They welcomed extra help, as they had been under staffed, and now there was a good flow of new talent to take advantage of. I joined the other young second lieutenants who had recently arrived: Keith Gascoigne, Tom Oliver, Freddy Evans, Tich Smart, and also Jim Bridge, Freddy Lewin, Ken Bradley, Ken Moore and Ken McKenzie who arrived slightly later. There were also three new Indian Officers arriving: PR Choudhary, Mohain Singh Power and Dost Mohammed.

We were all very friendly with each other and got on with life extremely well. I think the more senior officers welcomed us very well indeed, appreciating that our presence was lightening their workload. The senior Indian Officers, who were the backbone of the Battalion, were particularly good. The Adjutant, Maj BN Mittra - "Mitt"- was a gentle-mannered Bengali who had been a prison officer, and was widely loved and respected. He was very popular with junior British officers, and wrote a History of the Regiment in 1972.

Capt. LG Shinde was a splendid character who had been a ranker in the Maharatta Light Infantry, and though enormously experienced, was slightly shy in the presence of more sophisticated officers. He was much loved, and known, unofficially, as "Uncle" by the jawans (Indian soldiers). Capt. BN Upadhay was a very bright little Bihari. He was a brilliant footballer, tough as nails as he could kick a ball the length of the field with his bare feet, and was the best header of a ball that I knew.

Capt. MS Dhillon was a long-serving Sikh former ranker, and kept a tight ship as Quartermaster. Maj. Krishna Rao was immense. He commanded A Company and also acted as 2I/C. I always remember him proposing the Loyal Toast whenever we had an official dinner night in the mess. I was well over 6 foot tall, but I still had to look up to him, and he had a much more powerful physique than me. I had to look up to him intellectually as well, as he was far beyond me. Even in those early days, one could tell he was destined for higher things. What a privilege to serve such a person, and be accepted as a friend! In later years, he commanded the Battalion with great honour, eventually becoming Chief of Army Staff (COAS) of the Indian Army. The top man in every respect. He was looked on as the Father of the Regiment, and did more than anyone to enhance the profile and reputation of the Regiment. On retirement, he served India again as Governor of the three states of Manipur, Tripura and Nagaland. Subsequently, he was given the hot potato job of Governor of Kashmir, which he performed with distinction. I continued to get Christmas greeting cards from him throughout the years until his sad death.

The Subedar Major (SM) Bolaji Ranjane also deserves a mention. He had served with one of the Labour Battalions, which were the only military openings available to Mahars before the raising of the regiment in 1941. Previously he had been SM to 2Mahar from June 42 to October 43, and had come to 3Mahar on its raising in November 43, and remained as SM until September 49. He was a portly but good-humoured old sweat, who took his duties seriously, and kept junior British Officers in touch with how things should be done. The Head Clerk - Rajindernath Sibal spoke excellent English, and eventually retired as a Junior Commissioned Officer (JCO). The Battalion Havildar Major Dattu Kamble became a JCO, and was Subedar Major of 3Mahar later on, and eventually became an Honorary Captain. Good for him! It is also mentioning the Officers' Mess Havildar, Muniappa, whom we regarded as being a little too clever for his boots. They were all part of the family, so there was joy when people succeeded.

During my time with 3Mahar, there was a constant flow of officers coming in and out. It was hard to keep up with things. Other names spring to mind: Maj. Goddard who became a Company Commander, Maj. Ken Leacock came back from leave, but left after a short stay. He was a legendary drinker in the Mess, who could sink 20 whiskies a night without any distress at all. He lived in Canada after the war to a good age. Maj. Khalid Jan arrived, and he eventually took over as CO when Lt.Col Frier went home for some leave. Maj. Rawson-Gardiner from the Rajputana Rifles (RAJ RIFFS), who had experience with Medium Machine Guns – Vickers (MMGs) stayed a short time. I got the impression that he somewhat looked down his nose at the MAHARS as being very inferior to the RAJ-RIFFS. There was no loss when he left!

At the same time, we had a Capt. NA Nair MBE from the Madras Regt. He had been awarded his decoration when in the Merchant navy, having repeatedly dived into shark infested waters to rescue survivors of a torpedoed ship. I found him very over-the-top, anti British, and most difficult to get along with. There was also Capt. Bhandari - an eloquent and jovial Sikh, who commanded D Company. A Capt. Stuart Plomly - an Anglo Indian - spent a little time with us, as did Lt. Khan and Capt. Bush. It was hard to keep track of them all!

A Brig. JJ PURVES DSO MC commanded the Zhob Brigade. The senior infantry battalion was 1st Battalion (Wellesleys) Rajputana Rifles, commanded by Lt.Col Forbes, which we treated with great respect. It was one of the oldest units in the Indian Army, having indeed served under Wellesely, and it had a tremendous fighting record during the war. It eventually became 3rd Battalion, Brigade of Guards in 1949. The third Zhob infantry Battalion was 6th Madras. We treated them with considerably less respect, regarding it from our not altogether unbiased view as being distinctly inferior to the MAHARS.

Other units making up the Brigade were "A" Troop 10 Independent Light Anti Aircraft Battery when greater fire power was required; 69 Animal Transport Company (RIASC), whose mules were of great help to us; Zhobsigs - a small detachment of British other ranks, maintaining signal links and supplying other technical help when needed; 9 Independent Field Ambulance - they used camels for stretcher bearing, one stretcher on each side, which swayed alarmingly up and down. There was also a small repair workshop. There must have been 2,500 service personnel in all.

I was appointed as 2nd in command of D Company, under the control of Capt Bhandari. I was also given a choice of being Mess Officer or Finance Officer. I would have been useless as Mess Officer, so, with my background in banking, I opted for Finance Officer. I found it easy keeping the accounts in order, and being in charge of what we called The Treasure Chest, where all the hard cash was kept. Our lines, Suvla Lines, adjoined those of the Zhob Militia. I can still hear the drone of their bagpipes as raw recruits learned, with difficulty, how to march rather than covering ground with the long loping stride of the tribesman. They were very smart when fully trained. Our military routines soon developed into a regular pattern. This comprised morning parade, drill, weapon training, assault course and the like.

Afternoons were generally put aside for sport. In such an isolated spot, boredom could easily set in, and that would have been no good. Better to keep everybody occupied with a bit of competitive sport.

There was plenty on offer. We had pitches for football and hockey, and volleyball was easy to set up and very popular. I played all three, and enjoyed it. The Battalion played in the Murree Brewery hockey competition, and we reached the semifinal. I wasn't in the team, but our goalie got injured, and I stepped in to take his place. I played a blinder by moving out quickly and blocking shots before they could damage us. We were posted soon after so could take no further part in the event. I was always picked at volleyball. Being tall was an asset as I could dominate play at the net. We were keen on our athletics, and there were some really excellent performers.

Evenings were usually spent in relaxation, with the nightly distribution of the rum ration to the Jawans (Indian Soldiers) during the coldest weather. All these things took second place when the more important Brigade or Battalion operational activities were required. The Officers' Mess proved a haven of peace, and many happy hours were spent there. It wasn't a lavish Mess, but it had the bare necessities. A table tennis table was a favourite, and hours of practice can make for some good players. There was a good bar if one wanted to indulge. The occasional game of Mess rugby was played, which must be the most brutal game in the world, but we all survived. Halfway through our stay, we moved into the much superior Brigade Mess, which had fallen vacant. I can remember a solitary picture on the wall of a Mahar sepoy, drawn in pencil by Capt. Mortlemans. I wonder where it is now? I know it was used on a Regimental Christmas card some years later. The CO was always keen on playing the card game Bridge on several evenings a week.

All officers were more or less obliged to attend the games, which went on to the late hours. Small amounts of money were wagered on these games, and settlement time was monthly on the Mess bill. It was quite a complicated game with lots of strange conventions. If you knew them, you were in with a chance of breaking even. I had never played the game, and was totally ignorant of the rules. Those who knew the rules never had any incentive to reveal them, as they were always in credit at the month end. I never did know the rules, until many years later when I had tuition from an instructor. I realise now that I never stood a chance.

We were lucky also, that when the Political Officer was away from his home in The Castle, he allowed us to use the facilities there. He had a specially built billiard room, complete with a competition size table. Tiers of benches capable of seating 50 or so spectators overlooked the table. We spent many happy evenings with snooker and billiards. The table must have weighed a ton, and how they managed to get it in the remote location of The Castle, I will never know. He also had a very good bar there, plus a small pool for swimming, which was always very yucky, a squash court, and facilities for showing films. Lucky us!

The junior officers slept in Bungalows, with four individual bedrooms to a block. There was a good balcony stretching the length of the block. In summertime, it was ideal for sleeping outside under the stars. We smartened up our rooms by buying some good carpets. A camel train, carrying a great range, was travelling on the much-used trade route from the north into India, and camped locally for the night. Good bargains were struck, and many carpets changed hands. I had four of them, and I managed to get them all home in due course, and they were used for many long years. We also spent many long hours playing cards in our billets - nothing as complicated as Bridge, rather the simple games of Poker and Pontoon.

One thing we did lack was music. We were out of range of any radio stations, but luckily the battalion we relieved left an old wind up portable record player, with 8 old 78 records, which lasted for about 4 minutes for each side played, though several of the sides were scratched and unplayable. We also had no supplies of gramophone needles, and had to improvise. The records were played continually several times, on a daily basis, and were left behind for those who took over from us. The tunes are still etched permanently in my mind.

If I was ever invited to play my 8 favourite records on the radio show Desert Island Discs, my choice would be easy: one side of the overture to Carmen, by Bizet. It starts off all Spanish, but after a couple of minutes, there is a pause, and then another haunting tune is played. To this day I get goose bumps when I hear it, as I am drawn back to Fort Sandeman, with its isolation and the majestic view of high mountains. Next, the tune Panis Angelicus by Cesar Franck, which was a serious religious work sung in Latin. We couldn't understand a word of it, but it was very inspiring. There were two sides of Eine Kleine Nachtmusik by Mozart, always one of my favourites, then a very good rendering of O Sole Mio, sung by the Italian tenor Caruso. One side of a Gilbert and Sullivan operetta with A Policeman's Lot is Not a Happy One from Pirates of Penzance. Two sides of New Orleans jazz played by Jelly Roll Morton and his Red Hot Peppers, which was sensational. Finally, the newest and least damaged record of Spike Jones and his City Slickers, playing Chloe and Leave the Dishes in the Sink, Ma. He had a good bunch of musicians, who always started off sounding really serious, but soon changing to maniacal bangs, whistles, drums, tins rattling and doors slamming. There were, however, more serious matters to contend with than enjoying ourselves. The frontier was a dangerous place, which demanded our full attention.

Each week, there was a duty company allocated to dealing with any unusual activities around Fort Sandeman. With 12 rifle companies available in the Brigade, it was only one stint every three months. We had certain routine jobs to undertake during our period of duty. There were a number of concrete strong points around Fort Sandeman, capable of holding a company of soldiers, and to be used in the event of Fort Sandeman being threatened. They were provisioned with food and ammunition, and all of them were located in order to give covering fire to each other. There were plenty of firing slits in the structures, with range cards showing distances to prominent features. Each week, the duty company had to check the distances with a long measuring tape. It was astounding how many alterations had to be made. Many of the objects were huge boulders weighing many tons, and, at times, they varied by 30 or 40 feet.

Fort Sandeman was on a fault line, and was prone to earthquakes of big magnitude, which moved these objects about, and so the need for re-measuring so often. The earth moved a number of times during our tenure, but nothing as big as the Quetta earthquake in 1935. We also had to help with well digging. If a local village got the support of the Political Agent to improve the water supply, he called in the army to help out. We always used to have a platoon around to protect us at the site, whilst the jawans used spades and explosives to dig deep. You would thing the locals would show a bit of gratitude for the help given, but we didn't trust them an inch, and thus the defensive requirement all the time we were there. Another memorable occasion when we were called out was when the train carrying ammunition to us was derailed about 20 miles out from us. We had to speed to secure the train and transfer the supplies to trucks for the last stage of the journey. There was also the time we had to go to Quetta by road to exchange some trucks. We broke down about half way there, near Hindubagh, and had to spend a night in a guest hut until we could get on the move again. Hindubagh was renamed Muslimbagh in 1960.

I encountered one really serious incident towards the end of 1946. We had a call out late one afternoon to a nearby habitation, with a report that the small water pumping station had been tampered with. We drove out about 10 miles to the local Zhob Militia post, where we proceeded on foot up the valley to our destination. The pumping station was in a little concrete obelisk with metal door, which had a big padlock on it. My Subedar and myself, standing about a foot apart, had just come to the conclusion that it was a false alarm, when there was a rifle shot. A bullet, probably a regulation.303, passed between the Subedar and myself. It was so close that you could feel the changed air pressure. It hit the rock behind us, and ricocheted away into the air. I felt a wasp-like sting in my neck as both of us hit the ground and rolled away. The defensive platoon was soon firing back, and a hot pursuit ensued for some twenty minutes.

The sniper knew the territory, and went off at high speed, and there was no way we could have caught up with him. We were now a fair distance away from our transport at the Zhob Militia post, and the sun was going down quickly. We had no option but to admit defeat, and get back to Fort Sandeman before it became dark. An entry in the logbook ended the affair. That is, except for the banter at being so incompetent when I got back to the Mess!

No harm seemed to have been done, as there was just a small trickle of blood on my neck, which was soon wiped away. It was some ten years later, after I was married, that my wife commented on a bump on my neck, which seemed to be getting bigger. I went to see my doctor, by the name of Dench (father of the world famous actress Dame Judy Dench). He took a sharp scalpel and cut the bump, squeezed it, and out popped a slim metal fragment, which was as sharp as a razor. I kept it as a souvenir, but somewhere in a house move, it got lost. I still had repercussions some 50 plus years later, when I required a scan on my head. I had to sign a form to guarantee that I had never had any metal in my head. I had to declare my story, and was subjected to x-rays, which showed I was now metal free. I wonder what happened to the bad lad who fired the shot? I wish him well, and thank him for being such a rotten shot!

We had many of the usual military routines - a Battalion Camp, a Brigade Column, drafts of new recruits to be trained, and, towards the end of the year, a completely new role to be learned. Towards the end of March, preparations began for the Battalion Camp at Kapip, about ten miles from Fort Sandeman, on the Dera Ismail Khan road, which began next day with a march to the camp site. The idea of the camp was to practice the techniques used in frontier warfare on a Battalion basis, so we could fit in with the brigade Column, which was due in April. It was a case of learning to be advanced guards, picketing practice, and rear-guard and withdrawal skills. It ended with field firing and bivouacking.

The camp was marred by a very nasty accident, when one of the portable gas cylinders, used to heat the metal plates on which chapattis were cooked, blew up and badly burned one of the cooks. He finished off by being taken to Quetta for hospital treatment.

The first week in April brought a flag showing exercise, when a Brigade Column moved northward to Sambaza, from which a detachment went onwards to Gul Kutch, to link with Wana Brigade from Waziristan. This entailed a ponderous march along the road, in a kind of rolling box formation, with the soft units - medical, transport etc. in the middle, and the infantry battalions at the front and end of the column, and mounting pickets on the hills on each side. The leading Battalion would post the pickets in advance of the column, while the rear Battalion brought the pickets down after the main body had passed through. It was a tough job for the pickets, as some of the hills were very steep, and after getting down, they had to move smartly forward to rejoin their units. Each night, the entire column halted in a square defensive position, about the size of a football pitch, with pickets posted on surrounding hills. It housed about 2,000 men and 100 animals, mostly mules. A wall three feet high was constructed in next to no time, and when we left, it was demolished, ready to provide the stones the next time we were there. We ate our evening meal in the Mess tent by the light of lamps that attracted hundreds of large, vicious insects, whose corpses littered the table by the time the meal had ended.

Each morning, we stood to at dawn, weapons facing outwards for an attack by tribesman, which never happened. It was a column whose tedium was relieved by various incidents. There was one Subaltern who was detailed in the previous night's reconnaissance to take a company up on a long ridge, and move forward as a rolling picket keeping that side of the column covered. Unfortunately, the hill he chose was not the one pointed out the night before by Frigger Frier in his briefing. He was incandescent, and as the unfortunate lad came down again, he tripped and hurt himself. He always maintained he was right, and thankfully for him, the Old Man had calmed down by the time he returned.

The next day, as we moved on to Tor Ghundi, Bill Griffin, who was looking after the 3-inch mortars, had an altercation with the Old Man about the siting of his 3-inch mortars to give covering fire. Again, there was a very irate CO, but all ended peacefully.

At Sambaza, we had two nights' rest, recce and a Brigade field-firing scheme. Due to miscommunication, supporting artillery fire was called down onto a hill that a company just received the order to advance up. They received the order to cease-fire before anyone got hurt. Then, back via Tor Ghundi, Naweoba and onto Fort Sandeman by truck. This kind of column was repeated every four months or so, no doubt to impress on the locals that we were the bosses. I doubt they ever saw it that way!

A significant change came when a Battalion of the Maharatta Light Infantry arrived, replacing the Rajputana Rifles. We had some apprehension about this, as there was little love lost between the MAHAR and Maharattas, who all came from Maharashtra, where the Maharattas were high caste Hindus and the MAHARS were untouchables who did all the menial work. In the end, it worked all right, mainly due to army discipline and the efforts of two very good Subedar Majors. In the view of the young British Subalterns, we were superior, and we knew far more of frontier warfare than they did, and they had to learn from our example.

It wasn't all work, and we had various highlights such as sports' day run by the animal detachment. This was where I first saw the art of tent pegging by their mounted troops. We had a sports' day of our own on 1st November to celebrate our third birthday. I also remember Mooltan Day, celebrating a battle honour of the Battalion. There were big celebrations in their Mess. Frigger Frier decided, at some unearthly hour of the night, that we should go and spice up the celebrations. He took a load of us in a Bren carrier, which managed to wreck the door of their Mess. Nobody seemed to care, and we celebrated with them till the sun came up.

One other experience is worth recounting. It was the first Sunday in September 1946. It was a free day for me. The sun was shining, and I was dozing mid-morning with not a care in the world. I heard footsteps approaching, and found the Adjutant's runner fast approaching me. "Makan tost Sahib, Adjutant Sahib wishes to see you ek dum (right away) Sahib." The jawans always claimed that my name McIntosh was too difficult to pronounce, Makan (butter) and Tost (toast) was much better! They always seemed to have a smile on their face when they said it. I received Christmas cards from India much later, addressed in the same fashion.

Pretty good improvisation though, which never worried me. I reported to Mitt the Adjutant, who quickly told me it was the Old Man who wanted me. Gracious me, what had I done wrong? He wanted to know if I had ever sat on an Army Court of Enquiry (the answer was no). He had been asked to provide a junior officer to be third member of a Court of Enquiry to be held in Loralai on the coming Tuesday. Loralai was a Battalion outpost some 80 miles east of Fort Sandeman. I enquired what it was about, and he gave a vague answer of interference with army transport. I made a slightly facetious comment, asking if someone had been getting at the mules. He wasn't very happy with me, and in no uncertain terms indicated that I was slightly immature for such a venture. I managed, with a bit of pleading, to change his mind, and he relented. He dismissed me, putting the burden of all the arrangements on me. He also gave his very stern advice – "you are going to represent the Zhob Brigade and 3MAHAR, but most of all me. Do not let me down. My advice to you McIntosh is to follow the lead of the Senior Officer who will be highly experienced in these matters." So, my restful Sunday was over, and it was a frenzied rush to make all the arrangements.

The road to Loralai was just a dirt track, up and down high hills, round bends with big drops at the side, down into dried up nullahs, and the anticipated average speed would be about 10mph. It was all over restricted territory, where an escort was necessary. My own company could act as escort, but had to be back to base for nightfall, so could only take me halfway. I had to arrange with Loralai to send out a unit to take over as escort. Then there was catering, and contact with the Zhob Militia for their posts to track me. It was endless!

The Monday arrived, and the journey completed to plan with no difficulties. I met with the Chairman, who was a senior Major who looked very old and weary to me. He told me the case was about a damaged bicycle. I was aghast, as I had already expended enough money to buy a dozen new bicycles. He gave me a stern talk on how small things had to be put right to prevent bigger things happening, with the extra advice that I should follow his lead, just as the CO had told me. The other member was a Sikh captain. The next day, we met at 10.00am in a practically empty company office. It was bare apart from a table and three chairs for the Committee, and a desk for a clerk who was recording the proceedings. There was a paper pad and pencil for each of us to jot down our thoughts.

There were a number of witnesses, who all gave similar accounts of the incident. The Officer in charge of the Transport Unit, followed by the JCO, Havildar and the sepoy who had actually issued the bike. It was simple - the bike was in good order when it was issued, and it had been returned just a few minutes later damaged and unusable. Hardly rocket science, and no need for a pencil and paper. The miscreant, a very young sepoy who could have been no older than 18, was marched in at the double by a Havildar Major. He was trembling like a leaf, totally out of his depth. He said the bicycle had wobbled, and he had fallen off and scraped his arms and legs. The Major put forward a different scenario – "It wasn't the bike that wobbled, it was you that wobbled. I have seen it all before, you were drunk, and it was you that wobbled not the bike. Get him out of here," and he was marched at the double.

The Major then said that we would break for half an hour, and when we returned, I was to start the summing up. I had half an hour of sheer agony! No substantive evidence had been produced, and my nature could not possibly allow me to find against him. Yet, I was under strict instructions to follow the Major's lead. The CO would eat me alive if I returned having fouled up. I did not enjoy the break at all. We returned, and I was invited to start. Inspiration came on me, and I suggested that we have a look at the damaged bike before we proceeded. I knew little of the workings of military law, but I was an expert with bicycles, having had one from a very early age, and able to do repairs with my eyes closed. The Major reluctantly agreed this to. The bicycle was wheeled in, and stood against the wall. It was an old Raleigh bike of WWl vintage, in good condition, with a very large saddle and pannier bags around the back wheel to carry papers. The mudguards were very wide and substantial.

The bicycle was damaged in that both pedals were hanging to the ground. As soon as I saw it, I knew I was safe. I had seen the same on my bicycles. It was clearly a loose cotter pin, which hold the pedal in place. "Could I have a hammer, please?" One was brought, and I gave the cotter pin several good thumps, until it was solid as a rock. I suggested that I should give it a test, to see how it went, and this was agreed. I took it to the parade square just outside, and rode around the square. This attracted the attention of many jawans, as it was an unheard of event for a British officer to ride a bike round the square in Loralai. I was now on a high, and to show off my prowess, I rode round again, without hands, much to the amusement of the hundreds of jawans now watching. We then went back into the office, and I began my summing up. The damage was caused by a loose cotter pin. I recommended that a) better maintenance provisions should be introduced in the Unit, and b) the sepoy bears no responsibility for the damage. I now waited with bated breath for the Sikh Captain to give his verdict. Good fellow, he agreed with me, and the Major endorsed it. It was the great escape. I returned to Fort Sandeman the next day, and after a shower, I wandered into the Mess.

The CO was there, holding forth, but when he saw me, he stopped and gave me a hearty welcome. He had been kept up-to-date by the Brigade Major, and was elated. He said "We showed them McIntosh, didn't we," and immediately ordered the Mess waiter to bring me a Bara Peg, saying "Put it on my account," words never before heard in the mess! I was his blue-eyed boy after that, and had a very easy ride. This was a make or break moment for me. Luck? Or that Guardian Angel again?

A very major event came on 1st October, when The Regiment officially became The Mahar Machine Gun Regiment. Before this time, machine gun battalions - which had .50 Vickers heavy machine guns as their main armament - had been scattered through normal infantry regiments. Now, the Indian Army was catching up with the British, who had specialised MMG regiments. The Mahars were to be one of two such regiments in the Indian Army, the other being 15 Punjab. An MMG training team from a machine gun battalion of the Madras Regiment, under Capt Nair MBE, arrived in Fort Sandeman. Major Rawson Gardiner, who had been with an MMG battalion of the RAJ RIFFS also assisted in the intensive training courses that were held. Needless to say, the Regiment made great success of this new role, and served India with bravery and pride for many years, until returning to their original role as infantry.

It was also about this time that the CO and three of the young British Subalterns went on a two-week leave break to Kashmir. They stayed on houseboats, on a lake at Srinagar, and had a great time. It was talked about for weeks later in the Mess, and I felt quite envious at missing out on such a trip. I cannot remember getting any kind of leave at all.

Towards the back of the year, we were posted to join the 4<sup>th</sup> Indian Division at Kirkee, just outside Poona, and were relieved by the 4 Baluch Regiment. It was chaos for days as we moved lock, stock and barrel on a special troop train, which took six days to reach our destination. We thought it a great honour to join the Red Eagle Division, as it was the most famous of all Indian fighting forces in WW2. We considered it well deserved after our efforts on the frontier.

It was certainly a culture shock to move from the most barren, isolated and dangerous of places to the more cultured atmosphere around Poona, with its cultured lawns and gardens, and very upmarket facilities such as the Polo Club and Gymkhana Club. The temperature too was very acceptable, as winter had been falling on Fort Sandeman, and it was getting rather cold and bleak. Best luck to the Baluchis there, but I expect they were used to it. We were based in the premises and grounds of a very large Army Hospital, which had been constructed to accept the anticipated casualties from fighting to recover Malaysia and Singapore, and which of course had not been required. The Hospital was largely unused, but there was a small staff there, including half a dozen young British Army nurses. That was a pleasant surprise, as we had been unused to young female company for rather a long time! They helped us celebrate Christmas and New Year at our parties and festivities. Having a lovely swimming pool in the grounds, which was a popular meeting place, helped us.

The commander of the 4<sup>th</sup> Indian Division was Maj. General 'Pete' Rees, who had made a good name for himself commanding 17 Indian Division in the Burma campaign. He was a short, stocky figure, who was well liked by his troops. He had the nickname "Pocket Napoleon". He met and greeted us well on our arrival, and shook the hand of every officer.

The 4<sup>th</sup> Indian Division became the nucleus of The Punjab Border Force, which would give such good service later in the year. Apart from one Brigade field exercise, we spent all our time on crowd control procedures. Endless hours in the sun until everyone was a bit sick of it, but the training paid big dividends some months later. Khalid Jan was now our CO. "Frigger" Frier had been posted as Inspector General of the Assam Rifles in Shillong. He ended his military career there as a Brigadier, and finally left India.

With WW2 won and over, Britain now had a new Labour government, who recognising the changed situation in the world, put forward proposals to grant independence to India, something sought by Indians for a long period. As far as I was concerned, this was exactly the right policy for the changing circumstances that were upon us. My own observation, after my brief sojourn in India, was that there were plenty of highly educated and proficient people to run their own affairs, and the opportunity must be taken.

A high-powered mission from GB met with Mr Nehru and Mr Jinnah, of the Congress Party and Muslim League respectively. From those meetings, the 16th May 1946 Agreement was forthcoming, offering independence to a united India. This was never accepted by Jinnah, who was hankering after a separate independent state for the Muslims. He finally got his way, and India and Pakistan became independent on 15th August 1947. There was enmity between the two sides, and many communal riots took place all over, but mainly in border area of the Punjab. This was causing great concern at the start of 1947, and was the catalyst for starting the Punjab Boundary Force. It moved north to take up duties in the middle of the year, and proved necessary, as the civilian authorities, including police, were overwhelmed by the riots. 3MAHAR played a sterling role in this with exemplary conduct, saving many lives both Hindu and Muslim, and setting an example of what could be done that few other units attained. Well done the Mahars in India's time of need! Conduct that I may say has been repeated often in the short history of independent India. One of the bonuses of independence was that the Mahars were retained as a military unit. Without independence, I am sure the British would have disbanded the Regiment, which would have been a terrible blow.

With the future plans now set, it became paramount that all British personnel should leave India quickly. On 3rd February, myself, together with Tom Oliver, Ken Bradley and Bill Griffin, had to say farewell to 3MAHAR, as we were posted to Kalyan Transit Camp for repatriation. There was a big farewell, but with lots of sadness. I remember giving a farewell speech that one-day I would return, but really thought that it was a bit of a pipe dream at the time. The others followed by the end of March. What an impact it must have had on our colleagues.

I have given a lot of detail of by brief stay with the Mahars. It was a pivotal period in my life, which changed my whole outlook. I grew in stature, and left as a much better person. No period of my life was better than my time with the British Indian Army. There were 500+ of us, a mixture of British and Indian, black and white, rich and poor, highly intelligent to dim, Christian, Hindu, Muslim - a microcosm of the world itself - but we stuck together as if fixed with glue. We were a real family, who looked after each other, a regular Band of Brothers who would have died for each other. I hope I have expressed the flavour of the loyalty this small and junior regiment of the British Army inspired, and the pride that its former British Officers have felt over the years as they watched the Regiment's distinguished progress. There is a saying that "Great oaks from little acorns grow." We who were present at the planting of the Mahar acorn take enormous pride in its growth, and always wish every success to the Regiment as it adds to its glory now and in the future.

I was now back at Kalyan, two years after first being there. Nothing much had changed, as it was still a large sprawling base, being very arid with lots of baked mud and little vegetation. The exception this time was that the flow of troops was in the opposite direction, with the war long finished and Indian independence fast approaching. All my worldly possessions were in 5 kit bags and a bedding roll. Three of the kit bags contained the rugs purchased in Fort Sandeman.

Living conditions were slightly more agreeable, and dining at the Officer's Mess was a real bonus. After a three week period of nothing happening, orders were received to embark on the troopship 'Lancashire' in Bombay. This was greeted with many cheers, as we all wanted to get home and see our families. There had been some relief during the long delay, as Great Britain was in the grip of the worst winter weather for a long, long time, and after the warm conditions in India, we were not looking forward to that.

The 'Lancashire' turned out to be an elderly troopship of WW1 era, of some 10,000 tons, with a top speed of 10 knots if the wind was blowing behind it. It was, of course, overcrowded, but Officers did at least have bunks rather than the usual hammocks. Progress home was tediously slow, but when we saw land, such as the barren rocks of Aden and the Sinnai, it helped to plot our progress. Then, it was up through the Red Sea and to the Canal Zone, which was not much changed. The boredom of the journey was somewhat relieved by being able to listen, over the ship's loudspeaker, to the BBC Overseas Service, giving us news and music, and we did have film shows of ancient films every other evening. The BBC was reporting a lot of trouble in Palestine, which was still under our jurisdiction, and rumours spread that a number of personnel would be offloaded at Port Said and sent to reinforce our presence in Palestine. A number were indeed disembarked, but the majority of us were able to breath a sigh of relief. We continued to crawl through the Mediterranean, round Gibraltar and through a very rough Bay of Biscay, where we were tossed around like a top, and made very slow progress. Luckily, by that time we, we all had our sea legs, and there were very view cases of seasickness.

We arrived in Liverpool on a Sunday morning at the beginning of April. The weather was still bleak, and very cold with snow still in the air. I, with a group of others, was given a travel warrant to Stirling in mid-Scotland, as the regimental HQ of the Argyll and Sutherland Highlanders was in the ancient Stirling Castle. The place was overflowing with people, and we were quickly told there was no place for us to sleep there, and we could go on indefinite leave until they got it round to our turn. Joy unbounded! I was free to catch the train to York along with my 5 kit bags and bedding roll. It was a wonderful feeling being able to see the house where I was brought up, and return to the arms of my ever-loving family.

It was quite emotional to have me back home really, especially for my Mother who, in WW1 lost her twin brother James, who was killed on the western front in France in 1917.

She had always feared the worst and that I would not return. They were all looking fine, although the effects of war had not gone away. There was still very strict rationing of food and clothing, fuel was scarce and the winter had been and still was very cold. On the whole, everything was pretty threadbare, and my view was that I had had a much better deal over my time away than they had at home. My beautiful rugs were warmly welcomed, and took pride of place at home for many long years.

The deep snow that had fallen all winter was now starting to thaw, as the sun got higher and temperatures rose. York was always at risk of flooding from its two rivers, because it had some low-lying areas. Large areas were flooded, and walking into town became difficult, as you had to navigate a number of planks, which were sited just above the water line. One slip and ugh, you would be up to your waist in dirty water.

York was a garrison city, and home to thousands of servicemen. They were well tutored to salute any Officer they saw. I reckon the muscles in my right arm were over developed coping with the number of salutes I had to respond to. My Dad was still working for the Post Office, and was happy in his work. A lot of his leisure time was taken up with golf, and he was a top player at the Heworth Club, and had a range of cups to prove this.

My Mother was still a volunteer with the WVS. My sister had now spent over five years as a shorthand typist, but was just at the point of giving it up and becoming a Nurse. Our pet dog, a black spaniel by the name Nell, had not forgotten me, and gave me a really good welcome back home. She was of a nervous disposition and shunned strangers, but recognised me immediately. My family said I talked a little bit more posh than when I left. I did not recognise that at all, as I never thought of myself as posh.

I had plenty of time to meet up with my youth club friends (now called The Young People's Mission). Of course they were no longer young, most of them now being in their twenties. All were now leaders of our group, with a hundred or so younger children under their charge. After three weeks getting used to home life, a telegram came asking me to report for duty at 35 Light Anti Aircraft (LAA) Regiment, based at Hardwick Hall

Camp at Sedgefield, a market town ten miles north of Stockton in County Durham.

I reported by mid afternoon on the following day, and was met with surprise, as they had not been notified of my transfer. They were already carrying surplus RA Officers, and the arrival of an Infantry Officer serving with A&SH was just too much for them. But, there I was, and they took me in. The 35 LAA Regiment had been raised at the start of the war, but had been mostly wiped out or taken prisoner at the time of the Singapore debacle. They had been reformed, and now there were 500 personnel serving in three Batteries, each equipped with 4x40mm Bofors anti aircraft guns. Most of the gunners were just 18 year olds conscripted for two years service. Why I received this posting puzzled me, but I think it must have been due to my service record of starting as a gunner in the Home Guard. It was a total mismatch, of course, but there was no way of changing it.

They invented a job for me, with the important sounding title of Camp Commandant, and basically put me in charge of upkeep of the camp facilities, the turn out and demeanour of the other ranks, as well as off loading all the financial affairs of the Unit. It was an easy enough job for me over a period of four lovely summer months. They kept me well away from the Bofors Guns, and in my time there, they were never fired at all. There was plenty of whitewashing to be done around the site, and as far as the bearing of the gunners was concerned, they never quite achieved the standard, which would be expected in an Infantry Battalion.

They were strange days, and I can remember that every week we paid a visit to a bank in Stockton before payday. We always had an armed escort of half a dozen soldiers carrying rifles, and it did not seem to cause any concern to the general public who were just going about there daily business. Armed force was never needed, and if it were done in this day and age, it would have caused a riot.

The Mess was rather good at Hardwick Hall Camp, with good food in big helpings, much better rations than the civilians were getting at that time. The Camp was in the grounds of Hardwick Hall, which were well kept and open for us to use. We had plenty of space to take out a few golf balls and clubs to get a bit of practice. I also managed to get into Middlesbrough at weekends for relaxation. Ayresome Park, the home of the local first division football club was a must, and I saw some good games there, including a classic Manchester United with many famous internationals showing off their skills. Sedgefield itself was a nice quiet place, and there was always a good meal and company to be found at Hardwick Arms, the local hostelry. The stay there was good enough, but in no way did it match up with the MAHAR experience.

It was the beginning of August that I got the call to become the Adjutant of a new Territorial Army Royal Artillery Unit, which had been established a couple of months earlier in South Shields. So, farewell to 35LAA Regiment, which I think was slightly better than when I joined it.

I took over from a Capt. Parrott RA, who was being demobilised. We were based in a TA establishment in Northfield Gardens near the centre of the town, and the total strength of the Unit was 12 new volunteers. I was billeted in a hotel near the sea front - me being the sole service person and the rest civilians. Again, it was a strange situation, and back to civilian rations.

My task was to try to drum up far more recruits, to make it a viable proposition. It was a difficult task as everyone was war weary, and it was the last thing they wanted. Nevertheless, I persisted in my task, using press adverts, cinema shots in between films, stands in shops etc. There was limited response, with number rising to around 70 by the end of November.

Most days there was not much to be done until the evening time, so I had plenty of time to explore South Shields. It was much better than I expected. Part of it was on the banks of the Tyne, with heavy industry and shipbuilding and maintenance. Another part of the town was the seafront, with a magnificent beach, and plenty of attractive public gardens. The main shopping street ran for about a mile inland, starting from the beach, with all the big national shops represented.

One good aspect of the job was that I was able to take weekend leave all the time, travelling to York and back - first class on the train, of course! I was then informed that I was due for demobilisation as from 18th November. I was given the choice if I so wished, to stay on. A big decision easily made. I had been in uniform since 1942 when the country was in peril, but now everybody was looking forward to many years peace, and I opted to be out.

My last journey was back to Fulford Barracks in York, where I was formally discharged. They gave me a set of civilian clothing, a Ration book and a first class rail voucher to wherever I wanted. As I was only 2 miles from home, I opted for one to the south coast of England. It would pay my fare to have a few days holiday in London and on the south coast. So ended my active military duty. What an experience! I had seen the world at the Government's expense and become a much more rounded, knowledgeable person, and I had survived. My military connection with the MAHARS however ran very deep, and would remain so for my lifespan.

*Officer cadet, 1944*

*Fort Sandeman, 1946*

*Patrol on Afghan border, 1946*

*Fort Sandeman, 1946*

*At camp near Afghan border, 1946*

*Fort Sandeman stalwarts*

*Mahar Officers, Fort Sandeman, 1946*

*Fond Farewells*

*In Battledress at home, 1947*

# CHAPTER 4

## YORK AND CIVILIAN LIFE AGAIN

Now at the beginning of December 1947, I was a civilian again and my Army pay had stopped. I needed some quick action to get back into work in order to pay my way. It was my right, in law, to apply to rejoin the Westminster Bank, and I did this straight away. They had no option other than re-employing me, and a starting date was set for a couple of weeks before Christmas. This allowed me to have a few days grace to get used to the new way of living. I spent some of it having a short break in London and on the south coast. I booked three nights accommodation at the Regent Palace Hotel, just off Piccadilly Circus, which was very handy. London was a little more vibrant than I had found it at the turn of 1944, but was still plagued with untidy bombsites, and run down facilities. The sightseeing was good though, and I did get to meet up with Isobel, who was, by this time a Trainee Nurse at Hackney Children's Hospital, which was situated in a desperately poor area of London.

I also got down to the south coast for the first time, and found the seaside resorts were not a patch on the ones in Yorkshire. The beaches were made up of pebbles rather than the golden sand I was used to. On my return to York, I had time to reacquaint myself with all my old friends at the YPM, and found they had started to form into pairs: Jack Coward and Marjorie Walker, Chris Wells and Joyce Atkins, Douglas Greenfield and Joan Catton, Ken Wright and June Pollard, Tony Brook and June Easton, Reg Coward and Brenda Dunford, Dennis Allison and Brenda Calpin, Reg Hartley and Muriel Haxby, and more. They all eventually married. I had been left behind in my absence, and was a bit of a loner, although I was friendly with lots of girls, and my time had yet to come.

I started back at the Pocklington Branch of the Westminster Bank in mid December. Back to the old routine of getting up early to catch the first bus out of town, which was a little easier as I did not have to contend with crowds of airmen. Most of the Bomber stations had closed down as demobilisation had gathered pace. The great difference was at the Bank. Pocklington and the Bank premises were exactly as I remembered. Now, however, there were 5 staff at the Branch, with 3 junior staff assisting the Manager and Chief Cashier. I was the most junior staff member, and never got a sniff of working at the counter with the customers.

The workload was about the same as when I left, so we were grossly over staffed. A great deal of idleness and pointless jobs (logging the serial numbers of all the £5 notes that were issued or received) was not enough to satisfy me. I persisted until mid year 1948, when I came to the conclusion it was not for me. Such a shame, as it was a prestigious job with prospects of promotion somewhere in the distance.

It seemed like waiting for dead men's shoes. I was still happy in my free time, with sport being my main pastime. I was honing my table tennis skills, which I had started in India. I played tennis to a reasonably high standard, Badminton took up my Thursday evenings and football on Saturday. I had been a keen supporter of York City since I was an infant, and soon started to follow them again. I was astonished to find my old school pal Peter Pickering now playing for the first team. After leaving school I bumped into him again at Hollywood Barracks and also at Wrotham. We seemed to run a parallel course as he was also commissioned. He was posted to a Unit in York and never went overseas, and got the opportunity to get established in the York team. After about a year with York, he was transferred to Chelsea for a record fee, and reached the top flight. I was his standard at school and really envied him. With a little luck it might have been me, and life would have been different.

At about this time, the Government nationalised the electricity industry. The North Eastern Electricity Board (NEEB) was formed by merging some 50 enterprises covering Northumberland, Tyneside, Durham, Wearside, Teesside and North Yorkshire. By far the biggest operator was The North Eastern Electric Supply Company with its HQ at Carliol House in Newcastle Upon Tyne, and it took the lead in establishing the new enterprise. Many of the smaller firms were Municipal Authorities, who ran their own electricity supplies. York was one of these, with the electricity staff being of York City Council's workforce. They were expected to move over to the new Electricity Board workforce, but many preferred to stay put, and only a 50% transfer was achieved.

The York office of the Board was hopelessly understaffed, with the workload increased by the complexity of the change. My tennis partner was one of those who switched over. Knowing of my dissatisfaction at my job, he implored me to change jobs, as they were in desperate need of a cashier on the counter where the consumers paid their bills. A life-changing decision had to be made pretty promptly. I was offered roughly comparable terms for pay and conditions such as holidays, pension provisions and sickness etc. I opted for the move, which in the fullness of time turned out to be a great decision. I ended up working for over 40 years non-stop for the Board, and enjoyed every minute of it.

I gave my notice to the Bank, and worked out the statutory few weeks to complete my contract. For the final period, I was transferred to the York Branch in Coney Street. It was a high-class cathedral style bank where you talked in hushed voices when inside. How the mighty are fallen, as it is now used as one of the ubiquitous Coffee bars.

Getting to work was much easier now, and I seemed to have lots more spare time. The work was easy for me, and non-stop. I was a natural cashier, and did twice the workload of any of my colleagues, and this did not go unnoticed by my superiors, and did me no harm at all. It was a real fresh start for me entering 1949.

It was about this time I started noticing a young lady at meetings in the YPM. Our eyes met over a crowded room, and we were hooked. I'm sure my Guardian Angel had a hand in it. Her name was Patricia Josephine Moger, who I eventually married in 1953, a marriage that lasted over 50 good years. Pat was just leaving school, and had gained a place at Bingley Teacher Training College located in Yorkshire, which she was starting in the autumn. We spent all our time together for a couple of months until the start of her College Course, and then we parted until Christmas.

I got highly practiced in letter writing, which was the only practical way of keeping in touch at the time. This was all hard to bear, but the saving grace was the lengthy holidays she got between terms. Then, disaster struck. Pat's stepfather, who was manager of a shop in York, got transferred to a branch in Grimsby. Pat would now go home to Grimsby in her breaks between terms. Bingley was a difficult place for me to get to. It was only 60 miles away, but in those days without a car, it took forever by train and bus to go to and fro, and on a full Saturday trip, we only managed about an hour together.

It is very hilly in Bingley, and the college was right on the top of a hill overlooking Ilkley Moor, and required plenty of stamina to negotiate. Grimsby was a worse place to get to. It was 100 miles away, off the beaten track, both expensive and time taking to get there. One consolation was that Cleethorpes, a seaside resort, was nearby, and in the summer months, a York Bus company used to run day trips there on a Sunday, and I used this facility a number of times.

After a stint of a year as a cashier, I was transferred to an accounts office, where quarterly bills were produced and sent out. I had responsibility for calculating the bills for all the consumers in Malton and all the surrounding villages, following up the payment and issuing red reminders, and finally cut off warnings to non-payers. Again, it was interesting and time passed quickly. My colleagues then were Ron Fisher, Bernard Sellars, Ken Lancaster, Stan Wall, Charlie Boddy and Freddy Miskin. They were a good progressive bunch of fellows, all looking for promotion, and all rivals if any higher posts became vacant.

It struck me at this time that, if I wanted promotion in this new firm, I should really buckle down and get myself a professional qualification. I opted for the Association of Certified and Corporate Accountants. This would give the post-nominal letters ACCA, which were held by a few of the top managers at our Head Office in Newcastle upon Tyne. To qualify, you had to pass three examinations. There was an intermediate one of six subjects, a final part 1 of 5 subjects, and a final part 2 also of 5 subjects. These covered subjects such as accounting, income tax, economics, commercial law, executors and trust accounting and law etc.

This was all home study through a correspondence school. A tough assignment was ahead, which I would persist with for fully six years. This took up a lot of my spare time in the evenings, but good planning ensured that I did not neglect my multiple sporting commitments. I really had a busy life, with next to no spare time.

My Mother had a windfall from the estate of a long forgotten relative. He owned a farm in Aberdeenshire, and died intestate. All living relatives were traced by the solicitors, and got a share of the money that he had. My Mother got about £2,000 out of the blue, which was a lovely surprise. I think this triggered the next big event, which was a house move away from Sixth Avenue to 30 Monkton Road in Muncaster, York. This made my Dad very happy, because it was just next to his Golf Club. I was a little bit further from the City Centre, which made for longer walks and transport times. It was a bigger, better house in a nice location, and we were happy there. Things were certainly getting better for living. Petrol was taken off the ration, bread became more readily available, identity cards were withdrawn from use, and the utility furniture scheme ended.

The Festival of Britain was held mainly in London, which gave the whole nation a boost, as the various exhibitions displayed new and futuristic ideas. I managed to pay a short visit to London to enjoy the festivities. The first black and white television sets were also on sale. My friend Jack Coward's family had one, and I can remember the thrill of going round to his house to watch the FA Cup Final. The first Zebra Crossing was opened, and the first jet airliner - the Comet - took to the skies.

Progress indeed!

I also had the first opportunity to attend a Mahar Regiment Reunion dinner, at the Grosvenor Park Hotel in London, and renew acquaintances with my old buddies. Alas, after that, I lost contact because the Secretary failed to implement an address change, which I had notified to him. It was many years before contact was made again.

All was not good news. During this period, the King died suddenly, and we had a change of Monarchy. Also, the Korean War began. What a shock that was, as we were all looking forward to years of wonderful peace. On Christmas Day 1952, I proposed marriage to Pat, she accepted, and we were officially engaged to be married. By this time, she had passed out of Bingley Training College, as top student, and had started work as a Biology teacher at Carr Lane School in Grimsby.

Now, it was 1953, a very significant period of my life. Firstly, at work, a vacancy at a slightly higher grade in the Cashiers' Section came up. There was strong competition from a number of people, but as luck would have it, I got the job. It was just to my liking, with more money and a whole range of tasks involving banking of cash, issuing of cheques and generally looking after all financial problems that needed to be sorted.

It was a job that was going to last me four years. I also passed the intermediate ACCA examinations. At home, my sister Isobel returned from London as a fully qualified Nurse. She then got a job as a Ward Sister at York County Hospital. The normal sporting activities continued apace, as did my activities at the YPM. One big event of the year was the coronation of the Queen. I managed to see it on a friend's television, along with about 20 other people crammed into a room. In York, as in London, it was a wet, cold and miserable day weather wise. Everest was conquered for the first time on the same day.

I took every opportunity to meet with Pat at weekends in Hull, to perfect all the arrangements for our wedding. The date was set for August 8th at St Michaels' Church in Littlecoates, a part of Grimsby. We could not have picked a better day. It was cloudless, and the sun shone from dawn to dusk. Everyone who was invited got there, despite the difficult travel arrangements to get to Grimsby. Uncle Bob and Aunties Helen and Meg made it from as far as Aberdeen. Douglas Greenfield was my best man, helped by Chris Wells and Reg Coward. My sister Isobel, and Pauline, Pat's sister were two very attractive bridesmaids. They couldn't hold a candle to Pat, who was just a vision of beauty in her long, white wedding dress. Pat was always very attractive, with a smile to die for. She could have passed for a film star, with her long auburn hair and brown eyes. To add to that of course, she was a very clever, well-educated young lady. She excelled all her married life, being a loving, caring Mother, first-class cook, dressmaker, decorator, gardener and jack-of-all-trades. I reckon that I got a very good deal. Our reception was at a big hotel in Grimsby - not all that lavish, as we were still living in austere times. For our honeymoon, we spent a week in London at the Regent Palace Hotel. I remember a spell of very warm weather, with some ferocious thunderstorms.

We arrived back in York to live in a flat in Albermarle Road, just near the racecourse on the Knavesmire. It was just a short step from where my old wartime rocket battery was located. We didn't live there very long, as we wanted a house of our own. Pat, clever girl, managed to get a post as Science teacher at Knavesmire School, just across the road.

After a search around, we picked a smallish pre-war semi-detached house at Burnholme Avenue. For the magnificent sum of £1,600, we were on the property ladder. I paid a deposit of £150, with monthly payments set at seven pounds and ten shillings. A big commitment in those days, it was a cosy little house, with a nice front and back garden, plus a garage (no hope of buying a car yet).

We had an excellent life there for four and a half years, and soon adapted to our ways as a married couple. We must have set a trend, as shortly afterwards, my sister Isobel was married to Robert Chrystie, a dentist from Aberdeen, at the Royal Station Hotel in York. Also, Pat's sister Pauline was married to Geoff Leavitt from York. Isobel left to start a new life in Aberdeen, whilst Pauline and Geoff bought a house in Burnholme, about 100 yards away from ours. We at last got free from rationing, as the meat and sweets rations were dropped. Our usual routine activities continued with the addition of weekly visits to my parent's house, as they were feeling somewhat lonely after both their children had left at about the same time.

We were always keen on getting away on holidays, and spent time on Jersey, and visited Bournemouth, Ilfracombe and Morecambe. We also spent time with the Chrysties in Aberdeen, and had trips to Newtonmoor and Kingussie. Christmas was always spent in Grimsby. We added to our interests by taking up Scottish Country dancing, and spent many happy hours in the old Merchant Adventure Hall - a lovely setting. Other things that stick in my mind from those days are: the crash of the Comet (first jet airliner), the four-minute mile, York City reaching the semi-final of the FA Cup, and seeing Sputnik travelling across the sky over our house.

Other odd things were the first fish fingers, and the first self-service shops appeared. My Dad retired from his work at the Post Office (he got a medal for his long service), and spent a short time at Yorkshire Insurance Head Office, reorganising their mailing department. Not long afterwards, Mum and Dad upped sticks, and moved back to dear old Aberdeen. I managed to pass ACCA examination Final Part 1, after sitting it in Leeds over 3 days.

Suez dominated the news for a time, with petrol being rationed, and threats that ex-servicemen might be called back to serve. That would have put the cat among the pigeons, but it never came about. Further good news was that Isobel gave birth to Valerie in Aberdeen. So we came to the start of 1958, another very significant year.

*Lovely demob suit*

*Unicrux football team*

*Bruce looking good*

*Pat looking gorgeous*

*Pat and me in Cleethorpes, 1952*

*Wedding Day, August 8ᵗʰ 1953*

*Mother and Father at wedding*

*Mother and me at YPM outing*

*Together at NEEB dinner in Scarborough*

# CHAPTER 5

## WHITLEY BAY AND FAMILY LIFE

1958 was a life-changing year, with some very big decisions having to be made. I always remember the start of the year, because of the news of the air crash in Belgrade, where Manchester United had been playing a cup match. So many famous footballers were killed or hurt, that it made sombre news for many days, as was the main topic of conversation.

Pat and I continued to be very happy in our respective jobs, and all was going well. I sat the final part of the ACCA examination for three days in Leeds, and awaited the results. Meanwhile, my employers The North Eastern Electricity Board (NEEB), decided to start a training scheme with a name of Accountant in Training. I got one of these vacancies. I was still located in York, but for a three-month period, I was posted out to NEEB Headquarters located at Carliol House in Newcastle-upon-Tyne. Each week, it required a train journey to Newcastle, first thing on a Monday morning, a four-night stay in Newcastle, and a return to York late Friday afternoon. I stayed in a private guesthouse on Heaton Park Road in Newcastle, and was well looked after, though I missed the comforts of home life, and Pat's company so much.

The training was extensive, and not only covered the accounting routines at HQ, but also involved visits to another four Sub Area HQs. Although some nine years had passed since NEEB was formed, it soon became apparent to me that totally different practices were being followed in each place, based on the diverse local procedures from way back in 1948/49. For example, five billing sections based in Newcastle, Sunderland, Middlesbrough, York and Harrogate were producing some two million quarterly electricity bills. The accounts were as different as chalk is from cheese for all five of them. The same was true of the payroll, stock control, costing, and every other area of work.

It was at the same time, very interesting and confusing for me. At the end of the three months, I wrote a detailed description of what I had observed, and was very critical of the state of affairs. I think it was a bit of an eye opener to the chief officers of NEEB.

Meanwhile, back in York, I received the good news that I had passed my exams, and now I only had to serve a six month probationary period in an accounting post to be able to use the post nominal letters ACCA. Life was going well, then out of the blue, NEEB decided to set up a new department called The Organisation and Methods Unit (O&M), based in Carliol House in Newcastle. This was a small but very powerful group, reporting directly to the top management, which would look at all aspects, not just accounting, of NEEB's work. I was given the nod to apply for one of these posts. My dilemma was that it was not a purely accounting post, which I needed to get my qualification. On the other hand, it would be a great jump in status if I took the post. My salary would be practically doubled, and I would also get a car allowance to enable me to travel around. The doors to much wider prospects would also be opened. It would mean leaving York, which was a beautiful city, and all my friends and activities. What should I do? I had lots of discussions with Pat, as it would affect her life as well as mine, and, in the end, we decided to go for it. A wise life-changing decision no doubt influenced from above.

We would have to sell our house and buy another on Tyneside. We managed to get a quick sale of our house for £1,650, which we left with regret, as we had been happy there. Our search for property around Newcastle finally came to a choice between a newly built house at Ponteland, or a similar property in Whitley Bay. There was the lure of the sea and sand at Whitley Bay, and we bought a new house at 30 Garsdale Road for £2.250, which seemed a lot of money in those days. It was a good choice, as we lived there happily for 28 years. It was a nice three-bedroom house, with garden back and front, and included an inbuilt garage. It was just off the seafront in Whitley Bay, quite near St Mary's Island, and well within the range of the foghorn on the lighthouse.

Initially, it meant for me a 10-mile journey to the office, with a choice of bus or electric train, or a combination, which took about 45 minutes on a good day. I soon bought a car however, as my work territory was the whole North East of England. It was a second hand green Standard 8, which cost me £500, which seemed a fortune to me. NEEB paid for me to have driving lessons, as I hadn't driven since 1947, and my Licence had expired. I brought my bicycle with me to Whitley Bay, and stored it in the garage ready for use. Unbelievably, I never used it again, and gave it away to a local lad who was out of work, but who had helped me give the gardens their first dig.

We soon started to make friends in Whitley Bay, from the many young couples who bought the surrounding houses. We also joined the local Presbyterian Church (St Cuthbert's), which had a membership of some 500 people, which was a good source for more friends. In addition, Pat soon got a job as a Science teacher in a school in Tynemouth, so we made friends at our workplaces too. No sooner had we settled in than I was shipped off to London on a four-week course run by the Institute of Public Administration, to learn new skills as an O&M Officer. That involved travelling to London by train on a Monday morning, and returning on Friday evening. So Pat was stuck by herself again for long periods. She did, however, manage to come down with me for a week in London on her half-term break. I was a member of the Victory Ex Service Club near Paddington Station, which provided extremely cheap, but well appointed accommodation.

Back at home, we soon got into a regular routine, and I found my job very much to my liking, and my stint of O&M Officer was to last 4 years. It was hard, but very rewarding work trying to update old and complicated systems, and drag people from past to present. It was never very easy to get change implemented, as it upset so many people's lives and way of living. Trade Union Officials were especially difficult to convince when a simplified system required reductions in staffing levels.

No one was ever made redundant, as not recruiting, and natural wastage prevented this. All in all, we started to transform NEEB into a much more productive company in an amicable way. This was a long term project that would last forever really, as technology advanced and change had to come about.

Early in 1959, I started to go to evening classes at Newcastle University. They had just installed the first computer in Newcastle, and were trying to get to grips with this very new technology. Our little group was led by Professors Ewan Page, Brian Randle, Paul Samet and two or three other boffins, and we played about with electronic storage, input and output, together with basic programming. This was all brand new pioneering stuff, which was to stand me in good stead some time later.

We formed the first regional branch of The British Computer Society (BCS) in Newcastle in 1959. I got the task of auditor of the accounts which was a simple enough task. In the following years computing and information technology increased in scale, importance and complexity and finally dominated all aspects of our lives. The BCS was recognised as the professional body and learned society that represented those who worked in the industry. It was incorporated by Royal Charter in 1984 at which time I was awarded the professional grade of Member (MBCS) and the chartered status of Chartered Information Professional (CITP). Some compensation on missing out on the accounting qualification ACCA. In 1958. Two for the price of one and the hard choice I had to make in 1958 was vindicated. I am now an Honorary Member (it just means that I no longer have to pay the annual subscription).

Pat had to resign from her teaching post in the spring of 1959, as she became pregnant. Robert Bruce was born on Saturday 24th October. That was a real life-changing event, and we were both as proud as punch with our new little boy. Pat was in her element, and no one could have been a better mother. She was confident and on top of the situation right from the start. She had experience from earlier in her life, when as a young girl she was always tending to her young stepbrother Michael, who was born when she was around ten years old. Robert had a most comfortable pram, and Pat used to walk him into town almost every day. I did my bit at the weekend, and a walk to the lighthouse and back became my regular task. Of course, my Mother and Father came down from Aberdeen to see their new grandson many times, and continued to do so when Andrew and Christine were born. We soon realised that if Robert cried, he would stop as soon as he was put in the car, so we had many short trips round and about.

We were now at the start of a new decade - the 1960's - and the world was changing. WW2 was becoming a memory, and technology was advancing at a pace. Life expectations were changing, with a more affluent population willing to spend money to keep up with the front-runners. Pat and I were feeling very comfortable in our new house now with a family. We bought our first television set in 1960, and although it only had a couple of channels, and was in black and white, what an impact it had.

Also, although it was a new house we were living in, our heating was from a coal fire in the dining room. There was no such thing as affordable central heating, or double glazing of windows and in winter time ice would still form on the inside of the bedroom windows. We managed to install an electric night storage heater in the hall, which at least gave a small measure of background heat to the rest of the house. We topped this up with portable electric fires in other rooms to make them more comfortable. It was still a dirty business cleaning out the ashes of the coal fire every day, and having a dozen bags of coal delivered at regular intervals. It was so different in the summertime when the sun was high and warm, and the lovely sandy beach and sea was only five minutes walk away from the house.

The nearby coastline of Northumberland was stunning with its extensive sandy beaches, castles and fishing villages, and we made good use of the car at weekends to do some exploring. We also had a good-sized garden to work on in the early years. It was just a builders' plot to start with, but Pat had grand idea of what it would look like in the future.

1960 was the year the hard graft was done to clear it, dig it and level it. That was my task, with a helper there to do the first rough dig. Thereafter, the grand plan of design came from Pat. She had green fingers, and anything she planted and tended to seemed to flourish. I was put in charge of the lawns, from the initial seeding to the eventual weekly cutting and tidying. Pat's area covered the flowers, apple trees, fruit bushes and vegetables. Pat even knew the Latin names of all the plants and flowers, whereas I scarcely knew the difference between weeds and flowers. Woe betides me if I ever strayed from my territory!

My work continued to keep me very busy from Monday to Friday. Some of the assignments were vast, and lasted months, whilst others could be solved in a day. Armed with the 5 W's and 1 H (WHAT, WHERE, WHEN, WHY, WHO AND HOW) as questions, one could usually get to the root of a problem, and begin to chart a solution. We must have saved millions of pounds of expenditure by simplifying things or eliminating unnecessary work.

At times it was unbelievable that the strange and expensive habits hadn't been spotted and corrected many years before by the line managers. I suppose that was the main advantage of an independent, professional team to do the job. Way back at the end of the 1940's, someone at Head Office had decided to have a central filing system for the 500 or so staff based at Carliol House. The section employed 30 or so clerks to run it, and it needed a large office to house the hundreds of 4 drawer filing cabinets that held all the files. They were running out of space, as more and more filing cabinets were needed. We were asked to solve the problem, and it took weeks to trawl through the contents of the vast collection. Two major things we uncovered were that nothing was ever scrapped, and things that were history and no longer live would be kept forever. Secondly, the users didn't have much faith in the system, and they all had their own filing system and cabinets, duplicating the central filing system. Once the facts were established, it did not take a genius to work out the solution. Scrapping the central filing system and throwing away old records was soon accepted.

Instead of buying more filing cabinets, we had many surplus ones, which would last us for years to come. The saving of the annual cost of employing 30 clerks was an added bonus for years to come. The difficultly was the effect on the 30 surplus staff, and the reaction of their Unions. That was solved by not recruiting any more clerks until all 30 of them had been fitted into vacant positions. It was not only staff salaries that could be saved. NEEB was a big organisation formed from the amalgamation of many smaller enterprises. After 10 years or so, people were still buying locally in small quantities. The whole thing was in need of a revamp. We introduced central purchasing and tendering procedures. Instead of paying full whack for hundreds of small quantities, we got massive discounts for bulk buying, and saved ourselves a mint of money. There was never a dull day, and the workload stretched as far as one could see.

I still maintained my contact with the University, and carried on enlarging my knowledge of computing. In the present day, it would be looked on as a primitive machine, but at the time it was state of art. It was a Ferranti Pegasus, which we nicknamed Ferdinand. It had a $56 \times 40$ bit fast memory storage using Nickel delay lines. Storage was on a 5120 word magnetic drum. Input and output was by paper tape. Programming was just trial and error, and a cheer went up when something actually worked. There was enough evidence there though to suggest that this was going to be the way of the future. If you got the programming right, the machine could produce the results in double quick time, and it would always be 100% accurate. It was still part time experimental, but the germs of the ideas were beginning to form. This would stand me in good stead in the near future.

My social life was concentrated around my new friends at the Presbyterian Church. I joined the choir as a bass singer, and attended choir practice each week. It was a big choir of at least 40 people, equally spread over the four sections. I didn't think of myself as a good singer. I certainly couldn't sight read any musical score, but I was reasonable at picking up a tune, and following a strong bass line. In time, we sang some big oratorios at public performances, accompanied by soloists and orchestra. I can remember fine performances of The Messiah, Judas Maccabeas and Haydn's Creation. Because of my financial training, I became Treasurer of the Church, which was a big job. They were always short of money, and I helped introduce Covenant Giving - the forerunner of Gift Aid, where you can reclaim income tax paid to the Inland Revenue. This was new to most people, who looked on it with suspicion. When explained to them properly, they seemed very eager to sign on to get their money back from the Inland Revenue for the benefit of the Church.

I also talked to people about leaving legacies in their wills, to be paid to the Church on their demise. This again was highly successful, and tens of thousands of pounds were received and hopefully well spent. This was high-powered stuff on top of the weekly task of counting the collections. I was expert at it, but some of the helpers were clueless. Later on, my three children gave me help in this, and they were much better at it. It must be in the genes!

On 17th August, my second son Andrew was born with the same birthday date as Pat. What a joy again, but double the workload for Pat. She was well up for it, of course, and coped magnificently. I helped as much as I could, and there were well-worn paths that I followed along the sea front and to St Mary's Island with a pram with two little ones aboard. There were no holidays that year, but plenty of excursions in the car into lovely rural Northumberland.

1962 turned out to be another very important year as far as my work was concerned. My interest in computing was growing, as I could see the potential for their use within NEEB. One of the biggest problems that had been with us from the start in 1949, was that the system for invoicing our one million plus customers, which involved sending out five million invoices a year, was a mish-mash of archaic systems inherited from the many authorities that came together at the start. The income of several hundred millions of pounds was our lifeblood, and nobody really wanted the responsibility of upsetting that flow of money by tinkering with it. A computer was the ideal solution to our problem, and not only would it offer to help our billing processes, but it would also help us to break into the new electronic world, which the mass of people were totally unaware of at that time. The business press started running articles on these new fangled machines and the benefits they offered.

Luckily, our Chief Accountant put two and two together, and came to the conclusion that we should follow that path. A big decision was made at Board level to invest in a computer, and a brand new 'Computer Department' was born, with six staff appointed, including myself. That saw the end of my O&M activities for a few years.

Our first major task was to write the specifications of the main job (invoicing), which the new computer would be undertaking.

We could discount all the existing procedures and start afresh on a brand new set of procedure, with all bills being produced at our HQ in Carliol House. A total revolution was going to take place. The O&M mantra of 5W's and 1H was to the fore, so I was in my element. A big dossier outlining all our requirements to the smallest detail was sent out to six computer manufacturers who wished to tender for our business. They were all well known firms - IBM, Honeywell, Burroughs, NCR, Hollerith and ICT. This really occupied us full time for three months, as it was a big job.

Eventually, a shortlist of two was chosen to give us presentations before a final decision was made. We had a very detailed marking system for all the elements of the deal, such as cost, training, on-hands assistance, time scales, reliability and many more.

The final deal was done. It would be ICT rather than IBM. Both could have done the job with marks fairly even. The deciding issue was that ICT was a British firm, whereas IBM was American. Buy British was the policy of the government of the day, and that finally decided the issue.

We ordered a 1301 model, which was the earliest business computer available from International Computers and Tabulators. Its main memory came in increments of 400 words of 40 bits (12 decimal digits), with a maximum size of 2000 words. It was the first British machine to use core memory. Backing store was on magnetic drums of 12000 words, with a maximum of eight. Input was by 80 column punched cards. The machine ran at a clock speed of 1 MHz, and its arithmetic logic unit operated on data in a serial-parallel fashion - the 48 bit words were processed sequentially four bits at a time. A simple addition took 21 clock cycles (21 micro seconds), whilst hardware multiplication averaged 170 microseconds, and division was done by software. A microsecond is in fact one millionth of a second. People wouldn't believe that we were programming to such fine margins. In that day and age it was pretty good, but nothing compared to present day speeds.

The peripherals, such as a card reader was operating at 600 cards a minute, and the printer at 600 lines of 120 characters a line. A typical 1301 required 700 square feet of floor space and weighed 5 tons. It needed 13KVA of three phase electric power. The electronics consisted of over 4000 printed circuit boards, each with many germanium diodes, germanium transistors, resistors, capacitors, inductors and a handful of thermionic valves, and a few dozen relays operated when buttons were pressed. Integrated circuits and magnetic tape decks were not commercially available at that time. It was a powerful machine for its era, but for storage capacity, speed etc., it does not reach what a good mobile phone does these days. It did require a specially built air-conditioned room, as it generated an awful lot of heat. The console to operate it looked very futuristic, and in fact in later years, Dr Who could be seen sitting in front of a similar console on the *TV*.

To be able to program and operate such a computer was a mammoth undertaking. All six original staff members undertook six weeks of intensive training, firstly at ICTs head office at Putney Bridge, and at their training establishment at Bradenham Manor near High Wycombe. This was a bit of a hardship for our families. Pat was left on her own to cope with two young children for a long time. Weekends at home were very precious. Part of our training extended into 1963, when the winter months registered the lowest temperatures for a century.

The analysis of procedures and the programming were only part of our responsibilities. We were left to explain to all and sundry staff what was going to happen in the near future. Seminars and lectures to staff throughout the area, and the prospect of such upheaval left them stunned. It all started to come to fruition, and we were meeting the timescales, which had been laid down. We became expert programmers, using the 1301 machine code language in very inventive ways, which surprised the ICT experts. We had to, because NEEB were very stingy, and could only afford two blocks of 400 words fast store and two magnetic drums. The programs had to be kept in the fast store, leaving little room for the data, which had to be constantly transferred in and out to the drums, wasting a lot of time. We also found out very soon that the adage GIGO was very true - garbage in, garbage out. Any error in our programming, or faulty data could escalate in seconds throughout the whole system. Total accuracy was at the very heart of our jobs. Our documentation of programs was a state of art operation. In the event of a glitch appearing when we got to operational running, we needed to pinpoint very quickly and accurately what happened to cause it. We wrote masses of programs, and the only place we could test them and correct errors was on a machine at Putney Bridge in London. All six programmers went down for full weeks at a time for testing, which could only be done outside normal office hours, so it was midnight to 6.00am shifts for us.

Some three million punched cards had to be created from paper records to enable us to get programs operational. We employed about 100 girls for punching and verifying cards to get us on our way. Vast operational changes were needed to train for what was going to be a new occupation.

Some time near the end of 1963, it all came together, and we were ready to roll. The Chief Accountant seemed to get cold feet at the thought of this new enterprise starting up with the possibility of chaos. We had done our work well, with testing and parallel running showing the system was good and ready to go. Staff had been well trained, and all was ready for the start button to be pushed. Eventually, we got the nod, and the new system worked a charm. We were launched into the new computer age. Just luck again? It was the first commercial computer to be used in Newcastle. The old billing system was at long last dead and buried. Not only did we save loads of staff, but also standard bills were going out to everyone, and they received them just two days after their meters had been read. It used to take two or three weeks, as there was such a backlog. Interest rates in those days were around 10%. Because of the quicker payment our bank balance rose by £500,000, which raised a further £50,000 in interest as a way of a bonus.

During that year, my leisure time was restricted very much, and perhaps the family suffered a little. I retained as normal a routine as possible with my weekly activities. We even managed a fortnight in the Lake District at Braithwaite, in a caravan. By this time, Pat had become a Brownie Leader in the Girl Guiding movement, and was looking after a group at Church. She was ideal for the job, being a trained teacher, and having a good rapport with the young girls. I used to give her a lift to the Church and back, as she could not drive. I can remember picking her up at the end of one meeting just as the news of the assassination of President Kennedy was being reported.

1964 saw life returning to a bit of normality, which would last for several years. The stress and strain of pioneering the introduction of computers was becoming a memory. Life at work and home was far more relaxed, with the constant stays in London, which had so much disrupted my home life, no longer required. Three of my computing colleagues lived fairly close to me, and to make travelling to Newcastle and back easier, we organised a car-sharing scheme. It worked well for many years with a stint of a week as a driver and then three weeks being chauffeur driven. At a more leisurely pace, we started to transfer other big accounting systems to the 1301 computer. The programming was becoming more familiar to us, and we knew of the countless snags that we had to avoid. We also had a working computer on site for testing work, so life was much easier. The majority of our time was taken up trying to understand the countless clerical systems we were going to scrap, and then creating new procedures to supersede them on a one system fits everything basis. We recruited many more programmers, and this allowed us to spend our time on the more difficult analysis part of the job. It also helped free up time for the education and training of staff, and sometimes the difficult industrial relations problems that confronted us.

So we dealt with such things as Payroll, Stock and ordering procedures, costing, budgeting and many more minor accounting matters. By this time, other departments of NEEB, especially the Engineers, had seen the benefits of computerising procedures, and they wanted access as well.

Work flowed into the Computer Department, and in 1967, we were obliged to buy a second 1301 to handle the workload. In 1968, our currency changed to decimal. All the programs we had written thus far were in pounds, shillings and pence, and so, every program had to be amended. It was then that we reaped the benefit of the top class program recording system that we introduced from the start. Computer systems of course soon became out-dated, with technology advancing at a great pace, and in 1969 our minds turned to updating our computers.

Punched cards were out-dated for storing information, and were being replaced by electronic tapes and discs. Computer speeds had advanced, and our once world beating speeds in micro seconds were overtaken by nano second machines. After the usual work of drawing up new specifications, and going out for tender, we purchased an English Electric System 4 Computer. The program languages were, of course, different, and there was a vast job of converting all existing 1301 programs. I was not trained as a programmer on the new computer system, and we had lots of new graduates employed purely as programmers. My task was to draw up the specifications for them to work to. It was complicated work, but right up my street with my knowledge of how NEEB worked. It was successfully completed in 1970. My time in the Computer Department was just about to end. The top O&M job became vacant, and that was to be my future.

It was good to have a more settled life for a period. Both Robert and Andrew were doing well, and on 2/2/1965, Pat and I got the gift of a beautiful baby girl called Christine. We were on tenterhooks before the arrival of our baby. Would it be a boy again, which would have made a family of three boys and no girls, or our preferred option a little girl to make an ideal family of two boys and one girl. It all worked out very well for us, and Pat was over the moon. Both the boys were born in hospital, but for some reason, presumably shortage of NHS funds, it was decided that Christine should be born at home. This was not a very clever idea, for as soon as the Doctor left Pat after a morning visit, she went into labour, and the midwife only made it by the skin of her teeth. A very nerve wracking experience for both of us!

We now had our complete family, and the workload was certainly on Pat again, now looking after three little ones. She was great though, and took it in her stride. I was back to pram pushing again, and we got our monies worth out of the original pram we had bought. Pat kept it in pristine condition, and we sold it second hand for a good price when Christine was too big for it.

We continued with all our activities, and over the years added to them. I can remember taking all the children to the swimming baths in Blyth every Saturday morning for lessons. Later, we switched to a new Leisure Pool in Whitley Bay when it opened. Whitley Bay Ice Rink was also a regular haunt for us at the weekends. The children, I think, mostly enjoyed these activities without reaching Olympic standards. Later on, the boys joined the Boy Scout movement as Cubs, and then Scouts and Venture Scouts. I became Secretary of the Scout group for many years, and helped raise £20,000 to build a new hut for their meetings. Christine joined the Girl Guides as a Brownie and then a Guide, and eventually earned her Queen's Guide Award. She has since spent her life supporting the movement in quite senior posts.

Christine was also very taken up with music and dance, so I became her taxi driver, transporting her back and forward to her lessons. All the children attended Brierdene Primary School, which was a ten-minute walk away from home, past the Whitley Bay Golf Course. They later went to Valley Gardens Middle School and finally Whitley Bay High School, which were a good thirty minutes walk from home. Sundays were usually spent going to Church, followed by a slap up Sunday dinner made by Pat, and invariably a two to three hour trip in the car to see the sights of Northumberland. Our black and white television set was also popular with the children before bedtime. To let Christine have her own room, the boys slept in a double-decker bunk in the third bedroom.

I can recollect the exciting times when the first Moon landing was made, and watching it all on the television with the children. We always went away on summer holidays for a fortnight, using the car packed to the gunnels. The Lake District was a favourite for a number of years, and we stayed in a caravan at a site in Braithwaite, just the other side of Keswick. It gave us lots of freedom and the countryside was breathtaking. I can remember being there in 1966 on the Saturday England won the football World Cup. I tried to get a commentary of the match on an old portable transistor radio, but there was no reception because of the steep hills.

We later ventured further afield up to Pitlochry in Scotland, again in a static caravan. I remember a plague of earwigs invading the caravan at night, much to the distress of the children. The family also spent a few days in London looking at the sights, staying at our old haunt of the Regent Palace Hotel.

One year, I looked after the children on my own on a holiday to Scarborough, as Pat's Mother was ill, and she wanted to be near her over the holiday period. I took the children to a putting green to pass an hour or so. I recall sinking a putt of some 60 feet on a hole where a good number of people were sitting and watching in the sunshine, and getting a standing ovation! Later, we took to spending our holidays in University accommodation, and had lovely times in Stirling and Lancaster.

My Mother died in Aberdeen in 1970, and Dad came with us the following year to York University. It was a nostalgic visit back to the city where we had lived for many years. We spent a lovely day at Fulford Golf Course, watching golf stars in an international competition.

1971 was another significant year in my life. A vacancy for the head post in the O&M unit occurred at work. With my past experience from 1958 to 1962 in the Unit, and after a stint of nine years pioneering the Computer Department, I applied for the job and was promoted into it. The Unit had increased in staff numbers and importance. As well as the original O&M side of the job, there was now a large work measurement team to be looked after. The large industrial staff we employed had already been subject to work-study, with set times for jobs and incentive schemes applied. Nationally it had been agreed that similar schemes should be implemented for clerical and administrative staff. The first schemes had been started about a year earlier, but progress had been very slow, and was in need of a bit of impetus. The clerical staff were complaining that they had to wait too long for the chance to earn some bonus incentives. I went straight in at the deep end to try and simplify the measurement procedures to try to keep people happy. With the current rate of progress, it was estimated that it would take twenty years to complete the task, which was not acceptable. I set a new limit of 5 years, which was acceptable, and then had to simplify the measurement to fit the solution, whilst still maintaining accuracy.

There were about 1500 staff in around 100 measurable locations, and it was a big job. I took no part in the actual measurement processes, which were carried out by specialised work measurement staff. My task was to meet the staff in the locations to be measured, and tell them all about what was going to happen and why, and generally put their minds at rest. There was always the possibility that a measurement might show some overstaffing, or in some cases a shortage of staff. Again, we had a no redundancy policy, but it was still a worrying time for some. At my initial meeting with them, they always had the opportunity to refuse to be measured, or if they accepted, to get an immediate part payment of the set bonus. This was incentive enough for all of them to accept. I was also helped by the fact that all the schemes had been backed nationally by the Trade Unions, and the local representatives had to abide by the national decisions.

At the end of each measurement a report was produced showing the results, which laid bare all the times that had been calculated, and the mass of statistics, which finally led to staffing level being set. These were massive reports, and I had an uncanny knack of spotting arithmetic errors in the first drafts that had to come to me. It was then a job of trying to convince the staff of the veracity of the final report and get acceptance, which was sometimes hard fought for. I did have the authority to compromise on some matters of detail in order to make progress. They all ended successfully, resulting in more bonuses, with the obligation to have a monthly report to prepare showing work output against staff availability.

We were easily able to monitor the ebb and flow of work and revise staff levels in an instant. The Chairman of NEEB took a very keen interest in staffing levels, and insisted that I vetted any job vacancy notices before they were advertised. All this meant of course was that he came to my office and I could immediately advise him yea or nay from the very accurate records we kept. Later on, the same schemes were applied to shop staff. We had about 60 shops in the NEEB area, selling electrical items as well as dealing with payment of invoices and service enquiries. We had it all tied up, and knew exactly what was happening.

The O&M part of the work was also continuing nicely. Massive changes in management structure were made, eliminating unnecessary layers of senior supervisory staff, so there was a very lean and efficient outfit.

A lot of our efficiency came from investing heavily in up-to-date office equipment. It was my task to make sure we stayed ahead of the field. Whether it be photocopying, typing, data transmission etc., we always wanted the best. It was around this time that great progress was being made with electronic equipment, and all the manufactures' salesmen used to buzz around my office like flies vying for business. It came with its perils, as they were not slow in offering inducements. Offers of tickets for sporting activities and the theatre etc. were often made but always refused. We made seamless progress from mechanical typewriters to electronic typewriters to new fangled word processors, overcoming the fears of our many typists, who in the end welcomed the new machines. No wonder, as it must have been a relief to be able to correct errors without tippex, and to get rid of carbon paper.

One of our finest successes at work was to update our old mechanical Strowger telephone systems with new electronic exchanges. Answering incoming phone calls quickly was always a problem, and still is today even with internationally renowned companies. We had over a million potential callers and really no idea of how long callers took to be answered, or how many gave up in despair. The new equipment had the facility to log all this type of information, and we took full advantage of it. I was staggered to find out that so many callers gave up, and also the long times that people had to hold on before they were answered. We now had figures to show when peaks and troughs of telephone traffic occurred, and how you could fairly accurately predict the changes. Algorithms were soon written to give us the best solutions.

We also introduced three new features, which helped satisfy customers. If they were in a queue, we were able to tell them what position they were in the queue, and the approximate wait time for being answered, and they also had the facility to leave a telephone number for us to ring them back if they so wanted. We had lots of multi-tasked staff trained in telephone duties, who could be co-opted for work in peak periods. The whole thing was 100% better, and gave a level of service that many cannot match even today.

Another big subject that took up my time was the effort to rationalise the production of new forms. Everyone thought they had a need for a new form, and that they had the ability to design them perfectly. In reality, very few new forms were needed, and design wise they were rubbish. No new forms could be introduced without my say so. I was also in charge of the staff suggestion scheme. We gave a small monetary award to anyone who came up with an innovative idea that we could implement. We discovered that we had some bright people working for us at some lower level jobs.

A seed change in our approach to computing was also taking place. When we first introduced computing, it was mandatory that all computing activity should be under the control of the Computer department, rules that were strictly observed. We were now faced with the advent of personal computers, and access to remote terminals, which changed the whole philosophy. It was now possible to input data locally and pass it over the telephone lines to the mainframe. The saving in time and material was immense. I ensured that it was not a free for all, and that we had uniform systems in use.

The Electricity Industry had a staff college based at Horsley Towers near Guilford, just outside London. I was one of the lecturers they could draw on to talk about computing, work measurement and organisation in general. I got well looked after there, and it was a pleasure to do the job. From time to time, I was made a member of various working parties, trying to come up with solutions to tricky problems. For one of them, questions had been asked in Parliament on the number of times roads were being dug up by the various utility firms (Gas, Electricity, Water, Telephones and Highways Authority), sometimes within days of the roads being restored. A simple solution should surely be possible? Our little working party, with representatives from each utility, worked on it for half a dozen meetings, and found it not as easy as all that. We found that 95% of the digs were because of faults, which had to be repaired, and a tiny proportion were pre-planned events and nothing could be done to change that. We put a more efficient system in for advising each other of pre-planned work, but to this day roads are dug up in the same fashion when a fault occurs. You cannot win them all!

There was a Working Party formed to look at the computer requirements of all 12 Area Electricity Boards. We had all gone our own ways, and there was a multiplicity of equipment and systems in use. The question had been asked as to whether some uniformity could be achieved, as after all, we were all just doing the same job. We found that there would be no hope of uniform equipment and routines, as the present systems formed tentacles all over the country, which would be impossible to unravel. It was left that on a quarterly basis, each Board would report on its activities, and a combined statement would be circulated. Guess who had that job?

Another big job I was co-opted onto was the building of a very large central warehouse. We were really the forerunners of all the vast warehouse systems operating these days. Our problem was that we ran some 60 shops in town centres, with very limited storage space. You might display goods in the showroom, but if you had a sale, there was a delay as the goods had to be sent from the factory. Not a good way of doing business. A new central warehouse was planned for Washington, just on the south side of the Tyne. It was about the central point of our big area, and our delivery trucks could reach any part of the area in just over an hour. There were good "A" roads in all directions to help deliver quickly. It would also hold the masses of engineering materials we needed to maintain our systems. It was all automated; picking and delivery would be made the day after the sale, which was a vast improvement. It was a good two years in the planning and construction, but it worked a charm, and we were very proud of it.

NEEB was also a member of a Quango called Management Systems Training Council (MSTC). A whole range of large firms, both nationalised and public, supported it. Its aim was to increase productivity in the nation' workforce, by having properly trained managers in position. Somehow I got myself appointed as the User Group Secretary, which was a time-taking, but enjoyable task. One of the duties was to arrange a visit on a quarterly basis to a whole range of organisations, to show us the complexities of their work, and how they dealt with it. It was a day out each quarter, which was most enjoyable and eye opening to see how we compared to similar size operations.

We had visits to several nationalised industries - other Electricity Area Boards, Gas Boards, Atomic Energy Authority, Post Office, Local Councils, National Savings, as well as many well know private industries such as Marks and Spencer, Pilkingtons' Glass, Allied Brewery, Bournemouth Airport and many others. As well as being very educational, it was good fun, and let me go to various locations only the luckiest people get to. I have sat in the iconic Council Offices in Liverpool, and had lunch on the Mersey Ferry. I have been in the office where "ERNIE" the premium bond computer works. I have been on the underground railway that the Post Office runs between offices in London. And what could top a lunch given by the Allied Brewery at Burton? The overall opinion I formed by all these trips was that NEEB was at the cutting edge of technology and efficiency compared to the majority, which was most assuring.

In 1989, things started to change. The government decided that the electricity supply industry should be privatised. Surely they where not serious about it? But yes, the Electricity Bill 1989 was passed, and we were to be privatised. I thought it was a mistaken idea then, and I have not altered my views to date. We were a highly efficient industry, with all the profits being poured back in the form of modern equipment to keep it continually at the cutting edge. No more of that, as most of the profits would now go to paying dividends to shareholders. There was a depression hanging over all our staff. The first move was to change our name to Northern Electric. It was a massive pointless cost of changing all our letterheads and printed forms. In no time at all, foreign predators - French, German and American - were taking an interest in us, with a view to a take-over. "Experts" arrived en-masse to trawl through our affairs to prepare their bids. It was a hostile take-over, which they eventually won. I had had enough of it, and as I had got over forty years service behind me, I had the opportunity to retire on full pension. Even though I was only 62, it was too good to miss, and I was out of it. Lucky for me in many ways, as Pat's health was causing us a lot of trouble and anxiety.

1971 to 1989 proved to be joyful and tranquil years at work, and our home life was also very happy, although with a little anxiety growing over the period due to Pat's health. It was an ever-changing situation, with three children growing up with all their different needs and aspirations. I had my share of problems as well. In the winter of 1971, on a dark, cold and icy morning, a motorist behind me failed to see traffic slowing, and whacked into the back of my car on the A19 road near to the Coast Road. He pushed me into the back of the car in front of me before we came to a halt. The car seemed more damaged than me at first, and I thanked my lucky stars that I had escaped so lightly. Sometime later, I realised I was suffering from blurred vision, which was no doubt the result of the shunt. The outcome was that I had to have an operation on my left eye to repair the damage. A new lens had to be put in, and in those days it was a lengthy operation, and afterwards I had to lie still on my back with my eyes covered for seven days in the Royal Victoria Infirmary. These days, you are in and out in the same morning or afternoon. They inserted what was called a Binkhorst Clip, which was the state of art treatment at the time. It was only the state of art treatment for a couple of months as new things overtook it. It is still there in my eye after nearly 50 years.

Binkhorst and his famous clip are always mentioned in the medical textbooks that present day eye surgeons have to study for their exams. When new people examine me at the present time, they fall over themselves, as although they have read about it, they have never seen one. It results in telephone calls to all their colleagues, to come and have a look to complete their education.

With the children getting older, Pat and I decided to build an extension to the house, to give us more room. Pat was expert in drafting exactly what she wanted. The inbuilt garage was to be converted to an entrance hall. The lounge would be extended to include the old hall, which gave us much more living space. A new garage would be built against the existing outer wall, and at the back of it, there was room for a Utility Room. Above the garage and utility room, there was space for two good-sized bedrooms.

We installed gas-fired central heating all over the house. We no longer needed a coal house, so that space and the existing larder were incorporated into a bigger kitchen. Robert and Andrew now had separate bedrooms, and in addition, we had a guest bed room. We all felt the benefit of the extra space. Everything worked out to plan in the end, but it seemed to take an awfully long time. The children had plenty of animals as pets, and over the years, we had gerbils, hamsters, guinea pigs and stick insects. We had fun as the hamsters sometimes managed to escape, and we spent days searching for them. We were sold the guinea pig as a young male, and Christine was responsible for looking after him. Pat thought he was getting fat, and told Christine to feed him a little less. Christine got the shock of her life one morning, when she went to feed him, and found three guinea pigs in the hutch! We kept one of the babies, and gave the other to one of the schools Pat worked at. The stick insects were no trouble, but they were not very exciting.

The children were developing their own personalities. Robert was always out on his bicycle, and took a keen interest in cars. Even as a very young toddler, he could amaze people by knowing the make and model of all the cars that passed by. Andrew was always keen on dressing-up so he could be Batman, Superman, Robin Hood or a Sailor depending on his mood. He was also a bit of a boffin, who built a matchbox Crystal radio when he was very young. It worked too. Christine was always very keen on the arts. She attended Miss Quinn's Ballet school, and took part in many shows. She played the violin and piano, and passed exams at high grades, and played with the North Tyneside Youth Orchestra and the National Scout and Guide Symphony Orchestra. Christine also had a good voice, and in later years performed with Whitley Bay, Newcastle and West End Operatic Societies.

We continued to enjoy our annual holidays, with visits all over the place. We visited Wales, and stayed in Llandudno, with trips up and down the Little and Great Orme, visits to slate mines and loads of castles. We also visited Buxton in the Peak District, where we explored some underground caverns. We even managed to call in on Jodrell Bank.

Gatehouse of Fleet in south-west Scotland was also visited a couple of times, and it was there that we bumped into my Cousin Irene and her husband Chick who were also on holiday - a chance in a million encounter. The Lake District continued to be one of our favourite destinations, and we discovered a fairly remote farmhouse in Borrowdale, where we received a very good welcome. The boys also enjoyed camping with the Scouts and the Knoydart Peninsular in northwest Scotland.

When the children were a little older, Pat resumed her career as a teacher. She had no problem getting a job as a peripatetic science teacher with North Tyneside Council. They were woefully lacking in qualified science teachers in infant and primary schools, and Pat's job was to spend a day a week at five different schools. The objective was not only to give the children an interesting start to the subject, but also to encourage the teachers at the same time. Pat was very good at the job, and after a time, she lectured to teachers at the North Tyneside Teachers' Centre. We bought another car, a Hillman Imp, which she used in her travels around, and it was usually filled to the brim with all kinds of demonstration material that she carried with her.

Often at weekends we would go out foraging for stones, leaves, grasses, flowers, worms etc. for use in the coming week. There was one good occasion when she and her pupils built a hot air balloon, to demonstrate that hot air rises. The whole school came out to see the take-off, and it was sensational. It took off and went hundreds of feet in the air, and then drifted over North Shields. People were reporting an unidentified flying object to the police! How good is that in stimulating interest in kiddies? After some years, Pat then became the very successful Biology teacher at Valley Garden Middle School, and managed to teach our own children there.

Pat was having problems with her health, and was forced to retire early in about 1982. When she was quite young, she started complaining of stiff and sore fingers. She was eventually diagnosed with Rheumatoid Arthritis. It started affecting her other joints, and she eventually came under the care of the hospital. They started her on a new treatment, which was supposed to be a wonder drug. It was nothing of the kind, and it was withdrawn from the market following the deaths of patients, and other side effects. It made Pat's skin super sensitive, and it blistered in direct sunlight. The rays even penetrated clothing at times, and made life difficult. The side effects lasted many years, and curtailed our outdoor activities. Another catastrophic treatment was a gold injection. This treatment apparently worked well for most people, but it nearly killed Pat. It destroyed the platelets in the blood, which are vital to stop bleeding. Most people have a couple of hundred thousand platelets per cubic millimetre of blood. Some counts put Pat at 10,000, and her life was at risk to the extent that she had to have painful bone marrow transplants to boost her count. They soon understood that Pat had a very pernicious and aggressive form of Rheumatoid Arthritis, which was beyond their help. Pat's condition was deteriorating all the time, so I was thankful for early retirement to be able to help at home.

Robert left school after passing his exams, and got a job at NEEB. He worked for a time in the NorthTyneside District, and later at Carliol House. Andrew stayed on at school and passed his A levels, then went off to Salford University to study Computing. Pat and I went across to Salford for Andrew's graduation day, which was a happy occasion. Andrew then got a job at Systime, a computer firm in Leeds, and bought a flat in Leeds. Christine also sat her A levels, but was not successful in getting a place at Bretton Hall Music College in west Yorkshire. A big disappointment, but she recovered and went to North Tyneside College of Further Education, and qualified as a Nursery Nurse.

I can remember 1984 fairly clearly, as the Miners' strike affected the northeast very badly, with lots of hardship and enmity. It was a bitter affair, which started in March and lasted a year. It caused us a lot of problems in the electricity industry, with power outages and plenty of sitting in candlelight at home. It lasted a full year, until March 1985, and rankles many people until this day. I also remember this year for the first overseas holiday that Pat and I went on. We took a flight from Newcastle to Bergen, and spent a week in Norway, based at the Strand Hotel on the shores of the Hardanger Fjord at Ulvick. The weather was gorgeous, and the scenery spectacular. We went out on trips on several days, seeing Voss, Utne, Kinsarvik and many other great spots. It was our first taste of overseas holidays, of which there would be many in the future.

Around this time, Robert eventually bought a flat of his own in Percy Main, at 3 Fletcher House, St. Johns Green, and moved out for some independent living. Pat was paying regular visits to hospitals in Newcastle, so in 1985, we took the brave move and bought a newly built 3 bedroom bungalow at 5 Wells Close, Little Benton, Newcastle Upon Tyne, a move we never regretted despite spending thirty years of our lives in Whitley Bay. It meant making new friends and leaving lots of old ones. There was a lot of work to be done, as the garden looked like a building site. Pat had a pretty good idea of what the garden should look like, and with her design capabilities and knowledge of trees, shrubs and flowers, and my prowess as a labourer with a spade, the garden took shape over a couple of years.

Another major event was that Andrew was engaged to marry Geri Sidwell, also an employee of Systime, and they were married in Leeds on 14th September 1985, and bought a bungalow at 13 Wavell Grove, Sandal, near Wakefield. My Dad managed to get down for the wedding, and we also managed to get to Aberdeen in November to celebrate his 90th birthday.

1986 was also a memorable year for me. I remember I had a very bad back, which damaged itself when I was innocently sweeping the drive. I was bent over for days, and it was agony getting in and out of the car. I managed to stay at work, and just shuffled around. It took a couple of months of visits to the Chiropractor to put it right, but touch wood, nothing as bad has ever happened again.

Worse things happened to Pat. She had a replacement left hip and a new right knee put in at the same time, which took us a long time to adjust to. Another major event happened that year in April. I was sitting reading the paper, when my eye caught the ex service announcements - a reunion of the Mahar Regiment Officers at a hotel in Oxford. I had had no contact with the Mahars since I moved from Sixth Avenue in York in the late 1940s, so this was a complete shock to me, but one that raised my spirits. I wrote to the hotel to find out the address of their contact, which turned out to be Jack Webb, an old friend from some forty years ago. The Mahar Regiment was still alive and flourishing. Jack told me that three ex British Mahar Officers were planning to go on a visit to India in the autumn, and, after talking it over with Pat, I immediately signed on to go out there as well.

In October, four of us - Gordon Summers, Jack Webb, Bill Griffin and myself made the trip. I went to Heathrow on the overnight clipper service from Newcastle, and then by Thai Air to New Delhi. What an experience being back there in India, and being so warmly welcomed by the Indian Army. We were greeted at New Delhi airport by a whole galaxy of soldiers, and given army accommodation in New Delhi.

We then took a long train journey to Japulpur, where army transport was ready for the final part of the journey to Saugor, in Madya Pradesh, which was now the Regimental HQ of the Mahar Regiment. This location had previously been the Army School of Equitation, looking after the needs of Cavalry Regiments, and was a beautiful Cantonment with fine buildings and grounds. What a thrill it was to be amongst old friends, and see the advances the Regiment had made over the years. It was so much more smart and efficient than in my days. It had risen from 3 Battalions in 1947 to 19 Battalions, and had acquitted itself very well in defence of India against Pakistan and China, as well as giving great service to the United Nations' Blue Beret Forces. The Colonel of the Regiment was no other than my friend General Krishna Rao, who I knew as a Major in the 3rd Battalion, but was now Chief of Army Staff, the number 1 soldier in India.

They also had a number of Lieutenant Generals and Major Generals. The big military parade to celebrate the Reunion was mind blowing, much akin to the Trooping of the Colour on Horse Guards Parade in London. Dining in the Mess was a fantastic experience, and the wine waiters especially good at refreshing partly drunk glasses of wine without being noticed. It was altogether a top class experience. It was to be followed over the years with Annual Reunions at home, and visits to India every five years for a big reunion. It was a good job I was reading that paper and that my eyes were good enough to spot a connection back to the Mahars.

Pat and I still managed to enjoy times at the theatre, seeing both Kismet and Kiss Me Kate performed by the local amateurs. We were lucky to be able to get to Fort William in the Highlands of Scotland in August, even though Pat was still finding it difficult to move about after her joint replacements.

*Pat and me, retirement day, 1988*

*Thanks from the chairman after 40 years*

Example ICT 1301 Installation.

*301 mainframe computer, 1963*

*NEEB computer team*

*St Cuthbert's Presbyterian Church elders*

*The young family*

*The young family*

*The young family*

*The young family*

117

*The young family*

*The young family*

*The young family*

*Happy holidays*

*Happy holidays*

*Happy holidays*

119

*Happy holidays*

*Pat in her kitchen*

*Dad and me at Val's wedding*

*Andrew's graduation*

# CHAPTER 6

## NEWCASTLE-UPON-TYNE
## TO RETIREMENT

1987 started off in the same way as 1986 ended, with the main concern being Pat's health, and the way that the Rheumatoid Arthritis was slowly yet systematically destroying her joints. She had regular checks at the Freeman Hospital, being under the care of top consultants. Although they were making breakthroughs in all kinds of treatments, none of them seemed to work on Pat. She was steadily deteriorating. It was not only her main joints that were giving trouble, but also finger joints. She was in constant pain, and her movements were becoming very restricted.

Never the less, she had a never say die attitude to it all, with her mind and brain still at 100%. Her left knee was the next major problem, and had to be replaced with another long period of recovery. We always hoped there would be some kind of breakthrough, but we hoped in vain, and became reconciled to the fact that the disease would take its own course, but that we would fight it to the end, and try to keep as normal a lifestyle as possible. Pat got lots of visitors calling, and she was a good conversationalist, so there were still happy times to be had for her despite all of the difficulties.

We managed our summer holidays, with a week at Linden Hall Hotel, which is just north of Newcastle and has good facilities for disabled guests. Northumberland is a lovely county, and in the summer months, with good weather and very light traffic, was ideal for us. We also managed three or four nights in Harrogate, which is also a good touring centre.

The new garden was the source of a lot of hard work, but it was a joy to see its progress, and Pat's expertise with flowers produced first class results. We also continued to support the Amateur Operatic Societies, in productions of The Song of Norway and Half a Sixpence. It was around about this time that

Christine persuaded Robert to get involved back stage, and for a number of years he gave valuable support to Whitley Bay Operatic Society as Assistant Stage Manager.

Following my new found association with the Mahar Regiment; I attended the UK Reunion in Oxford in March, where I met several more of my old army friends. The annual reunion became a fixed date each year, around the end of March, and took me to far-flung places in England. Although wives were always invited, Pat was never able to come with me because of her disabilities. This was a great shame, as she would really have enjoyed herself in such good company.

My dad was getting into his 90's and living by himself in Aberdeen, so it was good to be able to visit him later in the year for a three-night stay. Isobel lived close by him and saw him most days, so I never really had any great worries about being so far from him. Nevertheless, I felt slightly uncomfortable having Pat by herself when I made the solo trip.

After moving to Wells Close in 1985, we still maintained our membership of Trinity Church in Whitley Bay - after all, we had been there since 1958, and it was very much part of our lives. It was only a 20-minute journey by car, and not much of a hardship to get there and back. I was the Church Secretary, and had a leading role in its running. Our long serving Minister, the Rev AP Dickey, who had been with us for 22 years, retired from the ministry, and we had a six month gap before a new Minister arrived. This was a very busy time for me, until a much younger Minister, the Rev M Armstrong, took over in the spring of 1988.

This was much to my relief, as 1988 turned out to be a hard year. Pat's right hand was in need of attention, and the surgeons at the RVI decided that all four knuckle and 4 main finger joints should be replaced. The bones in the hand are very complicated, and it needed endless visits to hospital for this to be done, and a long period of rehabilitation. We tried our best to keep things as close to normal as possible, and managed our normal holidays at Linden Hall Hotel in the summertime, and another one in Harrogate. I also had a solo trip to the Mahar Reunion weekend in the Bear Hotel in Street, way down in Somerset, which entailed an 800 mile round trip. Our visits to the Theatre were much curtailed, but we did get to see the Gilbert and Sullivan production of The Gondoliers. The most joyous part of the year was the birth of our first grandson, James, and we managed to get down to Sandal for his christening at the start of September.

My time at Northern Electric was coming to an end, as I had opted for early retirement after 40 years of service, mainly to devote more time to Pat, but also for not agreeing with all the impending changes in the organisation. For several weeks I attended a one-day a week pre-retirement course at the High Point Hotel in Cullercoats. My last day of duty was the 22$^{nd}$ March, and it turned out not so bad, as I had a nice retirement party at work, where Pat came along, and the Chairman made a presentation and a gracious speech. This was a watershed in my life, with me now approaching my 63$^{rd}$ birthday and having retired from work.

There were big changes in the offing for both Pat and myself, but we both relished the idea. Pat had her own routines of course, which I didn't want to interfere with too much, but we now had freedom to spend more time together, and have a bit of enjoyment. We seemed to cope quite well, and didn't get under each other's feet too much. We soon established some new routines, such as shopping in Newcastle every Wednesday morning, including coffee and jam doughnuts at M&S. We also set aside a day to have local trips in the car, taking a picnic with us, which was always a great success, whether it be at the coast looking out to sea, or in more rural Northumberland.

Friday morning was always the time for Pat's visit to the hairdresser. Pat was still blighted by operations, and the major one for the year was a right hip replacement. This one turned out to cause a lot more trauma for Pat. The anesthetic did not work properly, and for a short time whilst they were working on her hip, she could hear the surgeons talking, and feel them working on her. From her reactions, they soon knew about it, and saved the day by putting in some local blocks. I was all for putting in a complaint to the NHS, but Pat was against it, as she didn't want to fall out with the experts who had already given her good service, and on whom she would need to rely in the future. Following this, we were really forced to get a wheelchair for Pat so we could get around easier, and this soon became a fixture in our lives.

It was about this time that we acquired a kitten. Robert, who was living in a flat in Percy Main, was offered one, and he decided to give it a go. Robert was at work, of course, so it spent a lot of its time alone in his flat. It wasn't very happy, and wasn't eating at all, and got into a very weak state. Robert turned to us for help, and Pat and I responded by giving the kitten a home at Wells Close. She was a lovely looking calico kitten named Cal, of course, but was just a thin scrap weighing next to nothing. We couldn't get her to eat, and the only thing she showed an interest in was goats' milk. She would totally avoid any cat food that was put before her. The vet suggesting giving her chicken and fish, which Cal seemed to enjoy. After a time, we decided that the best thing for Cal was that she should stay with us for the company, and she became our much-loved pet for many years. She never did take to cat food, and always had chicken and fish. We roasted a chicken every week for her, and made regular trips to the fish quay in North Shields to get her supplies of fish. For a long time, Cal would not go outside the house, but eventually, she took a brave step and went out, and soon had a small territory, which she would defend fiercely against all comers.

Even when she was in the house, if another cat was seen outside, she would go berserk and throw herself at the windows, through the blinds. She always came in a night, apart from once during one summer, when she managed to get onto the roof, but was too scared to jump down. All efforts failed to get her off the roof, and it wasn't until the next day that she eventually came down. It didn't happen again, so she learned her lesson. She liked to go into the garage, and taught herself to bang the light pull against the door when she wanted to be let back in.

The new Minister at our church was much younger than his predecessor, and had new ideas about how things should be done. This was why we appointed him in the first place, to try to rejuvenate things. A number of people in the congregation were not happy with the changes, and made life very difficult for our new, young Minister. It was too much, and he resigned. I fully supported him, and after putting in over 30 years as Treasurer and Secretary of the Church, I decided to resign as well, and Pat and I moved to Christchurch, Forest Hall, which was on our doorstep. Pat and I were warmly welcomed there, and were soon taking part in the weekly activities. I joined the Carpet Bowls Club, becoming a good player as several cups and trophies testify, and still enjoy playing the game. This was a regular Tuesday evening event, and luckily it coincided with Pat attending a Ladies meeting, where she served as Chair lady for many years. I also became Chairman of the Finance Committee, so my expertise could still be used.

With the extra free time we had, with me being retired, we were able to have some nice breaks during the year. We were back at Linden Hall, which had become a firm favourite for us during the summer, and in the autumn we spent a week in the Lake District, staying at the Guyll Hotel in Ambleside. We also managed a week up in Aberdeen, staying with Isobel in Cove Bay, and managed a few good days out in the northeast of Scotland. For good measure, I also made another long journey down to Street, in Somerset, for my Indian Army reunion. We also did a bit of entertaining ourselves, with Pat's sister Pauline staying for a week. We had some lovely trips out in the car, including a beautiful day at Cragside, near Rothbury. Andrew and Geri came up with James from Wakefield for a few nights' break.

We had now reached the start of a new decade, the 1990s. Pat and I were into a familiar routine by now, made possible by my early retirement. Pat's condition never improved, and continued to slowly deteriorate. Hands and wrists seemed to be the bugbear now, with more or less weekly visits to the RVI and Freeman Hospitals. With the help of a wheelchair, Pat could still get round and about reasonably well. I still had spare time on my hands and was invited to help a couple of organisations on a voluntary capacity. We had joined the Newcastle Branch of Arthritis Care, which was a branch of some hundred odd members, all with the same kind of health problems, which met on a monthly basis. It was a talking shop really, where people could meet to discuss common problems, and pass on tips and hints that might be useful. We usually had some entertainment such as a speaker or music group, and we organised holiday breaks, and occasional trips out. They were short of Committee members to organise, so I was co-opted as Holiday Organiser.

Nationally, Arthritis Care had a few hotels adapted for disabled people, which branch members could book. It wasn't long before I was appointed Chairman of the branch, little knowing that I would be in post for well over 20 years, and that the workload would increase as the years went by. Nevertheless, it was a worthwhile job, which I enjoyed doing. At the same time, the important job of Treasurer for the Northern Province of the URC became vacant, and I was pressed to give it a go. This meant giving oversight to some 50 Churches in the north of England and Scotland, and was a sizeable job. It was well within my competence to do it, so I finally accepted the call. It certainly took up a lot of my spare time, but it was a worthwhile job that I enjoyed doing.

I had also started to attend the Brunswick Club, which met in Newcastle on a Tuesday morning. Attendances were about 110 to 120 men every week, with a top class speaker to listen to on a whole range of subjects. On one morning, the speaker was to be a top surgeon from the RVI, talking to us about his job. The meeting started at 10.30am and with a short coffee break included, ended at 12.00 noon. With about 5 minutes to go, a phone call was taken from him apologising that he was too busy to come. Then ensued total panic by the Chairman, who pleaded for someone to fill the slot. No one wanted to take on the challenge. I knew that I could easily speak for an hour off the cuff on my time with the Mahar Regiment in India, so I put my hand up and volunteered.

I gave them a good hour on the Mahars, and it turned into a great success. It was the start of something big, as my name was put on the Speakers' list which circulated between the many clubs on Tyneside, and bookings started rolling in. This continues to the present day, with a whole range of talks that are on my list, such as The Mahar Regt., Life in the Indian Army, Adventures on the NW Frontier, Round the World in 120 Days, Remote Islands, The Tropic of Cancer, The Tropic of Capricorn, Charitable Cruising, Not so Plain Sailing, Name Dropping, Mountain Passes, the Amazon, Life Story and so on. I do not need notes, so I can concentrate on the delivery, and can talk for an hour at least on all these topics at the drop of a hat. I usually get paid a fee, ranging from £25 from smaller clubs to £50 or so from bigger Rotary Clubs. I give all the fees I receive to a range of charities.

The big holiday of the year was a week in Cavtat, a small place just across the bay from Dubrovnik, in Yugoslavia as it was in those days before the Balkans' troubles caused the big war and subsequent break-up of the country. About 30 of the Arthritis Care Branch managed the trip, accompanied by a specialist doctor. The whole holiday was wonderful, with fine weather, good food and accommodation, and a bus that took us all over the place. Not bad for the first holiday I had organised. Most had never been overseas before, and had given up hope of ever flying away somewhere, so the whole thing was very worthwhile. It certainly gave me an appetite for travel, and seeing different countries and people.

On a more domestic note, Pat and I spent more time at Linden Hall, and also managed trips to Rothbury and Bamburgh with Church friends. The year saw the birth of Alex, in June, a brother for James, and we had a couple of trips down to Sandal to see the new family. I managed to see Isobel on two occasions. She was spending a few days at Seahouses, and Pat and I went up there for a day's outing, and we all had a good time.

Later in the year, Dad and Isobel spent a few days' holidaying in Newcastle with us. My Dad was well over 90 by this time, and was still remarkably fit for his age. Robert was now living in Brock Farm Estate in North Shields, an upgrade on his first flat. He was also now in a different position in Northern Electric, having been promoted to an Energy Advisor, with the whole of Northumberland being his territory. By this time, Andrew had also transferred jobs and worked with Tunstall, a firm who specialise in medical computing. This was just the kind of job Andrew wanted, and he has progressively advanced into the management of the company.

The year 1991 was now upon us, and it did not prove to be a very good one in term of world peace and harmony. The first Gulf War started with a big allied force ejecting the Iraqis from Kuwait. News programmes were full of terrible scenes of burning oil wells and mayhem. The Iraqis were ejected and soon defeated. The victory was never taken to its conclusion, and anarchy came back to haunt us again a few years later, and still to this day is one of the worlds biggest problems. To compound all this, unrest started in the Balkan States; with Serbia flexing it's strength, starting a war that again lasted some years. Wars seemed to be the flavour of the day, and the world has never been at peace since then.

Where did it all go wrong? The world leaders must sleep uneasily at night for allowing it all to fall into such a state. Prospects looked a bit brighter when, at the same time, the mighty USSR collapsed and split into 15 different entities. It looked at the time that the Cold War was ended, but even to this day, Russia is still looked on as the bogeyman. But who am I to make judgements on it all? On the brighter side of life, it was the year that World Wide Web was introduced, and the first website started. Who could have foretold the massive impact that it would have on our lives?

Meanwhile, our own domestic situation didn't change that much. Pat and I were into a regular routine that kept us occupied and happy. We were now reconciled to the fact that there was no miracle cure that would have stopped the Rheumatoid Arthritis, which was slowly destroying Pat's joints, and causing her much pain. The year saw more operations on her hand and wrist joints, and weekly visits to the hospitals for physiotherapy and check-ups.

By 1992 we were getting used to be a retired couple and life continued in a well established pattern. Pat was very much restricted in her activities because the dependence on replacement joints was inevitably taking its toll. Hospital visits were now well established in our weekly time-tables and over the year there were plenty of those. The main problem was a replacement right shoulder joint. Pat was now a seasoned veteran when it came to major surgery and was remarkable in her resilience in overcoming such things. Life was far from easy at times but we managed to live within our capabilities.

I was now doing far more household chores and getting quite proficient at cooking, shopping, cleaning and the rest. I still had ample time to indulge in my usual activities of looking after church finances and chairing Arthritis Care, Newcastle. As always my own church was getting into a poor state of repair and looking in need of some tender care and an appeal was launched for a target of £100,000 to enable it to be brought up to standard. This of course brought extra work in for me which lasted a couple of years before the target was reached and rebuilding started.

Holidays were of course a godsend to us and we managed a few in the year. The Lake District was near to us and we always enjoyed our visits there. We spent a lovely three nights at the Derwentwater Hotel in Braithwaite just a mile or so out of Keswick. Crieff in Perthshire is a similar kind of place with mountains and lakes all around and the pace of life more serene and a weeks holiday did us a power of good. We also managed to get in a weeks holiday in Largs on the Clyde estuary in Scotland. This was at one of the Arthritis Care hotels which was adapted to the needs of disabled people and was wheelchair accessible throughout. It was only a two minute walk from the sea front with glorious views over the sea to the island of Rothesay and further away to Arran and Bute. The Branch hired the Jumbo Ambulance for the week to give us trips around to Loch Lomond etc. The Jumbo was a bus specially adapted for wheel chairs and disabled people to use and proved invaluable to us. We also used it on a day trip to Whitby for our annual AC outing It is a lovely little seaside town and the fish and chips they serve are just the best.

I also spent a weekend in York for The Mahar Reunion dinner which was a very nostalgic return to my old home. Christine and I also managed the Great North Walk to raise money for charity. It was about 12 miles in nice open country and the fresh air and the views were welcomed. We had some visitors during the year with Andrew and Geri and the two young lads staying with us for a couple of nights. Also Pauline, Pats sister who had not been the best of health stayed a few nights also. We took the opportunity to visit some of the National Trust properties and English Heritage places which were in car driving distance. Our appetite for the local amateur operatic societies was still with us and we supported several shows including Charlie Girl and Kismet. The year ended with me spending a short time in Aberdeen to get up-to date with family news.

This was the year that Barcelona staged the Olympic Games and there was some wonderful television viewing to be had. My memory tells me we didn't do very well with the Spanish excelling on home territory. It was also the year that the UK signed the Maastrict Treaty to join the EU.

As we started going through the 1990s Pats medical condition continued to deteriorate and by 1993 it became clear that a wheelchair was now a necessity if we wanted to get around and about outside. Pat could manage walking inside the house and round the garden but beyond that it was too much for her. It was a step we were reluctant to take as it seemed another stage on a downward spiral but realistically we had little option. A new fold up wheelchair was purchased and good use was made of it. I was still very fit and Pat was very light so it took very little effort for me to become a very proficient chair pusher. It was kept in the boot of the car. It was a real boon when we paid our weekly visit in town to the Eldon Shopping Centre and a smooth ride round the shops was guaranteed. It was not so good outside on the pavements and roads especially if they were badly maintained and in need of repair. I had to slow down a lot as the constant shaking of the chair was not good for Pats sore joints. Access and passage through some of the older shops at times restricted where we could go and what we could do. Sometimes getting higher than the ground floor was impossible if there was no lift.

The other great drawback was that many people would never talk to the person in the wheelchair and always directed remarks to the pusher much to Pats annoyance. It didn't improve as the years went by either. The chair was especially helpful when we went on holiday and I walked miles along the flat promenades on the coast of Spain in Benidorm and Fungerola. It was also well used along the long corridors of the Royal Victoria Infirmary and the Freeman Hospital which we seemed to visit far too often. Pat had her left hand joints replaced in the RVI during the year which entailed a couple of weeks stay in the hospital and then seemingly endless visits for physiotherapy. We were determined not to let all this get in the way of our normal activities and so we continued to have some very nice holidays. We had a lovely week in Benidorm in January which took us away from the cold winter conditions at home into the relative warmth of southern Spain. The warmer weather seemed to lift our spirits and did us the power of good. We paid a visit to Bridlington in the springtime to visit Pauline who was Pats younger sister. The Lake District was also a favourite of ours and we managed a couple of nights at the Derwentwater Hotel in Braithwaite.

Arthritis Care also organised a couple of holidays during the year to stay at their customised hotels in Blackpool and Largs. We were part of a party of some 30 people from the Newcastle Branch and we used the Jumbo Ambulance for the week to take us on trips. Largs won hands down with some beautiful coast line around, plenty of islands and some wonderful Scottish country side. We had rooms specially adapted for wheelchair users and the Jumbo had a lift to cater for people sitting in wheel chairs. We finished our holidays for the year at another old favourite with some nights at the Linden Hall Hotel in Northumberland and a couple of nights at The Cross Keys Hotel in Kelso.

Pat was kind enough to let me get away a couple of times for brief stays in Aberdeen to see my dad, who was well into his 90's. I also went on a long journey to Overton Grange near Ludlow for their Mahar reunion. I went by car, it was a tedious journey but it was the only way I could get there. Thankfully we only held one Reunion at the place. A nice spot but many miles too far.

One would think that with all the holidays and hospital visits we had there would be no spare time for other things but in fact we kept very busy. Andrew and Gerri with their family visited us a couple of times and stayed with us. We had great times during the summer holiday visiting places in Northumberland and had great amusement playing. Tennis and Putting with the boys in the park at Morpeth. Pauline who had not been keeping too well spent a week with us in October and we made the most of the fine autumn weather out in Northumberland at places like Cragside, Belsay Hall and Wallington.

I filled my time up with the endless duties connected to my posts as Chairman of Arthritis Care and as Northern Province Treasurer of the URC and Pat and I spent plenty of time in Church activities at Christchurch Forest Hall. I can also remember visiting the Gateshead Games with Christine where some good international athletes were racing. All good fun. There were still wars in the world with a new one starting in Sri

Lanka where one of my fellow Mahar Officers won a posthumous Indian VC for bravery. On a brighter note the IRA called a ceasefire in Ireland after too long a campaign.

1994 started in much the same way as previous years with a two week holiday planned for the middle of January - this time to Benidorm in sunny Spain. Pat and myself looked forward to this break as it took us away from the snowy cold weather and short dark days of January at home in Newcastle. At this time of year in Benidorm the sun shines on most days with temperatures reaching the lower 20s centigrade. It was a time to relax, enjoy a change of food and culture and generally recharge our batteries after a busy time over Christmas.

Benidorm had a reputation of being over-run with crowds of drunken people causing trouble, but we never experienced this during our winter breaks. The majority of visitors were in fact Spanish old age pensioners who got preferential treatment at that time of year, Benidorm had two long promenades covering the north and south bays each of around two miles in length. They were absolutely flat which made pushing Pat in her wheelchair very easy. The beaches were beautifully clean and the sea sparkling with plenty of nice places to stop for a drink or other refreshments. However events overtook us as on our second day there we got a phone call from home telling us that Pauline (Pats younger sister) was seriously ill in hospital in Cottingham near Hull and was not likely to survive. The holiday had to be abandoned and we flew home next day courtesy of Air Portugal who had spare seats on a flight to Heathrow.

When we arrived home in Newcastle the news could not have been worse as we learned that Pauline had died the previous day. Death in the close family had not been a worry for us for the past twenty years so it was taken very badly. We managed a trip down to Cottingham where we met Peter and Peggy and the rest of the family but it was a distressing time. Paulines funeral was held in Sheffield a week or so later. Pauline had spent a few years living in Sheffield and along with her second husband Ron had made their home there managing a Public House. Curtis her son by her first marriage along with his family also lived in Sheffield. Pauline was sadly missed as she was a lovely lady. She had been an expert potter with her own kiln who made high class products which she decorated herself and sold in expensive outlets. I still have one or two of her pots and vases at home. To make the year worse my Dad also died in the middle of June in Aberdeen. This was not so much of a shock as he was 99 years old at the time and I knew from earlier visits that his health was failing. My Mother had died some 19 years before and Dad had lived most of his life after this in sheltered accommodation comfortably and content. He was very active right to the end and I am sure he had a happy life. Isobel of course lived close by and was constantly in touch with him so I never really had to worry much after his well being.

After the debacle on our holiday in January we did manage to have a couple of weekly breaks in Scotland. Firstly we went to Crieff Hydro in central Perthshire where the hotel was a lovely place to stay and it was ideal for touring around the magnificent scenery of the Highlands. It was in mid June and the weather was perfect - a little compensation for the lack of sunshine in January.

One day we went to Glamis Castle and spent the day with Isobel who travelled across from Aberdeen. Our second weeks holiday was with an Arthritis Care group at our old favourite spot of Largs, once again making use of the Jumbo Ambulance. Pat continued with her series of operation, this time being a replacement of her left shoulder. All these operations took a toll on Pat. We accepted that they were necessary, but each joint that was replaced caused a deterioration of the quality of her life and with so many joints being replaced she was really disadvantaged. Never-the-less we continued to live as full a life as possible under the circumstances.

We managed a day trip to Gilsland with Arthritis Care, a nice rural spot way to the west of Northumberland close to the Cumbrian border. Due to more pressing needs I failed to attend The Mahar Regiment Reunion. It was held again in Ludlow which was a little bit too far away for me. All our other commitments were kept, chairing meetings etc and attending the amateur operatic societies productions. I think it was Oliver that took pride of place. Christine and I made our annual pilgrimage to the Gateshead International Stadium to see some international athletes at their best.

As far as the outside world was concerned it was all still mostly gloom and doom. On a brighter note Nelson Mandela became President of South Africa and at long last the Channel Tunnel was opened. And an up-and-coming new technology firm called Apple was started. Why didn't I buy some shares when the going was good?

1994 had been a poor year for Pat and myself with the deaths of Pauline and my Dad. We looked to 1995 to be kinder to us and so it turned out to be. There were prospects of a wedding as Christine was engaged to a fellow called Colin Docherty and a wedding was scheduled for the middle of the year. Also we had seen an advert in the paper for a tour of the Canadian Rockies in the autumn specially designed for disabled people and we thought we would give it a shot. Both these events eventually came to happen.

The beginning of the year started off with a fortnight in Benidorm to get a little bit of summer sunshine. After the debacle of the previous years holiday in Spain, this one turned out fine with no problems at all. We were quite happy just to relax in the sunshine and take advantage of the nice walks along the promenades. Benidorm has two main beaches, with Playa de Levante to the north and Playa de Poniete to the south each with a lovely flat and smooth promenade of about two miles in length for each of them. In between them is the old town of Benidorm with its old harbour which not much earlier had been a small fishing village. There are plenty of places to sit down and rest with numerous trees to give much needed shade.

We also took advantage of one or two bus excursions which took us inland and where we saw picturesque and sometimes very old villages. It wasn't all plain sailing on the buses. They could easily store the wheel chair in the hold of the bus, but Pat had extreme difficulty getting into the bus as the steps were very steep indeed. Also at some of the stops the cobbled streets in many of the villages didn't make for a comfortable ride in a wheel chair. On top of that it was extremely hilly and a tough task for a wheel chair pusher. On many occasions Pat had also to miss out on some of the attractions as there were so many steps up to the entrance. This was particularly true of the old churches. Very often some of the stronger young men gave help and lifted

Pat and the chair up to the top so that she would not miss out. I was very thankful for their efforts.

We also had an excellent holiday in Largs with our Arthritis Care friends at the end of May with the weather in west Scotland remaining dry and warm which certainly does help when you are away from home. We turned down a chance for another holiday with the group a couple of months later to Blackpool as we were already booked for our adventure to Canada later on in the year. However, we did manage to get on a days outing with the group to Jedburgh on the Scottish border. It was a lovely trip through great scenery over Carter Bar into Scotland and for the ladies a chance to spend money at the many woollen mill outlets to be found in the locality. I had my usual weekend trip to The Mahar Regiment Reunion, this time a very long journey to The Mill House Hotel situated in the small village of Ashington in West Sussex. This was again most enjoyable seeing all my wartime friends again and having much fun and laughter over recounting incidents in our lives so many years ago.

One of the events of the year happened on Saturday 6th May at 2.00pm, which was of course the marriage between Christine and Colin Docherty at St Georges United Reformed Church in High Heaton, Newcastle. It was a nice service and I contributed by giving the main reading. Christine looked pristine of course in her long white wedding dress. Judy her friend made a good bridesmaid and the two Grandsons James and Alex were page boys. They were very young at the time and I remember them both wearing fancy waistcoats and bow ties but were well behaved and carried out their duties admirably.

The Reception afterwards was at the Holiday Inn at Seaton Burn and these are always happy occasions and one of the few times that all the extended family can meet together. Sadly I have to recount that the marriage, like so many these days, did not last very long and ended acrimoniously in divorce. Colin at the time seemed to be a reasonable fellow, although clearly not a high flyer, and he kept his real character well hidden at the time. When that came out, the writing was on the wall for the marriage. More on that later.

Pats health continue to deteriorate and the hospitals were our second home. This was the year for elbows and ankles as the rheumatoid arthritis tightened its grip. We did not let this stop us from planning a trip to Canada. Pat still had plenty of plenty of spirit and I was still fit enough to push a wheel chair and attend to everything that had to be done. Before the much anticipated trip to Canada there was another great moment for me in the year. On the 19 August a big military parade was planned in London to mark the 50th anniversary of Victory over Japan. The Queen would take the salute at the march past of some 10,000 military personnel who had served in the far east.

I received an invitation from the Indian Army Association to take part in this great event. Gordon Summers and myself were the only two Mahars flying the flag on the big day. It involved a long trip down to London for the day and plenty of stamina. It was one of the best days weatherwise for the whole year, with nonstop warm sunshine all the time. There were about 200 ex Indian Army officers in the detachment I marched with and we were ably led by Bernard Weatherall who had been Speaker of the House of Commons from1982 to 1994. He was a captain with King George V Own Lancers during the war before rising to the lofty heights of one of the highest positions in the land. We were very near the front of the parade with the Band of the Gurkha Brigade marching just in front of us. There must have been at least half a million spectators along The Mall and in central London having a fiesta time.

It was easy to march along to some martial music with heads held high and arms swinging receiving the adulation and applause of the massed crowds. The Queen and Prince Phillip together with Charles and Diana and their two small sons were on The Mall to receive our salute as we passed by to the tune of Colonel Bogey. It was a truly memorable never to be repeated event. It all ended at about four pm with a fly past over Buckingham Palace by around about hundred aircraft.

September came along and it was time for our much anticipated trip to Canada. We were both really up for it although we realised it was going to stretch Pats endurance powers to their limits. The party met at Heathrow for an Air Canada flight to Calgary and it was a mixed bunch with around half a dozen wheelchair users and others with limited capacity to move quickly. It seemed a long flight which I suppose it was. We made a quick landing in Edmonton which is also in Alberta before we reached our destination of Calgary less than an hour later. We were given a warm reception from our tour guide and the bus driver and were glad to book in quickly at our hotel where we were able to relax a little after the long flight. Our tour guide was a fellow called Gordie West and he was very knowledgable and nothing was too much trouble for him.

He was an extrovert who had his own disc jockey programme on the local media and always carried his guitar with him. He was an expert country and western singer as well as a raconteur and there was never a dull moment during the whole trip. He was ably abetted by Henry Franzeb who was an excellent driver as well as being a foil to Gordie all the time. After a good nights sleep we had a full day in Calgary. It is a big modern city which oozed affluence with its many magnificent houses and gardens. It had recently hosted the winter Olympic Games and they were keen to show off all the facilities they had provided. As well as being a centre for modern industry and technology Calgary had been a big cattle town and still prided itself for the Calgary Stampede which was a big Rodeo event and we had a visit to the big show ground where it was held. The Rocky Mountains could be seen fifty or so miles west of Calgary and that is where we headed in the evening for a two nights stay.

The weather in Canada was absolutely perfect with cloudless skies and warm sunshine every day. Banff was a small resort town in the centre of the Banff National Park totally surrounded by mountains and lakes, with hot springs as a bonus. It has a wonderful main street overlooked by the massive Banff Springs Hotel. We were in a smaller hotel situated at the other end of the main road. The big hotel was built by The Canadian Pacific Railways and the railways play a big part in the life of this part of Alberta and British Columbia. A train journey through the Rockies is still classed as one of the best rail experiences in the world. We managed to reach the summit of Sulpher Mountain at about 2500 metres which was the highest peak in the vicinity and I have a nice certificate to prove it. The views were of course magnificent and it was well worth the effort. We also managed a short stay at the Bow Falls which again was a breathtaking place.

The next stage of our trip was to Jasper situated in the Athabasca River basin surrounded by the Jasper National Park.

On our way there we called in at Lake Louise which is a wonderful picture postcard kind of a place with a most picturesque lake with a backdrop of mountains and glaziers. An hours walk along the banks of the lake is sufficient to make you think you are in heaven. It was there that I had a shot of playing a very long alpine horn with very little success. We also managed afternoon tea at the very prestigious five star hotel which is in the grounds at one end of the lake. Jasper is just a small isolated spot but very popular for its winter sports activities. It is surrounded by numerous lakes with wooded slopes all around. We took a particular liking to Patricia Lake for obvious reasons.

We also skirted Medicine Lake which was particularly low in water and Gordie said the locals didn't know the reason for it. We told him that in fact it was a spoonful of sugar that makes the medicine go down. There was also Maligne Lake where the colour of the water was incredible. Pat and I managed to reach the summit of Whistlers Mountain at around 8000 feet which is the highest peak in the vicinity. You could see as far as the lordly peak of Mount Robson at some 13000 feet over 60 miles away over snow covered mountains. Nearer to view was the township of Jasper away down in the valley some 5 miles away The effort was well worth it and they gave us a certificate of proof of our achievement which I still have. After a two night stay in Jasper we were off to Kamloops by way of the Columbia Ice Field. This was worth a long stop where we boarded a huge ice explorer vehicle for a tour of the ice fields.

There was proof easy to see with the eye that the ice field was shrinking way back in those days when global warming was not top of the agenda. We also spent a couple of hours at the very historical Cache Creek which was akin to going back to the time of the gold diggers at the end of the 1800s. After a nights stay in Kamloops we were off to Whistler. This is a high ski resort and very popular in the winter. No skiing whilst we were there as it was out of season. Never the less, it was a very enjoyable stay as it is a very beautiful location, very expensive and quite exclusive. There were many good shops for the ladies and a big choice of high class eating outlets. I even bought a nice winter jumper with the Whistler logo which I still sometimes wear.

The next stage of our adventure was a ride down through the mountains to the sea where we boarded a ferry and landed at Nanaimo up on the east coast of Victoria Island. It was a great journey on the ferry passed the many small islands that dominate that area. On the way to Victoria we called at the small seaside town of Chemanus for afternoon tea. This was a well kept little place noted world-wide for about forty large murals which cover many of the buildings. A couple of nights were spent in Victoria which has a big harbour and plenty of activity surrounding it.

One day was visited the Buchard Gardens which have a world-wide reputation for the range of beauty of their plants. The gardens seemed to be the home of all kinds of activities for groups interested in yoga and similar life enhancing exercising. Then it was back on the ferry and over to Vancouver. This is a big modern city with a large seaport and I would think that it would be a lovely place to live in. It has a huge open area called Stanley Park which was a centre for sporting and cultural activities. The City has also some unique older areas such as Chinatown and Gastown which were worth a visit. We also spent a lovely time at Capalano Suspension Bridge. This is in a wooded area just out of the city and it is a narrow pedestrian bridge which stretches over 140 metres traversing a 70 metre wooded valley with a stream in it. The slightest movement makes the bridge sway making for a very uncomfortable crossing. You always have the feeling that the bridge is going to let you down. I crossed by myself as Pat did not fancy it in the slightest.

After a night in Vancouver it was off to the airport for a nonstop flight to Heathrow. All in all a memorable trip with a few problems such as wheelchair access in hotel rooms being dealt with so successfully by our good guide Gordie.

So 1995 turned out to be as well as we could expect. We kept all our normal activities going including our support for the local operatic groups rendering of The Mikado, Paint your Wagon and The Sound of Music. However, I felt it necessary to resign at the end of the year from the not inconsiderable duties as Provincial Treasurer and Trustee. This was a job I loved doing but it took up a lot of time and my view was that Pat was owed more time.

After all the excitement of the previous year Pat and I were looking forward to a quieter and less eventful time. We had booked for our usual fortnight early in the year in Spain to get us away from the cold weather into some nice warmth and sunshine. For a change from Benidorm we decided to go further south to the Costa del Sol to Fuengarola.

It was an easy journey from Newcastle to Malaga on the plane and only half an hour onwards to our hotel. Fuengarola had been a small fishing village but like a lot of seaside places in Spain it had developed a tourist industry and was now a big attraction for holiday makers from Spain and other countries. It was not as well developed or popular as Benidorm and it had retained many of its attractive historical charms which were not as brash as the skyscraper environment at Benidorm. It boasted two long sandy beaches either side of its busy harbour and its promenades were ideal for pushing the wheel chair for Pat.

At the south end of the town there is a well maintained medieval Moorish Fortress called Suhail which dominates the landscape. With a good hotel and nice food and company it suited us admirably. Spanish visitors outnumbered all other nationalities which we found better than previous years when British visitors and their customs seemed to dominate. This spot was an ideal base for daily excursions on the bus.

In particular we had a lovely day visiting Ronda which retains a lot of its old Moorish historical charms. It is in a very hilly area and the old and new parts of the small time are separated by a 100 metre deep gorge which is crossed by an 18th century bridge. It is a very picturesque place but the cobbled streets didn't make for a smooth ride in a wheelchair.

We also spent a great day in Gibralter which was not all that far away. I had passed by Gibralter during the war on ships but had never landed there. It is just a dot at the end of the Iberian Peninsular and it has been a British Oversees Territory since 1713. The Spanish are still irked by the situation and the border controls and checks are rigorous and passing over the border can be very tedious and time wasting. It is also odd in that the road over the border crosses the runway of the airport which does not seem a good idea, but the space is so limited there is no alternative. It is a nice enough place in itself with lots to do and see but the main attraction is that is a tax free haven which makes shopping very attractive.

The holiday was going remarkably well, when out of the blue some three days before we were due to fly home, we had a phone call from Christine to tell us that Isobel, my sister, had died. The episode last year had been bad enough but for it to happen again made us think that fate had a grudge against us. There was little I could have done by going home straight away, so we decided to see the holiday out but it certainly put a damper on it. I flew up to Aberdeen the following week for the funeral.

Isobel had moved back to Scotland in 1954 when she married Norman. They had a happy life there living in Rosemount where they ran a Dental Practice. Norman was the dentist and Isobel with her nursing and secretarial experience gave valuable help especially on the admin side of the business. Isobel took a full part in Aberdeen social life. She was a city magistrate for many years, also the County Commissionaire for the Girl Guide Association and a leading light at the local Church. When Norman died she moved from the big house they had in Aberdeen to a smaller bungalow in Cove Bay where she lived happily for many years. In her latter years she spent a lot of time travelling to far away places and enjoyed herself. The spirit of adventure in foreign climes must be in the genes as I had similar ambitions to travel widely

The next big event was my 70th birthday and with me being still fit and healthy I rejoiced that I had passed the three score years and ten which was the biblical norm for a life. There was no great celebration but I think we did go out to a celebration meal which was followed by a visit to the theatre.

For most of the year we followed our regular routines. Monday, Wednesday and Friday were washing machine days and I usually did the weeks ironing on Monday. Tuesday morning was always taken up with a visit to the Brunswick Club. On Wednesday Pat and I always tried to get into town for two or three hours to trawl round the shops and morning coffee at M & S. Thursday evening was a bowls evening for me, whilst Pat was at her evening meeting which she continued to lead.

Friday morning was always reserved for the weekly shopping and a visit to Pats hairdresser. Weekends invariably were devoted to church linked activities. We always continued to have a good Sunday dinner followed by trips out in the car. By this time I was doing much of the cooking under strict control of Pat. Regular meetings were held with my Arthritis Care friends and the many duties connected with that continued unabated On top of these routine activities visits to the hospitals took up a large slice of our time. Pats health problems multiplied as she was having major trouble with her feet and ankles. Special shoes were needed provided by the Hospital and they never seemed to get them right. Pat always took great pride in her appearance and the hospital shoes were hideous which did not help.

I still managed to get to my Mahar Reunion, this time in Ashington in Sussex - yet another very long journey there and back. We also managed a trip to Wakefield to see the family and also spent a couple of nights in Grimsby, I must have been keeping fit as together with Christine we completed the Great North Walk again.

Our second main holiday of the year was to Nairn with Arthritis Care. We booked the Jumbo Ambulance again for the full week and had a wonderful time. It was first visit to Nairn which is near to Inverness way up in North West Scotland. Nairn is a small seaside town with a wonderful beach and promenade and looks out onto the Moray Firth as far as Dingwall in Ross County. The hotel was specially adapted for disabled guests with friendly staff, good rooms and excellent food. It was also an ideal base for trips out in the Jumbo Ambulance. It was all so relaxing and enjoyable. In addition to all this we managed a couple of nights stay at our favourite Linden Hall in Northumberland.

The year sadly ended in another death. Aunt Helen, my Dads sister, sadly died. Again I flew up to Aberdeen for the funeral.

World-wide the year was not that good. The Taliban took control in Afghanistan. Osama Bin Laden was issuing provocative statements, Troubles continued with civil war in the Balkans, France was test exploding nuclear bombs in the Pacific. Mad cow disease was reported in the UK. It seemed all bad news. One bright spot in the year was that Newcastle United signed

Alan Shearer from Blackburn for a record fee. He turned out to be worth it.

1997 turned out to be a year when my whole range of emotions was tested. The whole year turned on two events in December when I reached the heights of joy and plumbed the depths of despair within days of each other. Christine became pregnant early in the year and Pat and I looked forward to having a new grandchild early in December. Events did not materialise as predicted as the new arrival did not put in an appearance and Christine was eventually admitted to the Maternity Wing in the Royal Victoria Infirmary. At the same time Pat had not been well and she was admitted for observation and rest into the Freeman Hospital.

My life was dominated by hospital visits both afternoon and evening. Eventually on 19th December a new baby girl (Bethany) was induced and both Christine and Bethany received excellent attention, thrived and were eventually released home, although it had been a tough time for Christine. It was also a tough time for Pat, as being in hospital she was unable to give Christine the support she would have been able to give and also missed out on spending some quality time with the new baby.

All this was soon overtaken a few days later when I got a call from the Freeman Hospital to get there as quickly as possible as there had been a big downturn in Pat's condition. Her right leg had developed a serious infection which was threatening her life and the only solution to save her was a total amputation of her leg from above the knee. We were given just a few quick minutes to think about it as she was going down-hill very quickly. The only practical solution was to agree to the amputation which was carried out more or less immediately. It was an awful decision to have to come to. Pat's quality of life had not been great in the previous year or so but this was going to have a major influence on our lives. Pat was mentally very strong but very weak physically as all her major joints were replacements and she did not have much strength in her body.

We made a pact that we would fight on together and make the very best of the new circumstances. It had been a mixed year of health for Pat but it had started off in its usual fashion. We had our usual trip in January to the sunshine visiting Minorca for the first time. It was a quieter and probably a more refined place than our previous Spanish haunts but most enjoyable all the same. We also managed to fit in a week at Nairn. We had enjoyed the rest in Nairn the previous year and this visit reinforced our belief that it was a marvellous spot to holiday for a week. Also towards the end of the year we ventured to Peebles on the Scottish border for a few nights stay at the Hydro. It was a big old hotel but offering magnificent accommodation and service which was just what we needed. There were also plenty of places for a drive out in the car in the beautiful border countryside.

I also managed a couple of nights at the Mahar Regiment Reunion, this time at Moreton on the Marsh in Gloucestershire. Unfortunately because of Pats health I wasn't able to accept the invitation to attend the 9th Reunion of the Regiment held in Saugor, India later on in the year.

The other sad event for the year was that Auntie Meg, my Dad's sister, died in Aberdeen. She had been a very nice person and had been part of my life for seventy years.

Nationally two big events dominated the year. Princess Diana was killed in a car crash in Paris and her funeral dominated the news with the nation in mourning - a sad end for a very nice person who deserved a little better than that. Politically there was an earthquake with Tony Blair becoming Prime Minister. I always held him in high regard and still do so, although many hold different views.

Life seemed to lose its reality for a time with the impact of Pats leg being amputated. It was a life changing situation that confronted us but at least we had time to make our plans on how we dealt with it. Pat was in hospital non-stop for two months and gradually came to terms with the consequences.

I was now living a solitary life at home broken by visits both afternoon and evening to the hospital to see Pat. The shopping, cooking, laundry, house cleaning, gardening was now all down to me. Thankfully Pat had left lots of notes which were of great assistance to me. I learned quickly and seemed to cope alright. The cooking could have been my weak spot, but I had a note-book full of recipes and hints together with what temperature and for how long. Without that I would have been lost.

Pat, stuck in a hospital bed for the majority of the time must have had a most boring time. Her only highlight was that after around six weeks or so she was provided with an electric wheelchair which allowed her to get out of the hospital ward and at least see other parts of the hospital and sometimes even get a breath of fresh air.

The longer term plan was that she would be given a prosthetic limb which would enable her to walk again. This was pie in the sky in reality. It would have been difficult for a strong able bodied person to achieve any kind of competency in this new art of walking as it required the use of crutches in the early stages of training. Pat had artificial upper joints and very little muscle strength so it was totally impracticable. The prosthetic leg they provided for her weighed practically as much as the rest of her did and was held on by a series if straps which were most difficult to secure. It looked positively dangerous to me. Pat, to her credit tried hard to make it work but it soon became obvious to all and sundry that it was a non starter. This again was a real set back as one builds up hope that some limited mobility might be achieved.

Eventually Pat was released from hospital but for months had to go three or four times a week for physiotherapy at the out-patients department. Coming home with her new disabilities was never going to be easy for us, and it took a time for us to get into new routines which suited us best. I was now in effect a twenty four hour a day care assistant as Pat was totally dependent on me. Lifting, carrying and transferring position was now a major occupation for me. Thankfully Pat did not weigh very much and my back-muscles stood the test and did not let me down.

The pace of life was much slower for us now and best kept to a known regular routine. It soon became clear that some assistance was needed and very soon social services were providing a professional care assistant at both ends of the day. One usually came at 7.30 each morning for half an hour to get Pat out of bed and wash and dress her. Similarly, one arrived at 9.30 each evening for a half hours visit to get Pat ready for bed. This was an absolute boon for me and was a real life saver. Thankfully we lived in a good sized bungalow with all rooms wheelchair accessible.

We soon purchased our own small electric wheelchair and once in it Pat was free to go anywhere in the house under her own power. We also installed ramps to allow Pat to get into the garden which she loved. We also purchased a new electrically operated bed to enable Pat to change her posture in bed which was a real treat for her. We mastered the art of getting Pat into and out of the car and that extended our horizons a little bit more. The electric wheel-chair was too heavy for putting in the boot of the car so we continued to use the old manually pushed one.

Pat was always self-conscious that her disability was clear to everyone when she was being pushed in a wheelchair and she was not all that happy with this. This was overcome with the purchase of a light-weight cosmetic leg which was easily fitted to her stump. It was very realistic and sitting in the wheelchair it appeared that she had two legs and this overcame all the problems associated with appearance.

Over night was a bit of a problem as I had to be wakened up whenever Pat needed to visit the bathroom. A couple of times a night interference with sleep soon became the norm. By the middle of the year we were into a well established routine. All the activities we were used to before the amputation had been re-established. A trip to town to look around the shops took one morning a week. Thursday evening we both went out for Church based activities. I would drop Pat off for her Ladies Meeting at the community hut in Forest Hall and then go on for a couple of hours carpet bowling in the Church hall before going back to pick her up. She insisted in resuming her role of Chair-women for her meeting and this was indicative of her drive to get back to some kind of normality. Her body might be broken but her spirit certainly wasn't.

Friday morning was always taken up by a visit to Pats hairdresser and there was always the shopping to do. Thankfully the supermarkets provided specially designed trolleys to fit to wheel chairs which were a great help although a little cumbersome if the shop was crowded. Another morning a week was set aside for a cleaner to come in and spend three hours cleaning and tidying the bungalow. This was a fine help to me as for the previous few years I did all that kind of work.

Additionally Pat had lots of visitors who tended to come in the afternoon for a chat and cup of tea.

This was very welcome for me as it meant freedom for me as I could leave Pat in their care and do something for myself. I still had commitments both to Arthritis Care as its Branch Chairman and to the Church as its Finance Committee Chairman. Both took up time which at times I could ill afford but my rule was to never leave Pat alone for more than two hours at a time. This provided a good excuse to terminate many a committee meeting where people talked repetitively too often.

There was still a lot of important business to be transacted as the Church which was in a poor structural state required a £100,000 renovation and I had my finger deep in the pie. Because of all the upset over Pats health and all the stays and visits to hospital it was not possible to have our usual holidays away from home during the year. We did of course get out and about in Northumberland on half day trips in the car. The family visited us often and it was a joy to spend time with young James and Alex who had their usual stay with us. Bethany of course was here quite often and it was a particular joy for us and helped counteract all the negativity we suffered during the year.

For the world itself it was not a good year, with war in the Balkans and trouble starting to brew up in Iraq and surrounding countries.

Just one more year and we would be in the 2000s, which would be a bit of a miracle really considering what had happened to Pat. But it was another target to aim for and it is always good to have clear aims in life. Our horizons were of course sorely limited but we had our usual weekly routines which had to be maintained and over and above that was the opportunity to get away from it all with some good holidays geared to Pats needs.

We were quite adventurous really and still managing to go abroad. The Airlines looked after disabled travellers really well and we had no worries in travelling. It was essential that any hotels we used were properly equipped to deal with disabilities and picking new spots to go to was a bit risky. There were a number of cases where we were told that everything was OK but on digging deeper we discovered them to be totally unsuitable for a wheelchair user.

The majority of places forgot about steps. "It is only six steps into the dining room and we thought that would be alright." They didn't have a clue so we tended to stick to a well-worn path. We went for a couple of weeks to our usual hotel in Fuengarola to get a bit of winter sunshine. Pat always felt that bit better with a bit of warm sunshine on her and I was fit enough to do miles of pushing each day, so we got round and about and enjoyed ourselves. We also had a full week in Nairn in July with gorgeous weather.

Later in the year we had a long weekend break at Peebles Hydro. I well remember that as the Scottish Rugby Union International team were staying there at the same time and it was good to see and speak with some well known players.

I also managed to get down to the Crown of Crucis Hotel in Ampney Crucis near Cirencester for the Mahar Reunion. We were pleased to meet new members in Lt.Col Jack Hassett and his wife Carmen who came from Northern Ireland. As well as being in 2Mahar Jack had subsequently stayed in the British Army and had commanded a battalion of the lnniskilling Fusiliers. A good addition to our little group. Pat and I also managed a days outing with Arthritis Care to Gilsland Spa on the borders of Cumbria.

At home we did a little bit of refurbishment in our Bungalow. New carpets were fitted along with a new fireplace. The colour of the sofa and chairs changed from green to gold and two new airline style reclining chairs were purchased which were a little more comfortable than the ones they replaced. Pat spent half her time sitting in one of them so it was a bonus to her.

One event I remember vividly in the autumn was a total eclipse of the sun. We went into town that day and it became very eerie as darkness descended in mid morning. Other major talking points in 1999 were the opening of the new Scottish Parliament building in Edinburgh. It was a very futuristic in design but a most beautiful building inside. The Euro came into circulation also, which I thought an improvement from the old varied national currencies. The UK of course still retained the pound and did not join.

149

I sat up to see the new millennium in but Pat of course had been in bed since ten o-clock to fit in with the carer's routines.

2001 brought no new comfort to us. The year was again dominated with a lengthy stay in hospital and countless visits to outpatients departments for Pat. As always in-between times we managed to get as much out of life as possible. We maintained our links with the many friends at our Church and Arthritis Care and I was still actively engaged with the running of them. Our Church buildings had been refurbished with £100,000 spent on it so it was looking good. There was always a good stream of people visiting Pat at home as well.

I managed to get away to the MAHAR Reunion this time at the Stakis Hotel in Bath which was again a long journey for me. The occasion itself was as always very enjoyable but it did not turn out to be one of the best venues. It should have been as it was a reputable hotel chain and Bath is an historic and popular place to visit, but the service was second class. Because of lack of staff they were unable to provide a cooked breakfast on the Sunday morning before we departed. Following this Jack Webb wrote a real snorter of a letter complaining to the top management and managed to get a full refund for all who attended.

Following a stay in hospital for Pat we decided that a period of recuperation was needed and we booked a holiday for a week in the hotel in Nairn that we were used to. This time we were going on our own and not with a bus party as was usual. Nairn is around 400 miles north of Newcastle and by car it is a full day to reach, so we decided to break the journey at Crieff to make it a bit easier for ourselves.

We always enjoyed our stays at Crieff Hydro and we knew that the rooms would be good and easily accessible. The Nairn hotel was specially adapted for severely disabled people so we were assured that we would be well looked after for the week. Having the car was a bonus as it enabled us to get out and about under our own steam every single day. We had a lovely day trip out along the Moray Firth coast to Cullen which revived all my childhood memories. It was still as beautiful as ever with the lovely golden sands and the old gatehouse still being used as some-ones home under the railway viaduct. We also spent time down the Spey Valley as far as Grantown on Spey with whisky distilleries to be found every few miles along the route.

Inverness is only a stone throw away from Nairn and was an ideal place for Pat and myself to do a bit of shopping for woollens. We managed a visit to Campbells soup factory in Fochabers and an afternoons retreat at the Findhorn Community site near Lossiemouth. There are many interested sites around Nairn such as the Culloden battlefield and Brodie Castle which were worth a visit. We came home invigorated after our little break although driving all those miles was a bit of an ordeal.

Later in the year we managed two more holidays with a stay for a week at both Largs and Blackpool with Arthritis Care. We also managed to visit Wakefield for a day to see Andrew and Family. They also spent a week staying with us in Newcastle during the school summer holidays. This was a kind of a ritual every year and it was different to have the house full of life. Both boys slept in the small bedroom and one of them had to sleep on the floor on a made up bed. The only way we could fit them in was by taking off the bedroom door.

We had lovely days out each year taking picnics with us and using our membership of The National Trust and English Heritage to visit some of the best kept sites in north east England. I am sure that Fun Days at Wallington Hall, exploring old castles such as Warkworth and playing tennis and putting in Morpeth are etched in the memories of both James and Alex. We certainly had some good times together.

Bethany by this time was ready to start Ivy Road School which was just round the corner from where they lived. She had already had a stint at a Nursery in Forest Hall and was well up to starting school. This gave us an interest in Ivy Road School and an opportunity for Pat to display more of her talent. The School were asking parents to volunteer a couple of hours a week to help children who were finding it difficult to read. Pat was a born teacher so immediately signed on to this venture. I took her along to the School one afternoon a week even though she was so disabled. She had an amazing rapport with the young children who came along in leaps and bounds. It certainly raised Pats spirit and esteem as well and was most beneficial. I think she deserved a medal for her efforts.

Certainly the year 2000 had its ups and downs with the usual despair and triumphs but we had survived. One memory of the year was working in the garden. I was always the labourer and Pat the designer. We decided to lay a couple of patios in different parts of the garden. Gosh, I found those patio slabs hard work to lift and move and most difficult to make them level overall. Anyway, it was done and was a nice change from cutting the grass and weeding.

Pat and I started the year 2001 with the usual holiday in Fuengarola to relax and get a bit of sunshine. It was as good as ever but as it turned out it was the last overseas holiday we would have. Pats state of health was getting worse and getting insurance to cover ourselves on these trips was increasingly hard and was most certainly getting far more expensive. I was happy enough paying the costs of it all but we realised it was becoming increasingly perilous for Pat to be far away from the medical back up she often wanted. We had had a good innings mind you over the years, with trips to Norway, Canada, Yugoslavia and especially Spain where we loved Benidorm, Fuengarola, Majorca and Minorca. Without those kinds of breaks I don't think Pats quality of life would have quite as good as it turned out to be.

We managed a further holiday with our Arthritis Care friends for one week in Nairn in August and that was in fact the last holiday we had together. Scotland had been our favourite destination for holidays all through our married years. It was so close to where we lived and it was also so peaceful with beautiful countryside and hills and relatively traffic free roads. We had great times in every part of Scotland. The northeast area with Aberdeen, Cullen, Royal Deeside and the Don Valley were inbuilt into my genes and never failed to invoke feeling of pride of having my roots there. Everywhere in Scotland is beautiful and we spent great times in the Central Highlands in places such as Crieff, Pitlochry and Stirling. Holidays in the southwest took us to such places as Creetown, Gate House of Fleet, Port Patrick and Largs.

The Northern Highland saw us stay in places such as Nairn, Aviemore and Fort William. The Borders region which was just over an hours drive from home saw many stays in Peebles, Melrose, Hawick, Lauder, St Boswells, Kelso and Moffat. I must not forget Callander in the Trossachs where the family had some wonderful times. I suppose it is natural in life that all these good things come to an end and we had reached the end of that road, but there were so many happy memories to retain.

There was one big upset on our lives around the middle of the year. We employed a cleaner for three hours each Wednesday morning to polish, dust and vacuum the house and keep it in good order. She was a good worker and did a good job. However I kept finding that money was missing from the house. Nobody else had the opportunity to do any pilfering apart from the cleaner so suspicion fell on her. I set traps for a couple of weeks where I knew absolutely how much money was in a drawer and after she had left a quick check showed money missing. I complained to the Agency who employed her and told them that we did not want her back. The matter had to be reported to the Police who followed it up very thoroughly and they decided to prosecute her in the Magistrates Court. Another of her clients at the same time had reported her to the Police and so it seemed a relatively straight forward for them to link the two cases together and provide a cast iron case for the prosecution. I am not in the least bit vengeful but in my naivety the least I was expecting was for her to be given a caution and be told to behave herself in future. I now realise the law is an ass and what a waste of time it was to try to get a little justice. The defence solicitor argued that it wasn't fair to link the two cases together and he won his point which I thought weakened the case. The cleaner of course denied any blame for the missing money so it was left as a choice between her word and my word. The Magistrate let her off scot free and that was the end of that. British justice - don't make me laugh. We got a new cleaner in her place and she has been working well for me for nearly twenty years.

Christine volunteered to decorate our hallway and spent a full week painting and decorating for us. Her marriage had not turned out to be a happy one. Colin was far from the ideal man and a breakup was inevitable. He never really let go of his mother and spent more time at her house than his own families. He was also a compulsive buyer who could not resist a bargain and the house was full of piles of unwanted stuff. I can remember he had about 100 pairs of shoes some of which I would not be seen dead in. Also he had a tendency for bad temper and physical aggression which was unhealthy.

Robert also was going through a bad time. He had retired early from his job at Northern Electric and became the owner of The Village Gift and Coffee Shop in Alnmouth. This is a nice little seaside village on the Northumberland coast. It was something new for Robert but he put a lot of hard work and effort into the enterprise and ran it successfully for a number of years. He met up with and became a partner of Vivianne Cleghorn a young lady who gave a lot of valuable assistance to Robert in the running of the shop. Unfortunately her health was not as good as good as it should have been and she sadly died. Pat and I managed to get to the funeral in Warkworth and it was not a happy time at all for the family.

The Mahar Regiment celebrated its Diamond Jubilee in Saugor at the end of September. It was the occasion when 19 Regimental Colours were trooped before representatives of all the Battalions and the Centre - a truly spectacular sight. Alas I missed this Reunion as there was no way I could leave Pat in the state she was in. She was spending more of her time in bed resting with constant visits from nurses and required a supply of oxygen and a mask to help with her breathing. The resting in bed also added the danger of bed sores to her very fragile skin and this was to become a very serious cause of concern some time later.

I did manage to make it to the UK Reunion of the Mahars early on in the year. This was at a new venue at The Marriott Goodwood Hotel way down near the south coast. As always it was rereshing to meet up with all my old chums.

2001 was not a good year for mankind. The news was dominated by the 9/11 terrorist attack on the USA when the twin towers were hit by planes and collapsed. Why oh why is there such hatred in the world that such awful things can happen? Love, peace and tolerance is a much better option.

The year 2002 did not get off to a good start. For the first time it became clear that Pat was not well enough to venture off to Spain to get the benefit of some nice sunshine. Her general condition was deteriorating and I was spending far more time in caring for her and at the same time not getting sufficient sleep. My good health was starting to desert me with stress, lack of sleep and loss of weight all symptoms of my slow decline. The medical advice was that I needed a break from the effort I was putting in to assist Pat. Their solution was that Pat should have a two week respite stay in a Nursing Home which would allow me to get away on a holiday. We were not tremendously impressed with this, but in the end came to see the sense of it and agreed. We looked at facilities of a number of Nursing Homes around Newcastle and finally chose one in Fawdon which was nearby.

I booked a fortnight away in Majorca and for company took along Christine and Bethany. It turned out to be a nice relaxing holiday in a good hotel situated near the beach and sea. Bethany was only 5 years old and I remember she always wanted to be in the swimming pool and when she was in she certainly didn't want to be out. We had several trips out including a train journey to the north of the island which we enjoyed. We also went to a sea-life centre to see the dolphin display and Bethany was chosen out of the crowd for the honour of a ride in a boat pulled by dolphins. For a young lass she took to it quite well and we were really proud of her. The holiday rest did me a power of good, restoring my batteries so to speak and setting me up for the rest of the year to come.

It however was always on my mind that I had left Pat isolated in a Nursing Home whilst I was swanning away having a good time in the sunshine. Pat coped with it very well although admitting that it was not quite as good as home. She had plenty of visitors who called on her which must have helped and she was used to living in a communal atmosphere because of her long stays in hospital.

Even without trips away there was plenty to keep us occupied during the year. Andrew and his family stayed with us as usual and I remember Andrew coming up later in the year to take part in the Great North Run, a half marathon starting in Newcastle and finishing in South Shields. Robert had made friends with another young lady named Debbie Cummins which we were very pleased with following his recent misfortunes. Debbie gave

Robert a lot of assistance in running his Alnmouth Shop but was also in her own right a very gifted designer of jewellery and glassware.

I continued to carry out my responsibilities to Arthritis Care and the Church and Pat also put in a brave effort to keep attending the meetings as much as possible. She was not however well enough to continue her work at Ivy Road School.

I had to help sort out lots of difficulties associated with our Church. Having spent upwards of £100,000 refurbishing the property it became obvious after a very brief time that the basic structure of one of the retaining walls was not up to standard. We obtained professional advice which concluded that a major rebuild was required as some enormous cost was needed to rectify it. There was no way that money could be raised to finance it and it was agreed that the Church buildings were no longer viable. Talks started immediately with the close by Benton Methodist Church who we had friendly relationships with a view to joining together as a combined Church using the Methodist Church buildings. Both Churches, in common with most in the land had seen membership fall over the years and it made economic sense to combine.

After a lot of discussion this was agreed and a new combined church named St Andrews Forest Hall was started. The old church building was sold to a property developer who converted it into modern flats whilst still retaining some of the original church design. With this sale and also proceeds from the now unwanted Manse over one million pounds was paid to us and this was available to modernise and improve the new premises we were moving to. It seemed a win-win situation after so much worry about our old buildings.

One sad event of the year was the death of Uncle Bob in Aberdeen. There were also two royal deaths with the Queen Mother and Princess Margaret passing away. On a brighter note the country celebrated the Golden Anniversary of the Queen's reign.

2003 turned into a period of unremitting hard and stressful work as Pats medical condition fast deteriorated over the year. She needed constant 24 hour attention and help not only from me but also from a small army of carers and medical staff. By the end of the year practically all her time was spent in bed. Our second bedroom resembled a first aid post with all the medical gear that was required. I was totally worn out but received considerable support to keep me going to the extent of having an overnight nurse on alternative nights so that I could at least have a few hours of unbroken sleep.

It should have been a year of celebration as our 50th wedding anniversary fell due on August 8th, but nothing could be planned which was a big disappointment. Sometime later in the year we did manage a family get together but it was a rather muted affair.

My outside activities were much curtailed but I kept in contact with both my Arthritis Care and Church finance work. I was happy indeed when the proposed merger of the two churches took place mid-year and my responsibilities and the need for seemingly endless meetings ceased.

There were no possibilities for me having any holidays during the year, but I did manage to get to my usual Mahar Reunion with Christine covering two nights for me. This year it again was held a long journey away at The Crown of Crucis Hotel in Ampney Crucis, Gloucestershire. It was our pleasure to welcome Lt.Col Pradeep Bhatia, Indian Army Liaison Officer at the School of Infantry, Warminster, with his wife Ashmi. Another welcome "first attendee" was our latest "recruit" Rene Miroy, coming all the way from Florida. He had served a short time with 1 Mahar.

To offset all the poor news for the year we had a piece of good fortune in November. Pat and I had subscribed a pound each week to the National Lottery each using a set of six numbers chosen way back from when it started. The chances of winning anything were practically nil but half the money went to good causes so we were reasonably content. I had a phone call one week mid morning out of the blue. It was from the National Lottery Head Office informing me that we had shared with five other winners in the first prize. Even a sixth share paid out a good dividend which would certainly have an influence on the rest of our lives. Just Luck? I think not.

Pat and I decided that we were in no position to have a spending spree on ourselves. We immediately decided to give 35% to the family and invest 60% in long term investments which would be passed on to the family when we were both gone.

We were relatively well off before this, with me having a good company pension and both of us getting state pensions as well. The extra now was just a little bit of icing on the cake which would allow us to be a little extra generous when required which was in both our natures. I took financial advice from Coutts Bank on the investment front which turned out to be first class as one would expect from the Queens bank.

*Mahar reunion, UK*

*Mahar reunion, UK*

*Col. Ashok Choundry, CO 3Mahar*

*Ashok with Bill Griffin and myself*

*Holidaying in Ulvick*

*Holidaying in Ulvick*

*Pat and me relaxing at Linden Hall*

*Pat at Linden Hall*

*Cold day at Cragside*

*By the river at Warkworth*

*South Bay in Scarborough*

*Pat and her beautiful garden*

*Pat and her beautiful garden*

*Pat and her beautiful garden*

*Pat and her beautiful garden*

*Chairman of Arthritis Care, Newcastle*

*Chairman of Arthritis Care, Newcastle*

*Chairman of Arthritis Care, Newcastle*

164

*Happy Birthday Pat*

*Always happy on holiday*

*Nice smile, Christine*

*Dad and Pauline at Andrew's wedding*

*Andrew and Geri with two smiling boys*

*Happy family group of Pat, Isobel, Dad and Robert*

*Dad's 90<sup>th</sup> birthday in Aberdeen*

*Dad's 90th birthday in Aberdeen*

*With young Bethany*

*They look happy with the meal*

*Christine and Bethany*

# CHAPTER 7

## A SAD END AND BEGINNING
## A NEW LIFE

The year 2004 got off to an awful start. On January 10th the nurse who was going to stay overnight to keep an eye on Pat arrived at about 10.30 in the evening She expressed concern that Pat was not coping very well and suggested we called for some medical assistance. An ambulance duly arrived and agreed that Pat should be taken to the Accident and Emergency Department at the City General Hospital. This turned out to be a nightmare experience.

It was a Saturday evening and the place was overflowing with people, the majority of whom were suffering from excess drinking or drug problems. The place was bedlam with shouting, screaming and swearing young people of both sexes who had indulged too much on their evening out. Because of the numbers to be dealt with there was a wait of over two hours for Pat who was on a stretcher on a trolley waiting to be assessed during which time we were subject to a constant barrage of noise. It was the last thing in the world that Pat would have wanted and there was no escape for us.

Pat was finally admitted to a medical ward at about 03.00 am on the Sunday morning and I was able to get home and catch up with some sleep. It was clear to me that Pat's days were coming to a close and I tried to reconcile myself to the thoughts of her passing on. The next day she was transferred onto a medical ward in the Freeman Hospital where she was sedated to the point that on my visit there was little reaction from her.

The next morning I had a call from the hospital saying that she had been moved into a private room with the likely outcome that she would not survive the day. Christine and I visited the hospital from around 2.00pm and found Pat sleeping peacefully and we sat talking to her and holding her hand for around two hours till we realised that she had stopped breathing and the doctor confirmed that she had passed away.

I recorded in my diary "the worst day of my life." Pat and I had known each other for over 55 years and we had been married for over 50 years. Although I knew that her death would come sooner than later it was still a dreadful shock as the bottom had fallen out of my life. I was pleased that she had such a peaceful death after her long years fighting a painful disfiguring illness but the grief was intense and tears came easily. I was so thankful that Christine was with me and that we could console each other.

I realise it was just as bad for the children and grandchildren as it was for me and it was no easy task to spread the news to the rest of the family and her many friends. Although I was heartbroken I felt the right course was to get a firm grip on myself get rid of any self pity and show a firm resolve in the difficult days up to the day of the funeral. There was plenty to attend to following the death where my mind had to concentrate on other matters but I found none of it easy.

We had decided beforehand on cremation rather than burial and a private family cremation service took place at 10.45am on Thursday January 22nd at the West End Crematorium and this was followed at 11.30am by a service of thanksgiving for Pat's life at St Andrews Church Benton with the Church overflowing with family and friends. I was so grateful that Andrew volunteered to speak a tribute to his mother for about ten minutes as the highlight of the service. He did so very well and eloquently and I doubt I could have managed it without breaking down. Both Pat and I had a strong faith and I am convinced that Pat's soul and spirit still exist even though her body has gone and that she is in a much better place still looking over us.

Life for me now was so different. I was now alone at home with seemingly endless hours each day which had been previously spent caring for Pat with nothing to do. Clearly this was no good and a major lifestyle change was required pretty smartly. I quickly came to several major decisions for activities which would eat into my spare time. I always loved travelling to far-away places so I pledged to travel the world on voyages of discovery. I was always a fellow keen on sport and this had been neglected for a few years. This was sorted by getting a season ticket to follow Newcastle United with a prime seat in the 1892 Bar premium area situated in the main Milburn Stand. A lot of new friends were to be made there and I followed Newcastle United in triumph and adversity for many years.

I was still fit enough for sporting activities and I chose bowls playing at the Blue Flames sporting club in Benton. This was an inspired move as I made scores and scores of very good friends and turned out to be a reasonably efficient bowler. I also enjoyed my odd speaking engagements and decided to greatly increase the number of them. Since leaving work I had no time to spend on my computer skills. Now was the time to buy a desktop computer and start again. Computing had advanced by light years since gave up work and even though I was a Chartered Member of the British Computer Society with the letters to prove it I now had no skills even to the point of not knowing even how to switch the desktop computer on. Even young Bethany at 6 years old knew how to do that so I had a lot of catching up to do.

I bought brand new car - a Vectra 1.6 5 door saloon to do my travelling in. So it was a new phase of my life I was starting on and I looked forward to the future in anticipation.

I managed to get in three holidays abroad in the remainder of 2004. Firstly, at Easter time, Christine, Bethany and I had a stay for a week in Madeira. This was our first visit to this island and we were very impressed with it. We stayed at the Hotel Palacio in Funchal which was a top class hotel. It was perhaps a little too posh for Bethany with its fine menus not being to her taste. She was only six years old and she just liked simple food, not the sophisticated dishes they served up. But we managed and they tried their best to keep her happy.

The climate of course was just to our liking with plenty of warm sunshine to enjoy; amazing though, with Madeira being just a small island we encountered snow when we took a bus trip up to the hills in the centre of the island. We stopped off at an inn where they had a roaring open fire to warm us up which was most appreciated as we were in summer clothes. We took a trip in a cable car to the top of some slopes just outside Funchal and took a basket ride down the very steep 2 kilometre slope to the bottom of the hill. It was quite a white-knuckle, hair-raising few minutes but what an experience. The baskets were in fact wooden sledges supervised by two runners who pushed us to start and were with us all the way down guiding us round bends in the road and eventually stopping us at the bottom. The scenery on the island was magnificent and we visited the levadas a system of irrigation channels which are unique to Madeira.

Later in the summer I flew to Saltzburg in Austria for a stay for a week amongst the hills and lakes. The weather was beautiful and the scenery breathtaking. It was in the region of all the winter skiing slopes, all the snow had gone but the views from the top of the slopes were tremendous. I saw a lot of hang gliding taking place but I didn't take the opportunity to join in.

The party who I was with had a coach at their disposal and we did a lot of touring around the area seeing lots of old castles and historical places. We managed to get to the magical location of Innsbruck and also Berchtchesgaden where Hitler had his home overlooking the small town. I spent an afternoon down a salt mine which was a great experience as the entrance was down a chute with a drop of a couple of hundred feet so you achieved some high speeds on the way down.

The hotel I stayed in was some two hours drive to the airport on Saltzburg and on the return journey a lady suddenly realised that she had left her handbag which held her passport at the hotel when we were half way to the Airport. We had a frantic return journey to pick it up and white-knuckle ride back to Saltzburg where the flight was already boarded and waiting to take off. They managed to scramble us through all the control points at high speed and we made the flight with seconds to spare. It was a memorable holiday and I would really like to go back there.

Later on in the year I went on a group holiday to Italy flying in to Marco Polo Airport in Venice. It was then a bus tour to Tuscany an eventually staying for a few nights in Monte Catini Terme which is a Spa town. I managed to spend a day in Florence with all its ancient architecture with magnificent buildings and bridges. Thereafter I saw Pisa with its famous leaning tower but also the imposing buildings around about it. I had a lovely day in Sienna where I climbed the clock tower overlooking the famous square where horse racing takes place. Lucca was also visited with its wonderful town walls and ancient buildings.

On the return journey there was day free to see Venice and have a walk along the canals and bridges as well as having a gondola ride. Well worth a return visit at some future time. I met some good friends on that holiday including Alan and Jean who are still in touch with me.

In addition to all these travels I did get away down to Ampney Crucis for the Mahar Reunion. I also visited Peter and Peggy in Humberston for three days and also visited Andrew and his family in Wakefield. Nearer home Bethany started a new school being transferred from Ivy Road to Linden in Forest Hall where the opportunities were a little better for a bright young girl. Also a weekly visit to the Swimming Pool in Byker was the norm, as Bethany was having swimming lessons.

So the eventful year came to close and I looked forward to the next adventure starting in 2005.

The highlight at the start of the year was a world cruise from the beginning of January to the end of April on the Saga Rose, the flag ship of Saga cruising. It was a comparatively small liner of some 24500 tons catering for 600 passengers served by a crew of 350. The majority of the crew came from the Philippine Islands and they provided first class service with a smile.

I embarked at Southampton on 7 January ready to set off just before midnight. We were delayed for 24 hours because of a south westerly gale blowing directly at us from the Channel. A similar sized cruise liner named Aurora set out just before we were due to go but was forced to return because they couldn't make headway. The ship developed an engine problem and the world cruise had to be abandoned. We thought we were unlucky to be delayed but that paled into insignificance compared with the Aurora passengers who had to pack up and go home. The weather was playing havoc all over the world and the main topic of conversation was the dreadful Tsunami which had devastated coastal areas all around the Indian Ocean just a few days before.

I had a lovely comfortable twin bedded cabin so I had plenty of personal space to retreat to when tiredness took over. I soon got used to the roll of the ship and suffered no sickness or discomfort for the entire journey. Equally I settled well into the social activities on board and soon was making friends. Most passengers were married couples with few single people making the trip and I am sure Pat would have loved to have been there with me.

There were plenty of activities to keep you occupied between all the fabulous meals which were served. I opted to join a passenger's choir of some 70 members and I was part of a very good bass section. We practised every day under the direction of the choirmaster who was a Welsh lady and she knew her stuff. We eventually gave a few concerts in the evening to entertain the passengers.

There were two Bridge instructors on board so I joined the beginners class and that is the first time I had played bridge since my Indian Army days. Once I had mastered the rudiments of the game and the complicated bidding system, I soon understood why I had no chance of winning anything in those long ago days.

To keep fit I managed to walk a couple of circuits of the ship around the upper deck and there were always masses of people doing the same thing. It would have been so easy to put on a lot weight on with the regular large meals on offer. The evening dinner was the climax of the day with every one dining together at the same time and in the same room. You had to dress appropriately according to a timetable. Sometimes casual clothes, other times a suit and collar and tie and on the posh occasions a dinner suit and bow tie. The ladies of course were in their element when it came to elegant gowns for the formal dinners. There was always plenty of entertainment by guest professionals onboard and endless dancing and quizzes.

Off we went through the Bay of Biscay to our first port of call which was Funchal in Madeira. This was familiar place for me now since my holiday in 2004. I opted for a jeep safari which went to the remote parts of the island I had not seen before and I was well pleased. Then it was southwards again to our next stop - Porto Grande in the Cape Verde Islands. These comprise a number of small volcanic islands which are trying to promote a large tourist trade but have lacked for investment in their infrastructure. They have potential to be a most attractive destination with good scenery, fine weather and a friendly population.

We then had to make a detour to Ascension Island to drop off a sick person. This is a small isolated island in the mid atlantic ocean with a population of less than 1000.It is not a holiday island and its main use is as a communications base and it is covered with military radar masts and antennae. It has a military airfield in the centre of the island and was well used as a staging post during the Falklands war it is called Wide Awake Airfield because of the noise made by the number of birds in the surrounding trees. There is no indigenous population there and the UK and USA military people are serviced by casual workpeople coming up from St Helena.

There was a big ceremony when we crossed the equator with everyone having to pay respect to King Neptune. This involved a lot of water being splashed around and kissing of fish with a considerable number of passengers ending up in the swimming pool. All very good natured and no one came to any harm. Then on to Recife a large sea port in Brazil. It is the fourth largest city in Brazil with a population approaching two million and was formally known as Pernambuco. It has become known as the Venice of Brazil because of the number of waterways and bridges to be found there. I opted for a day trip around the city taking in all the major sightseeing places and was quite impressed with my first encounter with South America.

Next stop was Rio de Janeiro which we reached just after day break and what a magnificent sight it was from the ship. It is one of the most beautiful cities in the world and is renowned for its annual carnival and beaches such as Copacabana and Ipanema. It is a major cultural centre with a majestic beauty, nestled between two dazzling beaches on one side and an abruptly rising mountain range covered by luxuriant tropical forest on the other. I was able to get up Sugar Loaf Mountain by cable car and later in the day took the cog wheel railway to the remarkable Christ the Redeemer Statue which is perched on Corcovado Mountain and stands 98 metres tall. This has become the symbol of modern Rio and from the terrace surrounding the statue you can take in breathtaking views of the entire city. This was a real highlight and well worth all the effort.

Next stop was Montevideo the capital of Uruguay lying at the mouth of the River Plate famous for a naval battle at the start of

WW2. It is a picturesque city of colonial Spanish, Italian and Art deco styles and has a distinctive European feel about it. As Uruguay's cultural, political and commercial centre the city boasts a good number of monuments, museums and impressive buildings. As well as having a tour of the city highlights I managed to have a few hours at a cattle ranch in the country side with a good barbecue, a wagon ride round the ranch and demonstrations of horsemanship.

Our next stop was Buenos Aires the capital city of Argentina a really big place with a population of over 13,000,000 people. I was shaken by the infrastructure of the place with six lanes both ways motorways and still facing traffic jams. A bus tour took in all the main sights of the city from the Presidential Palace to the enormous Cathedral. Then it was out again to a Ranch for yet another barbecue and entertainment from Gauchos showing off their many skills. The Ranch was in the middle of a wine producing area with facility to help your-self to the varied products on offer. Our cruise continued southwards and the weather was getting much more unsettled and colder. Next stop was Port Stanley in the Falkland Island where there were no port facilities and we had to use tenders to reach shore. The seas around Port Stanley are rough and only a small percentage of cruise liners are able to transfer people to land by tender because of the risks of transferring when there is a big swell. We were lucky as the weather was reasonably calm on the day of our arrival and I managed a full day on the Falkland. I opted for a battlefield tour to visit the places which were in the news during the Falkland war.

The landscape was one of miles of treeless fields filled with sheep and it was necessary to keep to the road as there were numerous signs indicating minefields left over from the battle. Not many people live there so it was many miles between the isolated hamlets. We took in Sapper Hill, Wireless Ridge and Mount Tumbledown. The most nostalgic place was Bluff Cove, scene of the disastrous attack on the St Galahad. The sun was shining on the cove which was as calm as a mill pond and it was hard to imagine that such a disaster could happen at such a remote spot. There is a beautifully kept war grave there in pristine condition with fresh flowers to remember the individual units who suffered losses in the battle. The War Grave Commission must employ locals to keep the site in such good condition but we could only see a couple of cottages in the vicinity of this remote spot.

Port Stanley itself is a distinctive small town with rows of houses with different vividly coloured roofs and it reminded me so much of the TV pictures from the place during the war. The weather remained calm and so we were able to get back to the Saga Rose in time for dinner. We were told that sometimes the weather deteriorated during the day and some cruise passengers were forced to stay overnight in Port Stanley. I would not have minded that happening to me.

Saga Rose was now heading due south into the Ross Sea and the Antarctic. The Ross Sea is one of the roughest patches in the world with the waters of the Atlantic and Pacific oceans meeting up causing a lot of disturbance. We were warned to expect some discomfort and we certainly got it. Evening dinner was just starting and it was one of the posh evenings when everyone was dressed in their Sunday best clothes. The tables were set like an official dinner at Buckingham Palace with countless sets of cutlery and at least three glasses per person. It had been rough during the day but now was the time for an extra big wave to hit us and it shook the ship to its foundations and it seemed to stop still for a moment.

In that split second everything on the table set for eight seemed to travel in my direction.

Bowls of soup, glasses of water and wine and assorted cutlery landed on my lap or seemed to whizz past me. I was trying to catch them like a slip fielder but with little success. Then in the next split second my chair over-turned and I performed a double backward summersault ending up on my back looking at the chandeliers. Another thirty or so people who were sitting in the same direction as myself suffered the same fate. Luckily for me, I suffered no ill effects but several people were badly shaken and we all had to have a check-up from the medical staff. It certainly was a talking point for a few days and was a memorable dinner.

The ships laundry did a good job of cleaning all our clothes - free of charge as well. We eventually reached the Antarctic waking up one morning with snow on the deck and the sea as calm as a mill pond. Our first port of call was Half Moon Island which we stood off and tenders took us to the island. It was just a small place with no inhabitants apart from thousands of penguins, a number of seals and sea lions and countless nesting birds. We could only land 50 people at a time on the island so our time was restricted to less than an hour ashore. We had to obey the Antarctic convention that no rubbish was left behind and most important of all penguins had the right of way over humans.

The noise on the island was deafening with the constant calls of the birds as they tried to steal the penguins eggs and the penguins responded to them. The penguins stood in massed ranks on the slopes of the island and they seemed to have formed gangs. Their intention seemed to be to pinch pebbles from the snow and ice of a rival gang and take them to their own patch where it was then pinched by a member of another rival gang, all of them making as much noise as possible. They disregarded the humans and would willingly walk over our feet to achieve their ends. The smell of thousands of closely packed penguins is horrible and before leaving the island we had to have our wellies scrubbed clean with disinfectant.

It was a wonderful experience seeing raw nature in these cold surroundings and well worth the effort getting there. The sea around the islands was a magnificent azure colour with lots of icebergs floating by. At times the whole island was vacated by the penguins who all dived expertly into the sea as a group and proved first class swimmers. Our next port of call was Port Lockroy at the edge of the landmass which was a British Government Research Station manned by two people. They run a Post Office from their premises which is the most southerly post office in the world. They sold post-cards and gifts in the shop and I bought six postcards to send to family and friends as well as a Antarctic tartan tie and hankerchief. They did a roaring business and I am sure that it was highly profitable. None of the postcards arrived home and it was too far away to go back to complain.

The following day we paid a similar visit to Waterboat Point where Chilean Air-force had a weather station. There were plenty more penguins to be seen but the Chilleans did not put in an appearance. We were told they had a shop which they opened for visitors to buy local curios but there was no evidence of that. We came to the conclusion that they had a riotous party the night before and were still sleeping it off.

One feature was a sign-post in the middle of the island with arrows pointing all over the world with vast distances given by the mile. Unique in its way I should think. The next stop was Deception Island which had been formed when a volcano exploded way back in time and had left a lagoon in the middle of the island with just enough open water to allow a liner to enter the lagoon. It used to be an old Norwegian whaling station and one or two derelict buildings still survive. The big attraction was the thermal pools which bubbled up on the shoreline. Those brave souls wanting to go and swim had the opportunity to do so and I signed on for the experience. Getting ready and into the water presented no difficulty as you could put your swimming trunks below your clothes and it was easy to be ready to swim. Getting out was the bad part as the change of temperature was extreme and trying to dry oneself and get dressed in double quick time is not easy. Never-the-less it was accomplished and it was a once in a lifetime opportunity which could not be missed. It adds to my list of conversation items which comes in handy at times. Then we had enough of the cold icy weather and the Saga Rose set sail north-wards to Ushuaia.

Ushuaia is the world's most southerly city and it is set on the island of Tierra del Fuego which is separated from the mainland of South America by the Magellan Straits. Its remote location in the Tierra del Fuego National Park, which is an area of outstanding beauty, adds to its charm. Active volcanic mountains, glaziers and rushing mountain streams make it an adventure playground. I visited the old Penal Colony which existed until 1947 and which was reserved for the worst of the worst. They had a rough time with their hard labour being the cutting down of trees. The area still shows tens of thousands of tree stumps as evidence of their hard work.

I got to the Penal Colony on a narrow gauged railway which used to transport the baddies to their work place. I also walked along the last half mile of the Great American Highway which starts off just north of Vancouver. The road comes to a halt with a wooden barrier in place with a sign saying "This is the end of the World." Not strictly true as my trip to the Antarctic proved.

Our stay in Ushuaia was followed by four days of cruising along the Magellan Straits, the Beagle Channel and northwards through the fjords along the coast of Chile. This was a visual spectacle with great views of the Andes mountain range, mighty glaziers, thundering waterfalls and a wide range of birds and marine life. The liner docked for a day at Puerta Montt and I was able to make a trip to what is termed the Lake District of Chile. You could see the reason why, as it bore resemblance to or own Lake District with its gentle hills and lakes.

We ended our journey northwards up the coast of Chile docking at Valparaiso. Santiago the capital of Chile was fifty miles inland and I managed a city tour taking in all the main attractions. The city has a beautiful backdrop of snow capped peaks of the mighty Andes. The first third of our world voyage was over and many passengers who had just booked for the first leg disembarked and flew home being replaced by newcomers. Our choir was broken up but I organised a farewell party for the group as many were leaving and we had become such good friends.

Now we were heading westward into the mighty Pacific Ocean to visit a chain of isolated islands with days of cruising in warm sunshine and calm waters between the islands. The first place we reached was Robinson Crusoe Island. Just about everybody has read the story of Robinson Crusoe with its pictures of a golden beach with lots of Palm trees and streams running down to the beach. It was nothing like that at all as it was a volcanic island with black rocks and little black sand patches. We landed by tender in the small bay where there was a statue of Robinson Crusoe standing. It is a small isolated place with less than 1000 inhabitants who make their living at fishing. The crabs and lobsters on show were impressive. I managed to get up the cliff side to see the famous cave where Crusoe had made his home but it was pitch black dark so there was not much to see.

Anyway it was Alexander Selkirk who was actually marooned on the island on which the story of Crusoe was based. One historical fact was that during WW1 a German cruiser named "Dresden" was sunk just off shore with the loss of around 1000 sailors. There is a very well kept war grave cemetery overlooking the site of the sinking which is a credit to the island. Whilst I was there along with several friends we went to a little kiosk on the shoreline for a cup of tea. One of my friends who was the ex main tea taster for Lipton's teas was with us and he always wanted that brand. What a surprise when we found that they were using Lipton's tea bags. He was always extolling the prowess of the salesmen who had managed to get the contracts in the worlds remotest places. It became a bit of a joke that we searched for Lipton's tea bags wherever we went and we never failed to find them in the most unlikely of places. He always wore a tee-shirt with the motto "Buy Lipton's tea bags" on the front of it and "My pension depends on it" on the back.

Easter Island was our next stop, again landing by tender for a full day visit. There was a strong sense of mystery and history at this stop. The island is best known for its 900 or so giant Moai Statues, some weighing up to 150 tons located in groups around the island. The Moai building period, relating to ancestor worship came to an end at the back end of the 17th century and was followed by a period of warfare and extreme poverty. The Moai were quarried from the side of a extinct volcano on one side of the island. They were carved fully in the cliff face till they were finally just held by a slight sliver of rock. Hundred of logs were placed under the carving and when the sliver was cut they fell onto the logs. They were then transported by the rolling logs to their location sometimes miles away on the island. The downfall of their society was because they cut down every single tree on the island. This left them with no wood for their boats to be made, so no more fishing was possible and famine resulted. This was compounded by the loss of birds and eggs on the Island. Civil war broke out and the island was on its knees and would have succumbed had it not been for the very fortunate sighting by a Dutch ship that was passing on Easter day, hence it's name. It gave much needed assistance and slow recovery started.

At the present day the island is still short of trees. I paid a visit to the extinct volcano where they did the quarrying and there is ample evidence of the work which went on there. Some finished Moai are still lying on the ground and a number of partly completed Moai are to be seen on the quarry face. The day was made memorable by a big barbecue that was organised on a lovely beach location. Local people were giving demonstrations of their culture with lots of music and dancing and many people were taking advantage and having a dip in the sea. After a day of non-stop sunshine, in the late afternoon a dark cloud appeared overhead and this turned into thunder and lightning with a torrential downpour. It happened so quickly that most people were taken unaware and were soon drenched. The day ended in chaos as we quickly made our way back to the safety of the Saga Rose.

Three days later we reached an isolated speck of Pitcairn Island famed for its association with the Munity on the Bounty. It is a difficult place to land because of the big swell but we were again lucky to have a fairly flat sea and managed to get ashore. Pitcairn is only 2 square miles in size with a population of 50 people almost all of them being called Christian. They live in the township of Adamstown at the top of what is called the hill of difficulty because of the steepness of the rough road from the jetty to the properties at the top. It is a pleasant little township with well built and kept houses. They have a well kept Church in the village square and WW3 nearly broke out whilst I was in it.

One lady visitor took great exception to a gentleman who would not take his hat off and it just about came to blows before the gentleman retreated outside. Also in the square there was the post office. As a boy I remember collecting stamps and a Pitcairn Island stamp was a prized possession. It was a must that I had to send 6 lovely stamped postcards to my friends which by the way all arrived at their destinations. This was a big improvement on the performance of Port Lockroy. The original anchor from the Bounty was on display outside the Municipal Office.

The prison buildings were half a mile away and were empty. The Prison was specially built to house half the male population who had been found guilty of incest. It was an open Prison where they went to sleep. They were all needed during the day for their normal duties of fishing and farming. What an odd situation. The islanders were very pleased to see us as a lot of money changed hand for tee shirts baseball caps etc which they were selling. The whole population of the island turned out to give us a choral farewell.

Three days later we docked at Papeeti the capital of Tahiti. There are over 150 islands in French Polynesia but a lot are uninhabited and Tahiti is by far and away the biggest and most important island. The island is well known for its association with Gauguin the famous French artist who settled there and that was acknowledged by a visit to the Museum full of his life story and artistic works. The whole Island with its savage beauty and laid back living style was a joy and you could see the attraction for someone to move there to live.

Two days sailing took us to Bora Bora docking at the small township of Vaitape. Bora Bora is usually featured in photographs of Polynesia because of its outstanding beauty. Ocean waves brush the barrier reef and the lagoon beyond has colours of all hues and it is lapped by a perfect crescent of a beach. Usually whispy clouds cover the summit of the volcano at the centre of the Island. It is a premium holiday destination and it was a joy to visit for a day. During WW2 it was the southern-most base for the USA forces in the South Pacific and signs of the fortifications were still visible. It never saw any action and it must have been a dream posting for the lucky few there. At the end of the war a lot of personnel were most unhappy at having to leave the island. An airstrip was constructed during the war and this is a great boon to its tourist trade. It takes a long time to reach.

After six days at sea following our visit to Bora Bora, in which time we had crossed the International Date Line, we arrived at Auckland on the northern island of New Zealand. I had always wanted to go to New Zealand as all the write ups for the place seemed to indicate that it was well worth a visit. We visited three ports on the northern island and two ports in the south and the place lived up to its billing.

Our first port of call was Auckland which is New Zealand's largest, most cosmopolitan city and it enjoys a stunning location overlooking a natural harbour. It is often called "the city of sails" because of the large number of yachts moored in the harbour. I had a coach trip around the city and its surrounding countryside to get the flavour of the place.

Then it was southwards to Napier a small city with a lot of art deco buildings overlooking Hawkes Bay. This is the centre of the sheep industry so time was spent at a farm where we enjoyed demonstrations of sheepdog handling and sheep shearing which looked a real back breaking job. The ship then called at Wellington the capital city which could easily be mistaken for a typical English city. The ship sailed onto Lyttelton the port for Christchurch the capital of the southern island. This is the most English looking city you can imagine with its grey Victorian buildings and again with just a short time to see it a coach trip round its famous sights and the countryside was the order of the day.

The final stop in the South Island was at Port Chalmers for Dunedin. This is called the Scottish City as the majority of its people seemed to be of Scottish descent. I also found it very hilly with some house built on really steep slopes. It has many lovely buildings such as the University of Otago and the old Edwardian railway station. I had a half day excursion along the peninsula to visit Larnach castle and also called in at an albatross sanctuary where they were most worried about the shortage of young albatross in the southern seas and they were doing their utmost to preserve them.

The following four days were spent in the Fjords round the south of the island and then northwards towards Australia. I was most cold an icy at times and there had to be a helicopter-transfer of an ill passenger when we were in Milford Sound which is a very picturesque but quite isolated place.

The next stop we reached was Sydney the state capital of New South Wales and the largest city in Australia. Everybody was on deck to witness our entry into the harbour as it is one of the great sights of the world. We berthed at the main pier just by the side of the Sydney Harbour Bridge and a few hundred yards away from the iconic Sydney Opera House. When I looked out from my cabin the only thing I could see was the Opera House. We had a two day stay in Sydney but it was really not long enough for all the activities I had on my list. I booked on a trip northwards to see the Blue Mountains and the wild life park and had a good cable car ride over the landscape. I did most of the things I had on my list to do including climbing the Harbour Bridge, a boat trip round the harbour (some of the houses were just out of this world) and a visit to Bondi Beach. I suppose the highlight was an Gala evening at the Opera House for a performance of Aida. I could have easily spent a week in Sydney as I loved it.

Our next stop was southwards through the Bass Straits to Hobart in Tasmania the most remote Australian territory. It is a very pleasant place although the place I chose to go to was the notorious Port Arthur Penal Settlement. It closed in 1877 but it is kept in pristine condition. It was a very strict regime reserved for the most recalcitrant of prisoners deported from England and they must have despaired for life. I also managed to get to the Tasmanian Devil Park. I wouldn't like to meet one of those fierce little creatures on a dark night.

The next step on this fabulous world cruise was Melbourne the capital city of the State of Victoria. It is a big city built on the banks of the Yarra River and is a good combination of old well preserved Victorian buildings and modern architecture. I saw most of the local attractions including visits to the famous Melbourne Cricket ground and the excellent Royal Botanical gardens. One of the highlights was having a posh three course evening meal on a converted 1930s tram. The tram features all the modern conveniences of a first-class restaurant including comfortable velvet seating, brass fittings, fresh flowers on each table and a comprehensive menu to choose from. It rattles round the city tram network for a couple of hours so that you see the sights as you dine.

Then it was on to South Australia and its capital Adelaide which was another beautiful city with acres of green parks and elegant houses and buildings. I disembarked here for a short stay in Australia and then rejoined the cruise liner some days later in Perth. I spent a lovely half day at the small seaside town of Glenelg which could be reached by a ten mile trip on the local tram system. This place had a lovely sandy beach which was being used by all the local schoolchildren for their annual sports day and it was most entertaining. I also spent time again at the Royal Botanical gardens and the famous cricket ground which began to feel mandatory for every Australian city I visited.

After an overnight stay in Adelaide I went on a day tour of the local wine making area which is very extensive and included a visit to Jacobs Creek one of the better known wine brands. I also visited a smaller estate run by an old German man in his nineties who had retired some years earlier but his zeal for wine making had got the better of him and he started a new business. He was selling a product called "Old Papas Port" which he extolled as the best in the world. He was so convincing that I among others bought a couple of bottles.

That evening out small party boarded the Ghan Express the iconic train which has a long journey north to Cairns via Alice Springs in the centre of Australia. It was named the Ghan because the original route was a camel track with the camels and their keepers originating from Afghanistan. It has a reputation similar to the Orient Express for quality and good service. It was a long journey over pretty barren land taking 24 hours with a comfortable bunk to sleep in. Alice Springs is an isolated spot in the middle of nowhere but around 10,000 people live there. We saw all the local sights including the Flying Doctor HQ.

Then it was off to the local airport for a flight to Ayers Rock to an overnight stay. At the airport one of our party put his bottles of port in the airport trolley he was using and sadly the rungs were a bit damaged and his lovely port wine went right through and smashed on the floor. Great hilarity. My bottles were in my overnight bag which I had with me which had to go in the baggage compartment. When I collected my bag at the Ayers Rock a slow trickle of red liquid was seeping out from it. This produced even greater hilarity this time at my expense.

Then it was straight off to a first class desert hotel some 5 miles from the world famous Ayers Rock for an overnight stay. I was put in a large air conditioned room with a King sized double bed for my use. When I opened my bag I found everything in it was damp and red. All my pyjamas and change of clothing were ruined amidst the broken glass and all my port had gone. I lay all the clothes out on the bed in the vain hope that they might dry out but that turned out to be wishful thinking.

It was then immediately out to see Ayers Rock as the sun set followed by a barbeque, an unsuccessful attempt to play a didgeridoo and a very interesting explanation of the star lit sky. On returning to my room after midnight it smelled like a brewery and the clothes were still soaking. We had to be up early and packed in the morning to see Ayers Rock at sunrise and then spent an interesting time at the Rock and its museum. I wish I had a pound for all the flies that seemed to be there.

Then it was off to the airport and a flight to Perth where our ship had docked. The security at Perth airport is very strict with many large security men with sniffer dogs. Alas when my overnight bag appeared I think every sniffer dog in the airport was attracted to it and I was given a thorough going over by security guards who eventually saw the funny side to it all. Needless to say I was the butt of countless jokes when I got on board ship because of my escapades. The cruise Hotel Director heard my story and the generous sole thought it was so good that I was surprised to find 6 bottles of assorted spirits in my cabin as some recompense for my misfortune. I managed a day in Perth which again is a beautiful city set on the Swan River with acres of green parks and sporting facilities. I rated Australia very highly and looked forward to the next time I could get there.

The ship was now on a long journey westward and it would be eight days before we had our next opportunity to get onto dry land. It was a pleasant and relaxing time with lots of on board activities to keep us occupied. The highlight was an afternoon Charity Fayre. Saga, the company owning the cruise liner ran a Charitable Trust the proceeds of which were used to help disadvantaged groups throughout the world where-ever Saga holiday makers went. The object of the afternoon was to get as much money as possible from the relatively well off passengers to add to the trust funds and as a bonus the Saga bosses agreed that they would match the proceeds from the Fayre, so doubling the money. The crew put their heart and soul into organising all type of activities from Sales tables, games, quizzes, raffles and other assorted ventures and the passengers responded well.

Over £12000 came from the passengers so in the end the Trust benefitted by nearly £25000 in all. I had my hair cut by a crew member for a donation and he was first class at being a barber. I also bought an oil painting of an old sailing ship in an action sale and this had been painted during the voyage by a chap called Steven Card who was a well renowned painter of maritime scenes. It hangs proudly in my lounge at 5 Wells Close. I always had an interest in charitable affairs as I considered myself to be a very privileged person on this earth and there as so many people around the world in desperate need of help. The Charity Fayre brought me into close contact with the Trust and I formed close links with them on future cruises where I gave hands on help in places throughout the world.

In no time at all it seemed we had docked in Port Louis the capital of the lovely island of Mauritius. The island is the centre of the sugar cane production in the South Indian Ocean as well as being a very popular holiday destination. The island became an independent member of the British Commonwealth and became a Republic in 1992. It is a densely populated island with the majority of the population coming from India and there is a vibrant Hindu community spirit to be seen. It has lovely sandy beaches with posh hotels on the coast to cater for the tourist trade and is reasonably well kept. Inland however they are not so lucky and much of the infra-structure was in need of up grading.

I took a bus tour round the island which is very volcanic in parts and visited the sacred lake of Grand Bassin, also known as Ganga Talau – the Ganges of Mauritius and centre of pilgrimage for the Hindu Community. On the following day we visited Reunion Island which is still under French control and which receives finance from the European Union. It is a well kept island with all its infrastructure in pristine condition far in advance of Mauritius. It is extremely volcanic in nature with large barren areas of grey lava and eruptions still happening on a regular basis.

A couple of days later found us at Richards Bay on the east coast of South Africa the busiest cargo port in Natal. What makes it attractive is that it is the gateway to some of the outstanding South African folklore and wildlife experiences such as game parks and KwaZulu the home of the Zulu warriors and dancers. I disembarked for a night and went on a two day safari to Hluhluwe-Um Folozi Game Reserve I stayed overnight at the Ubizane Tree Lodge which was a great experience by itself and spent two days on the Reserves in a jeep looking for the "big five" of lion, elephant, leopard, buffalo and rhino. I am still waiting to see the elephants for although they were all tagged with radio and the drivers had direction finders more than 200 of them managed to keep out of sight for the whole period. We were always in contact with drivers of other jeeps who kept reporting that elephants had been sighted but by the time that we got there they were always gone, quite amazing really as they are big creatures but I reckon very clever also. I keep telling people that the best way to see elephants is to pay a visit to Edinburgh Zoo.

I met up with the ship again at Durban which is a big, prosperous city with a very good seafront and miles of golden sands. There was still plenty of Zulu culture around the area and I headed for the Valley of the Thousand Hills which is the area surrounding Pietermaritzburg and reached the Zulu Village of Phezulu where we received our full fill of local culture. Another couple of days cruising down the east coast found us at Port Elizabeth known locally as the friendly city and which is the centre of the South African car making industry. It is the gateway to an area called the Settler Country a place which has seen numerous wars between British Settlers and the Xhosa tribes.

I spent most of the day on the Kariega Game reserve with lots of giraffe, zebra. rhino and antelopes to be seen. Also included in my time- table was a couple of hours cruising up and down the Kariaga River. Two days later we docked at Capetown for an overnight stay. This is an iconic city laid out beneath the majestic Table Mountain which invariably has a cloud covering its peak. There is too much to see in just two days but I managed the best I could with a bus tour around the magnificent city and a cable ride to the top of Table Mountain where there are beautiful views down below of the city and its surrounds. I spent just about the best two hours of my life in the Kirstenbosch Botanical Gardens on the eastern slopes of the mountain. I spent it sitting in an isolated garden surrounded by lush vegetation all by myself with the hum of insects being the only sound. It must have resembled the Garden of Eden. My only contact with the outside world was for the last fifteen minutes when an elderly black garden worker sat by my side for a rest from his work. We managed to put the worlds to right in just a quarter of an hour before I had to be on my way. Idyllic!

I also spent on evening on Signal Hill another piece of high ground overlooking Capetown where I watched the sun go down over the South Atlantic whilst having a glass of nice South African wine. The cruise proceeded up the west coast of Africa toward Namibia where we landed for the day at Walvis Bay. Namibia used to be a German territory up-to the end of WW1 and the old German presence is still to be found there. I went on a day trip to the Great Namibian Desert taking in the great sand dunes on the Skeleton coast when the evidence of many ship wrecks is to be seen every so many miles. It seldom rains in the area where we went and it looked completely barren. When it does rain the whole area turns green and lush as the seeds lay dormant for many years. Our guide demonstrated it by pouring a few gallons of water on an arid patch of sand and within ten minutes the patch was green with new growth. There is an awful lot of sand there and we were shown the locations where the film Lawrence of Arabia was shot.

Our next call three days later was the very remote island of St Helena with Jamestown its capital. It is not a big place as it only covers 48 square miles and has a population of 5,000 people mostly living in Jamestown. It was not big enough for the ship to dock and we were transferred by tender. It is probably best known because of Napoleon Bonaparte being exiled and dying there. Jamestown fits like a wedge into a long narrow valley. Most of the municipal buildings and shops are at sea level but the majority of the population live in the township at the top of the steep hill overlooking the small quay. It is a couple of miles journey by road to get from bottom to top of the hill. They have built some steps called "Jacob's Ladder" with 699 steps to reach the top 900 feet up so they are high steps indeed. And the ladder is only six feet wide with a handrail on either side of it. I was ashore with Johnson Ferrier, a friend from Edinburgh, and we decided along with many others to climb it. It was a tough task with about 90% of people failing even to reach halfway up. We managed it to the top and had the benefit of some great views of the lower town and quay. Getting back down was just about as difficult as the steps were very sheer. We reached the bottom in a state of exhaustion as it had been hard hot work.

There was an enterprising fellow selling certificates of proof of climbing Jacobs Ladder for a one pound charge so I do have proof that I managed it. Sitting at the bottom getting our breaths back we overlooked the small island police station and managed to read the crime statistics for St Helena for the previous month.

There were twenty cases in all made up of one drunk and disorderly man, three cases of thefts from shops including two footballs from the sports shop, a case of counterfeit money being passed (a cruise line passenger perhaps). Three cases of animals being hurt by dogs and the balance all traffic offences. Their full complement was a sergeant and six policemen which covered Ascension Island as well which is hundreds of miles away.

We then went for a drink at the Royal St Helena Yacht Club and got into conversation with a couple of locals sitting at the next table. One turned out to be the Assistant Governor of the island who was in total control as his boss was in London attending a conference and the other was the Attorney General. I think he must double up as the traffic warden as there is not much work to be done. They both extolled the place and the Assistant Governor who was due to retire told us he was staying put in the island rather than going back to the UK.

An essential visit is firstly to the graveyard where Napoleon had been buried and which is a small plot of land with the French flag flying over it. It is kept in good condition by a French Honorary Consul who lives on the island even though Napoleons body was taken back to France many years ago. Secondly we paid visit to Longwood House where Napoleon lived out his last few years. He had a lovely spot there with a good garden and even had a billiard table for his own use. Not bad, but still a bit of a come down for someone with such big ambitions. They have a nine-hole Golf Course on the island and the locals offered us golf clubs to have a game have a game, but because of lack of time we had to decline. We also had a good look over the Governors residence at Plantation House where we met a tortoise well over a hundred years old by the name of Johnathon. Altogether it was a great day out on a lovely remote island and I vowed to revisit it.

By this time it was the middle of April and we were moving north up the west coast of Africa towards home. Our next stop was Dakar the capital of Senegal which is practically the most westernmost point on the African continent. It still has a very French influence on it and is a mix of modern skyscrapers and old fashioned African buildings but was in a very dirty state with lots of litter everywhere and in the need of a quick lick of paint. In some ways it was very menacing with lots of gangs of youths standing around. I did a panoramic tour of the area by bus and visited some markets. I even bought a top of the range Rolex watch which after a lot of haggling I paid for with five pounds. It looked like the real thing and the source of much amusement at the dinner table.

The penultimate port of call was Agadir in Morocco. This was a seaside tourist town which was totally destroyed by an earthquake in 1960. It had been wonderfully restored with plenty of luxurious hotels and public buildings and was really back on its feet. I paid a visit to the old walled city of Toroudant some miles inland and amongst other things saw a memorable display by tribal horsemen and Berber folklore troupe. The final port of call was Casablanca the biggest city in Morocco and the most significant port as well as being the centre of commerce and industry. I paid a visit to the Palaces and Souks as well as spending time at the Hassan 11 Mosque a most impressive modern building situated right on the long seafront. It is 655 feet high and dominates its surroundings and no money was spared when it was being built. The Prayer Hall is the size of four football pitches with an overflow area to house a further 80,000 worshippers.

After that it was just a short trip up to Southampton and home. The trip had taken nearly four months and I enjoyed it immensely. As well as seeing a lot of the world, I made many long lasting friends who I am still in contact with and I vowed that as it had been such a good experience I must have more of it in the future.

It was strange being back at home again and living alone yet there was plenty of things to do to keep me occupied. A large quantity of mail had built up over my four months holiday and that took a long time to read and reply to. I was able to see the last few games of the season at St James' Park and renew my visits to Blue Flames Club to play bowls. My work for Arthritis Care was still there for me together with all my Church activities. Christine moved into a new house in May and I also attended the Mahar Reunion get-together in Alfriston, East Sussex, a later date than usual just to fit in with me. It was good to meet Col

Pradeep Bhatia and his wife Ashmi once again before they returned to India later in the year. I also managed to get a trip to York to look at some of my old haunts and also spent a day of two at Chester le Street to watch some international cricket at the Durham County ground with Robert.

There was not a dull moment in the year which was to finish off with another cruise, this time a month in the Caribbean during November and December to try to escape from the cold weather at home. I flew down to Southampton and boarded the Saga Ruby the sister ship to the one that I travelled round the world on. It was almost an identical ship with the same brilliant service and a mainly Philipino crew.

Our first stop was at Port Delgado in the Azores which is noted as a prime spot for Whale and Dolphin watching. The Azores are Portuguese and used to play a prominent role when transatlantic liners were still the vogue but are now a bit of a backwater. There are numerous islands forming the Azores, all with natural beauty and enjoying a relaxed way of living and just a lovely place to live. We soon reached the Caribbean and began visiting all the holiday islands making up the chain. They were places of natural beauty with gorgeous beaches, lovely sunny weather and a relaxing holiday atmosphere. We called at St.Lucia, Grenada, Margarita Island, Trinidad, St Vincent, Barbados, Tortola and Antigua. Then it was back home via Horta in the Azores and finally calling at my old favourite of Madeira. I got back just in time for the Christmas preparations and so ended a very adventurous 2005 which certainly was an unforgettable experience.

2006 promised to be another year for travel and adventure. After my experiences in 2005 I quickly booked for another cruise, this time on the Saga Ruby the sister ship of the one I was on last year. They were practically identical ships so I felt very much at home again.

Mid-February I flew to Singapore and spent three nights in Singapore at the Novotel situated at Clarks Quay. This was my first sight of Singapore and I found it very much to my liking. I had two free days before I boarded my ship and made the most of them by touring the highlights of the place. It is a very modern city with a nice climate and is both clean and well run and would require more than two days of sightseeing to do it just ice. I soon settled into the relaxed atmosphere and activities on the ship as we sailed northwards.

Our first stop was Sihanoukville one of Cambodias premier seaside resorts. This allowed us time to have a tour in the area and also time to spend time on the white sandy beaches which ran along the coastline at the Sokha beach resort. The next destination was Thailand where we called in at Bangkok for an overnight stay. This is a vibrant colourful city not to be missed with so many attractions to see and the opportunity to taste some different food. It has a lot of history and I paid a visit to the Temple of the Golden Buddha to see the world's largest solid gold Buddha at 13 feet and dating back to the 13th century.

The highlight of the day was a tour of the Grand Palace and Wat Phra Kaeo complex located at the heart of the old city. Built as a residence for the king and as a home for the sacred Emerald Buddha it is an exquisite and remarkable site with so many magnificent Temples. One lasting memory was going into one of these temples and having to leave my shoes out side. Whilst I was looking around it there was a heavy thunder storm outside and when I recovered my shoes they were full of water.

Part of the day was spent on a boat cruising along the Choa Phraya River and having a slap up meal at a riverside restaurant. This still allowed plenty of time to browse through the many markets where incredible bargains were on offer. Not to be missed also was a six hour elephant trek through plantations of cassava trees and rice fields. The elephants seemed happy enough to have us on their backs so long as you gave them a constant supply of bananas which they relished. Then it was on to Ho Chi Minh City in Vietnam formerly called Saigon. One could have expected the Vietnamese to be hostile to us after the long war they had been through with the West but this was far from the welcome we received which was most friendly.

It is a chaotic City in respect of its roads and transport with every one seeming to own at least a motor scooter. Even on the smallest scooter you could see two parents and two children on board with no safety helmets. I saw the Reunification Palace and Museum of National History where they extolled the triumphs of their recent war. I had an hours' white-knuckle ride through the centre of the city on a manually pulled rickshaw which was an amazing experience.

After an overnight stay I spent the next day at the Cu Chi Tunnels famed for its intricate network of tunnels outside the city where the Viet Cong Fighters were based. In all 120 miles of tunnel was used. I went down a tunnel through a trap door measuring one foot by one foot which was very hard to spot. It was a straight drop down for around six feet and then a crawl along a very restricted tunnel on all fours in pitch black darkness. There was no way I could stand up as the tunnel height was never more than four feet high. It was just a matter of following the person in front by touch and voice for about two hundred yards of winding tunnel until after about a quarter of an hour later you could spot a bit of light coming from the exit trapdoor. It was hot dirty work and not to be recommended. How they lived so long in those conditions seems remarkable.

It was nice to be outside again in the fresh air and to stand up straight again. We came out on a rifle range where we were each given a Kalashnikov machine gun and provided with bullets at one dollar a shot to test our capability for shooting. I was reasonably accurate and at least it provided a livelihood for the enterprising people who ran the tour. After all this excitement it was time for relaxing on board the ship for a couple of days on the way up to Hong Kong.

Sailing into Hong Kong is one of the greatest experiences one could have. The scenery in the harbour and the hills and buildings surrounding it are breathtaking and you could stand on deck mesmorised by it all and in awe of all the developments. After a quick look around the place it was off travelling 40 miles to the north to Ghangzou to the airport. I have never seen so many skyscrapers which were visible non-stop for the full 40 miles journey. It was a brand new very busy airport with planes coming and going at one a minute. All except my flight to Xian which was the only one on the board with any delay. The plane was due to fly out at 14.30 and it was around 20.00 that a note came up showing the delay was caused by deep snow on the runway at Xian. It was about 80* in Hong Kong but about minus 20* in

Xian. We eventually took off at 23.00 and reached our hotel in Xian in the middle of the night.

On 28 February as planned I landed at Xian on a bitter cold late night, looking forward to seeing the Terracotta Army. The next day we had to travel on an icy road for about 20 kms to reach the Terracotta Army site. There were several vehicle accidents all along and contrary to the warm weather I expected, it was freezing cold. The display of artefacts was amazing. Whilst there I met the old Chinese farmer who had discovered the site around 1974 comprising 3 pits. He was busy narrating his story and selling his book - a source of big fortune. At Xian we were honoured by being given the freedom of the city and treated to a cultural programme of traditional dance and music.

An interesting feature was that Xian had a formidable fortress like wall with ramparts and a road for vehicular traffic to move around it. Despite the freezing cold I thoroughly enjoyed the visit I then flew into Shanghai - the most modern, developed and affluent city with a staggering architectural high rise skyline, The Yangtse River which flows through the city has a waterscape of intense river traffic of all types almost nudging one another. It was a one day stay taking in visits to a Buddhist Monastery and a carpet factory. We flew into Beijing next, back to severe cold with wind chill and snow on some of the peaks around for a two day stay.

On the first day we went round places of interest like Tianamen Square, quite an area with all of us under tight security surveillance, and then to The Forbidden Palace (now thrown open to visitors), a Chinese Tea Ceremony and local favourite Peking Duck for dinner. What struck me most was the sight of millions of bicycles thronging the City amidst seeming chaos. Day two was an eventful visit to the renowned Heritage site of The Great Wall of China - running almost endlessly for 8850 Kms. We treaded a rather steep part of it for about 2 Kms followed by a visit to the Ming Tombs, the Ming Animal Walk adorned with stone carvings of all types of animals, a Jade factory and Emperor's Summer Palace. As we headed back to our ship we were in for a nasty Chinese surprise - about 500 people who had boarded were pulled out for a recount as one of them had made a probable miscount! This was bizarre experience of 2 hours in miserable cold in the open air. It left an awful distaste of Chinese misdemeanour.

Our next port of call was Kobe and Osaka. The day was spent on a general tour. As we sailed to Ngoya, we were given a royal welcome with a Brass Band playing martial music-indeed a very impressive, moving and memorable time. At Ngoya we visited the majestic, ancient Royal Castle of lnuyame. This was followed by a by a full day in Tokyo, where I visited the Emperor's Royal Palace and Gardens. Tokyo is a flourishing vibrant and wealthy city of high rise structures, and was a dynamic city of highly talented, trained and efficient people-receptive, courteous and helpful.

After several days out at sea, we touched two small islands Midway(2x3kms) and Sand (1x1km), both American military bases battle-scarred during WW2. We were lucky to have visited them, the only ship to have done so that year. All the American forces had left except for about 20 wildlife caretakers looking after a unique population of about one million Albatross pairs with a chick each, with no predators, and a mile-long coastline with bountiful fish. Interestingly it has been found that one main cause of their death is plastic from the sea! One had to tread with great care for fear of trampling on the chicks with barely any space for human intruders. The Americans were rather cordial and sought only one item - ice cream from the ship as their machine had broken down.

Around 18-19Mar, we touched Honolulu and Hailo, part of the Hawaian Islands. It was here at Pearl Harbour that the Japanese airforce made one the most daring and devastating attacks to sink practically the entire US fleet on 07Dec1941. We paid our homage at the poignant Memorial. After a fairly long voyage we reached San Francisco sailing under the famous Golden Gates suspension bridge for a full days visit. Highlights were a visit to the now closed notorious prison of Alcatraz and a journey on the famous street cars which go up and down the steep slopes of the city.

Then it was onto Los Angeles the home of Hollywood and mecca of the cineworld. It was most exciting and interesting to see their world renowned film sets and the footprints and galleries of legends and celebrities.

The next stop was San Diago, an important US Naval Base. We had the rare privilege of going on board the USS 'MIDWAY' a famous nuclear aircraft carrier now a unique museum. There was an imposing display of all the types of fighter aircraft on the flight deck. I had the rare honour to get onto the Captain's Chair on the Bridge, and later in the cockpits of the fighter aircraft! It was indeed most memorable. The ship then went on to the famous seaside resort of Acupulco, where we were treated by the daring cliff divers, to their spectacular diving from 200ft high cliffs into the sea - absolutely breathtaking and unforgettable!

Our next port of call was Puerto Quetsal in Gautemala and Puerto Cabiara in Costa Rica. On 06Apr, we sailed through the Panama Canal during the day - an experience to cherish.Towards the last few days of our cruise, we spent time in Miami, the Bahamas, Bermuda (both very rich) and the Azores. The highlight was the alligators and ever glades of Miami. Finally, we were homebound and reached Southampton on 23Apr, after a memorable and enriching cruise.

In mid-July Christine, Bethany and I set out for a holiday for a holiday in Majorca, a beautiful island in the Mediterranian. It was a welcome break for them. The next few months I was busy giving talks sharing my experiences, managing my voluntary job with Arthritis Care, playing bowls and following the Newcastle United football team. In December I had the privilege to be with the Mahar Regiment for the Xlth Reunion in Saugor (MP) along with Maj. Rene Miroy (of 2 Mahar and who also served with the US army). It was wonderful meeting and celebrating with our Regiments fraternity. This time I was honoured with the unique gift of a walking stick carved from Kashmiri walnut wood with an ornamental silver lion knob - a priceless momento indeed and my prized regimental possession.

2007 started with another cruise, this time on the Saga Rose from Southampton to Singapore lasting nearly seven weeks. As always, I had a super time with a lovely cabin and plenty of new friends to make. This cruise was somewhat different as for the first time I started to undertake charitable work for The Saga

Charitable Trust during some of the stops at various ports. It is only a small Trust set up after a lot of passengers expressed a wish to give help to mainly young children in great need which they so often saw when visiting the ports along the way.

I was friendly with Lady Jo Blanchard who was my bridge partner and one of the prime movers in the Trust who enlisted my support. I paid a return visit to Madeira which was always a nice place to spend time and then on to Dakar in Senegal with a visit to the Pink Lake. The unusual colour is caused by algae and the lake is super salty and a small local industry has been established which provides enough salt for the areas needs. The lake is noted for being the finishing point for the annual Dakar Rally the notoriously difficult long distance car rally. It was also a pleasure to revisit St Helena a few days later but this time I did not try to go up and down Jacobs Ladder.

The next stop at Walvis Bay was my first shot at hands on charitable work. Rather than going on an organised trip to see the sights of the local area, I went off on a trip to a small shanty town by the name of Mondesa to visit a creche set up by two young ladies some time previously which had come to the Charities attention as being in the need of help. On board the Saga Rose we had a cabin full of goods which we could take out as presents such as clothes, toys, books, pens and pencils, brushes and combs, soap and tooth brushes, cans of soft drinks, sweets, knitted teddy bears, balloons etc. These were all things had been donated big national retailers from their unsold stocks and which they willingly gave to the charity. I went out laden down like Father Christmas to see what help was needed.

The journey took me through the prosperous old German town of Swakopmund to the township of Mondesa and then on to the shanty town of Mondesa which was clearly down market. The two ladies were looking after about twenty youngsters all below five in a corrugated hut with one 40 watt bulb as its lighting and no water supply nor toilet facilities. There were some small desks and chairs of poor quality and a desk leg fell off whilst I was there. The children were left at the creche by their mothers who went into Mondesa or Swakopmund to find domestic work at around 7.00am and were picked up in the early evening when they returned. No food was available during their stay and the nearest water tap was some hundreds of yards away which charged on a meter.

Despite all these disadvantages the children seemed happy and content and sang some well rehearsed songs for me. They were overwhelmed by the presents they received and were in a state of wonderment at their good fortune. The two ladies were just about managing financially with a small payment per child per day but it was hard going for them. I wrote a one page report on my visit, praising the efforts of the leaders and recommending some help be given to the creche. The upshot of this was that the Charity gave them support, which enabled them to pass an examination on their proficiency which enabled them to claim support from the Namibian Government. They moved subsequently to a new building with running water and kitchen facilities and are now thriving - magic.

Later in the week we reached Capetown for an overnight stay which gave us two full days to explore its delights. I spent one day visiting Kaleysha on Charitable work and the next day enjoyed a cable car ride to the top of the Table Mountain and a stunning afternoon in the Kirstenbosch National Botanical Garden. I sat alone for about two hours in this most idyllic place with glorious views in warm sunshine in total silence apart from the sound of the bees in the flowers.

The next port was East London where I made a visit to an old Xhosa village to participate in the local customs. The ship then sailed northwards up the east coast to Durban, a thriving seaside resort with a magnificent beach. Once again I spent my time there on charitable duties visiting a creche for young Zulu folks some 40 miles from Durban. They gave a wonderful display of Zulu dancing and were richly rewarded with lots of presents. After leaving Durban we cruised to the Comoros Islands and landed for a day on Mayotte which remains under French jurisdiction although the rest of the islands gained independence. A strange event happened at we neared Mayotte with an elderly lady being taken seriously ill. She had to be left in hospital in Mayotte so we were all most concerned about this and felt bad at her misfortune. This was made worse a couple of days later when we were told that she had died. However, it turned out that the lady was no stranger to Mayotte. She had lived there for some years with her husband who was a diplomat and he had unfortunately died in service there some years previously. She was buried next to him in the British Cemetery a few days later. Truth is sometimes stranger than fiction it seems.

Then it was off to Mombasa for an incredible visit to an Orphanage along with the Captain of the ship, some of the senior officers and a handful of charity volunteers. The Orphanage which had already received a lot of support from the Saga Trust had been started by an English lady some years previously and catered for the needs of about 30 children with HIV. The management there now included 2 Sikh Restaurant owners who provided a lot of the finance and a Lieutenant Commander (Medical) of the Kenyan Navy who input a lot of medical expertise. On this visit the ships storeroom had been raided and tons of food and supplies were donated along with carpets and furniture. A most enjoyable time was had by all and it still continues to flourish. After that it was a case of cruising in the Indian Ocean to the exotic islands of Seychelles and Maldives. We also spent a day on an uninhabited island which was rented out for the day and taken over by the ships passengers for swimming, sunbathing and picnicking. A neighbouring island belonged to Roman Abramovich the Chelsea Manager who had his yacht moored nearby. Our ship was bigger than his. All too soon we reached Singapore and the long flight home. It was a good cruise and my bridge playing improved out of all measure.

Life was still full of interest at home, with a lot of talks to be given, the football team to be supported, bowls to be played with much Arthritis Care and Church work to be done. I also managed a trip to Ampney Cruscis for the annual Mahar Reunion.

Cruising however, was still the order of the day and this time out of the Tyne with the Saga Rose bound for the Baltic Sea. My friend Johnson Ferrier came down from Edinburgh to join me on the trip. We left the Tyne in a gale and I remember Christine waving goodbye to us from the bank near the mouth of the Tyne. We rode out the gale and were blessed with fine and sunny weather for the rest of the trip. The first port of call was Copenhagen a city with lots of canals and bicycles and home of the Little Mermaid which we saw. Two days later we were in Stockholm an impressive city with a strong maritime history and many interesting buildings. After that it was a short trip to Helsinki, the capital of Finland. It was a vibrant seaside city of beautiful islands and great green parks. Amongst other things we saw the old Olympic Stadium which is still in good condition and the Sibelius Monument. The highlight of the cruise was a two day stay in St. Petersburg which is a great city with miles of waterways to explore. We visited the Hermitage the great museum for a number of hours but you could really spend a week there and still not do it justice as it is so extensive. Luckily we managed to get a visit to the Kirov Ballet for an evening performance.

The next day found us in Tallinn the capital of Estonia. It is an old walled and cobble street city with lots of historical places to see and plenty of squares filled with cafes and shops. Two days later we docked in Warnemunde a Baltic Port around 100 miles north of Berlin. We had a bus tour to Berlin which was an excellent day. Berlin is a beautiful place with its parks, canals and famous sightseeing spots. We visited the Reichstag, the Brandenburg Gate, the old check point Charlie and what was left of the infamous wall,

The last port we visited was Aarhus in Denmark a quaint old seaside place where we visited an exceptionally fine museum. Then back to Newcastle upon Tyne after a fine cruise. As part of the entertainment on board there were a number of singers on board from the English National Opera. One evening at about midnight Johnson and I were making our way through one of the public rooms when we passed some of them singing "A policeman's lot is not a happy one" from the G &S comic opera. I joined in as we passed by and we were pounced on and asked whether we would volunteer to do a bit part in one of their shows as foolish policemen in The Pirates of Penzance. We made the show with lots of daft antics fully dressed as old coppers with truncheons and really enjoyed ourselves as did our audience.

Holidays for the year were not over as a fortnight in July was spent in Cyprus with Christine and Bethany. I remember it being super hot but still very enjoyable.

In October I spent a weekend in Sonning a lovely spot in Berkshire on the Thames as a guest of George and Angela Deanes, two of my cruising friends. We were all Newcastle

United fans and Newcastle were playing away to Reading. I treated them to a lunch and watching the match from a box which was a treat although it was a bit of a boring one all draw. Also at the end of October I was in hospital for a day for a hernia operation and by chance met up with Margaret Watson another of my cruising friends who by chance was being treated on the same day as myself. What a small world it is.

The rest of the year was well spent on bowling, watching Newcastle United play and numerous talking engagements. All in all a good and interesting year travelling the world and making lots of friends.

Cruising is a fine way of meeting people you would not normally meet when living a quiet life in Newcastle upon Tyne. I have been able to meet and interact with a number of well known people who have become good friends. For example who would ever have thought I could have Michael Shay (Queens Private Secretary) and his wife as a close friend. Or Lord David Hunt, a member of Margaret Thatcher's Cabinet, Lord David Steel the Liberal Democrat, Edwina Curry, Terry Waite, Katherine Jenkins - and many others.

2008 turned out to be another fine year of cruising and adventure. I was on the move in the middle of February when I flew out to Sydney to join the Saga Rose which was half way through a world cruise and making its way back to Southampton. This cruise was dogged by difficulties but turned into one of the best and most adventuresome. I flew from Heathrow making use of the new Terminal building which was newly opened. It was along flight to Sydney and quite a few weary travellers on getting off the plane were given a letter apologising for our luggage which was still at Heathrow. The new procedures were not fully understood by the staff there and the Terminal had major difficulties over one or two weeks before it was running to plan. They gave us comfort in that they guaranteed the luggage would soon follow us and would be delivered to us within three days. Much use that was for me as my ship would be around the Great Barrier Reef area by then with great difficulty anticipated in getting cases delivered to a ship way out in the ocean.

Thoughts turned to a shopping spree in Sydney to at least get the necessities in the short time before the ship sailed. Such was the confusion that about an hour later they found our luggage was on the plane after all. Situation saved but what an awful start. I soon settled into life on the ocean waves as we made our way to the north with stops at Cairns and Whitsunday Islands with their beautiful white sandy beaches. Then it was a day at the Barrier Reef sailing in a luxury catamaran with marine biologists on board. We then had several days at sea making our way to Port Moresby in Papua New Guinea. This is one of the world's least explored and most culturally diverse countries. It is also bottom of the list of poor countries in the world. Prior to joining the cruise, I had been giving a talk to the ladies meeting in the local Anglican Church and I mentioned in passing that I would be visiting Port Moresby on my way. At the end of the meeting a lady approached me to say that her son had been working in Port Moresby for a few years and was still there. I immediately offered to meet him and invite him on board for lunch. Only after I had made my offer she disclosed he was The Anglican Bishop of Port Moresby by the name of Peter Ramsden which came as a bit of a shock to me.

I had never met a Bishop before and was worried about the protocol to follow, but his mother put my worries aside by saying he likes to be called Peter and his wife is Sue. The great day comes and Peter and Sue arrive on board the Saga Rose where I have organised a lovely lunch with some friends and ships officers. Afterwards, Peter and Sue took me on a guided tour of Port Moresby and served tea at Bishops Palace. This had a grand name but in reality was a bungalow built on sticks and was far from being a Palace. One could pick bananas as they climbed the outside steps to the front door. I saw the Cathedral which was a modern building but on a small scale and met many of his parishioners. I also visited a very modern Parliament Building which must have cost them a fortune to build and which was surrounded very substandard low grade housing. It was a memorable day out which we all enjoyed.

On leaving I gave him a small donation for his work, being money I had saved by cancelling an organised tour I had booked for the day. Some months later Peter was back in the UK attending the Bishops conference at Canterbury. He came back to the local Anglican Church where he used to work and gave a talk with slides on his work in Port Moresby to which I was invited. I was staggered to hear that my small donation had been used to provide a water pump at a remote village and saved the people travelling many miles a day to collect polluted water which they previously used. A little goes a long way in some parts of the earth.

Our next stop should have been Ambon Island, part of Indonesia but we never made it. We were sailing northwards in the tropics in lovely calm water. It was Sunday afternoon at about two o'clock and most people were relaxing on deck after a good Sunday Lunch. Suddenly the noise of the engines stopped and the rhythm of the ship halted. A short time later the Captain informed us that we had lost all power but it was being worked on by the engineers. After about an hour the Captain came over the intercom to tell us that it was a more serious problem than first thought. A large diameter water pipe had sprung a leak way up near the top of the ship and the water had flooded down the decks through a few public rooms and cabins and had reached the engine room just over where the electrical panels serving the whole ship were situated and this had caused the whole electrical system to fail. And of course the generator which should have cut in immediately failed and we were left with no power.

The position was now serious. There was no lighting below decks. no cooking facilities, no air conditioning, no water supply and we were miles from the nearest port where we could get help. This was an emergency situation with no easy way out. We were banned from going below deck and this meant sleeping in deck chairs overnight on the open decks. No great burden with this as it was the tropics and the air was balmy and with no air conditioning the temperature below decks was far too high. We were each given a supply of water bottles and a flash light and portable BBQ's were set up on deck to give us some food. There were no washing facilities and very limited toilet facilities were provided. So much for luxury cruising!

Twenty four hours later a limited electrical supply was re-established which helped a little. On around half-power the ship made its way to Cebu in the Philippines, the nearest major port.

This was music to the ears of most of the crew who were mainly Philippino's whose homes were near to Cebu. We reached Cebu after a couple of days voyaging and everyone had to be disembarked and sent to hotel accommodation for a couple of nights whilst the ship was repaired and cleaned up. I was allocated to the Cebu Hilton Holiday Hotel along with two bus-loads of passengers numbering around 100. Being single, I held back whilst the reception desk was besieged by a rugby scrum of others wanting quick attention.

I was the last person to be served and they did not look happy when it was my turn. They had run out of rooms due to a slight miscalculation. As it was only a couple of nights I said I would sleep in a broom cupboard if they gave me something to lie on. This was not good enough though and after much debate they came up with the ideal solution. They had four penthouse suites at the top of the main block on floor 13 and one was free. It was mine for the two nights with its superior location, ambiance and view. In the end I had it for five nights as the repair of the ship took longer than expected with parts having to be flown in from Japan.

We were given daily trips round Cebu Island which is a lovely spot. On one day they suggested a trip to the nearby island of Bohal which required a ferry journey of some 20 miles. The computer did the booking and because I was in the Penthouse I was booked into first class on the ferry whilst everyone else was in steerage. Talk about the last shall be first! Bohal was a great visit with two must see things being The Chocolate Mountains and the Tarsir. The Chocolate Mountains were nice enough but they were just chocolate coloured earth and not the real thing for eating. The Tarsirs were great and I became an expert and admirer of this much endangered mammal. It is a small furry animal about the size of a tennis ball with big ogley eyes the size of table tennis balls. Their sight is around 160 times clearer than humans have and they can turn their heads around 350 degrees. They can also jump around five feet from a standing start.

They were housed in a sanctuary where the staff are trying to protect the species from extinction. There were about 50 of them sitting in branches of trees very silently and still. The gift shop had replicas of them on sale and it just looked as though some of the replicas had been glued to the branches. Then one of them winks and you know they are real.

During my stay in the Penthouse on the top floor the lift always took me past The Business Centre on the 12th floor. On the last morning I thought I would have a look at it and on my way up from breakfast I stopped at the 12th floor. By this time I was looking very scruffy as we had only planned to stay 2 nights in the place. The door opened up into a plush well carpeted and furnished place and there was a reception desk with a gorgeous young lady dressed in a long gown with a split up the side, who looked on me with disdain and said you cannot come in here. I said I was just passing and wanted to see what the facilities were like. As it was still early and no one else was around she relented and said I could look at the place for 5 minutes.

It was a typical business centre with computers and easy chairs with copies of the financial papers of the world scattered around and some dining facilities. The lady told me it the best views over the island and I disputed this with her as mine on the 13 floor were better. When she realised I stayed in the Penthouse her attitude changed and she said she would be delighted to see me there at anytime.

All this happened just because a water pipe had leaked. Our next stop should have been Hong Kong, but time was against us now and that was cancelled so we were now bound for Saigon or as it is now known Ho Chi Min City.

I had sailed up the Saigon River previously for a one day visit but this trip had a one night stop there with two days available to look around. I decided to spend the first day on organised trips and reserved the second day to do some charitable work. There was plenty to see in this vibrant city and my trips included a rickshaw ride for an hour around the commercial centre which was pretty hair raising as the traffic is just beyond belief with everyone seeming to own a motor scooter. Then it was a bit of shopping with many bargains on offer and a trip to the Chinatown area and a visit to an impressive pagoda. The evening was spent on a cruise along the Saigon River with a good meal and local entertainment on board.

The next day was a great visit to "15 May School" which was an orphanage where 200 children were looked after, it one of the poorest areas in town. I raided the supply cupboard on the Saga Rose and arrived with masses of goodies for the children. I found it a well run school equally divided between boys and girls with good supervision and teachers. The Saga Trust had been told that the water supply was in need of update and looking into that was my prime aim. It turned out that Coca Cola of America had already financed the renovation of the water supply and Monsato Chemicals had given a big donation to build a proper stage in the place as the pupils were very keen on putting on entertainments.

Saga had previously financed the building of a hairdressing saloon so I concluded that this was a rather well financed organisation. I had a long talk with the Principal who was most impressive and who had all the facts and figures on hand from computer printouts he produced. He was over the moon that one of his boy pupils had just received notice of acceptance for University entry. His main object was to give all in his care a good formal education and also to provide training in skills to enable them to get work when the time came for them to leave. This was concentrated on hairdressing for the girls and mechanics training for the boys in view of the large numbers of motor scooters in the city.

All the children were well dressed and cared for with white shirts and blouses and grey trousers and skirts. There were 4 classrooms with 25 twin desks in each and a fully qualified teacher in each room. All the students were very eager to show me their books and explain to me what they were doing. After having been on the ship for a long period my hair was rather unruly and the girls decided that I needed some expert attention the hair salon and I was given first class treatment by half a dozen of the girls and left looking smarter than when I arrived. All in all an excellent visit with no demand for more charitable money required. Then it was down to Singapore missing out China which put us more or less back on schedule.

The very moment we docked at Singapore, the lights went out with a major power failure - the whole nightmare was back - the temporary repair on the water pipe had failed and it was a repeat of the Cebu experience. There is no better place to be stranded than in Singapore and it turned out to be another four nights stay in very good hotel accommodation in central Singapore. There was a lot of sightseeing to be done and amongst other things I visited Changi Jail, the Johore Battery and Sentosa Island. I was also given the option of a flight to Hong Kong or Kuala Lumpur for a one night's stay. I opted for Kuala Lumpur as I had already been to Hong Kong and because of the new breakdown the visit to Kuala Lumpur had been cancelled.

I found Kuala Lumpur a beautiful city and well worth the effort of flying to and from there for an overnight stay. The hotel was top class and just over the road from the twin Petronas Towers which at that time was the highest building in the world. Our next stop on the cruise was now Colombo in Sri Lanka. Once again I decided to do a days' charitable work in place of the organised trips. This time it took me to the Wira Wara School some 80 miles north of Colombo. This school was situated very near the sea and in the 2004 Tsunami it had been deluged with water and most of its equipment had been lost. Saga Trust had already financed the replacement of musical instruments which had been washed away and this had been a great loss for the School as they prided themselves at their excellence at music.

On this visit I took along 5 desk top computers and a load of text books to help restock their library. It was Easter Monday and the children were on holiday so I didn't have the joy and giving them any presents and missed out on hearing the band play. They were making good steps towards a full recovery from the disaster.

Our next port of call was the teeming Indian City of Mumbai which I was very familiar with having been there several times already. This seemed to be another opportunity to do further charitable work. I had the choice of two projects and opted for a visit to the Zion Children's Home rather than the Mumbai Railway children project. The Zion Children's Home was run by the Salvation Army and had already received support from Saga Charity funds on a previous occasion. It was a long taxi journey out to Home taking me through some very downmarket areas on the way. Once again I was laden with all sorts of gifts for the 120 so girls who lived there.

It was a well run establishment with good living accommodation and the girls were obviously happy. Their dining room was in need of a bit of redecoration and there was also a need to form a hatch between the kitchen and the dining room to facilitate the serving of the food. I arrived late morning so I was invited to have lunch with the girls. I sat on the floor cross legged eating my rice and dhal with my fingers and talking with the girls. They spoke to me in English and I tried my best to speak to them in Urdu which made the time very interesting. However, after an hour on the floor I needed their help to untangle my legs and stand up straight again.

The Salvation Army and Saga Charity both declined to give money for the proposed alterations claiming lack of funds, but I paid for the job to be done and received a photograph some time later showing the completed job. It only cost coppers anyway but made them happy.

Because of the time spent in Singapore a one day stay in Muscat was cancelled to let us get on schedule again and our next stop was at Salalah in Oman. I spent the day in the lost city of Uber in the middle of the vast sand deserts of Oman. This was a place which was very prosperous a couple of thousand years ago but was abandoned and lost and became a fabled place. Many expeditions were made to find it in the 1800 and early 1900s including one led by Lawrence of Arabia who called it "the Atlantis of the Sands" but it was never found. It had to wait until the 1980s and the advent of satellites before it could be pin pointed.

It was easy for me in an air conditioned land rover to reach it and have a look around. Some excavations have been done and lots of old ruins have been found under the sands. There was also a cave with a narrow entrance which revealed a lake of pure water and this was no doubt the attraction when it was in its prime. No hidden treasure has yet been found there.

There was some excitement on the next part of our journey passed the Gulf of Aden. It was a Sunday afternoon just after lunch when a French Navy helicopter flew over the ship at low altitude and made off to the south where a few fast motor launches were getting nearer our ship. They turned round and made off and a couple of hours later a French destroyer went passed at high speed in the same direction. It was just the period when a lot of high-jacking was happening in these waters and we

210

must have been a target. We managed to get away safely up into the Red Sea for our next call at Aqaba in Jordan.

It was there that I opted for a trip to the ancient city of Petra. This was another city that had been lost but is now a world heritage site. It can only be accessed through a long narrow passage way and it is tough going to walk there. It has lots of well maintained old ruins including the famous Treasury building and came to prominence when a film about Indiana Jones was produced there.

There was a day's stop at Sharm El Sheikh on the southern tip of the Sinai Peninsula. It is a popular holiday these days with its fine weather and good beaches with rugged mountains as its back drop. I went on a trip to St Catherine's Monastery located at the foot of Mount Sinai. We visited the spot where Moses received the 10 Commandments and the site of the burning bush. It is dangerous country side and our party was accompanied by a number of armed guards.

Before going further north through the Suez Canal we stopped for a day at Port Suez on the southern point of the Canal. This enabled me to have a day trip to Cairo visiting the famous Museums and visiting the Pyramids at Giza. I managed to be on the bridge as the ship made its passage through the Canal bound for the port of Piraeus for a day in Athens. This was a pleasant day in an ancient city with the highlight being a visit to the Parthenon. Then it was homeward bound via Valletta the capital of Malta which is an interesting World Heritage site. A further two stops at Cadiz and Lisbon concluded a most interesting cruise, full of surprises and excitement. For all the changes that had to be made and the hardships we were given a 30% discount on the cost of the next cruise we booked.

Towards the end of the year, the travel bug must still have been with me as I flew off to South Africa for three weeks for a mixture of relaxing in the sun, playing bowls and bridge, doing a little exploring and some charity work. It was a long air flight via Heathrow, Johannesburg and Durban then on by car to Scottburgh a small seaside town some 50 miles south of Durban. It was a charming little place with a lovely beach and friendly local people.

The bowling green was in good condition and many happy hours were spent on the green, although thunder and lightning did at times curtail the games. It was a good centre for venturing out on day trips to the interesting spots nearby. I was able to spend time renewing my acquaintance with Durban with its lovely sea front and many beautiful gardens. I also visited Oribi Gorge in the KwaZulu-Natal Park with its amazing scenery, and spent a day in PheZulu Safari Park with its amazing range of animals with the crocodiles taking centre stage.

The most exciting trip was to Lesotho via the Sani Pass. Lesotho is a high altitude, land locked kingdom encircled by South Africa. The Sani Pass is some 9 miles in length with the gravel road having gradients of 1:3 and restricted to 4X4 vehicles. It is very dangerous and lots of wrecked vehicles can be spotted along the route. The road is not wide enough for passing traffic and passing points are few in number. Vehicles coming down have priority and it is hair-raising to have to reverse for some hundreds of yards at times to let people pass. The summit is at 10,000 feet and most of the journey is done in clouds and mist.

At the very top we got above the clouds and the sun was shining but it was very cold. There is a small village at the top and I think the people have a hard life up there. They live in big communal huts and all the children go away to further in the country for schooling coming back at weekends. They had an inn up there which claimed to be the highest pub in Africa. It was very popular as it had a big roaring fire.

Later I spent a good deal of time visiting Saga Charitable projects in the area including the Word of Hope Creche in ZimbaIi Lodge and Pennington which is a big centre of activity with ladies being taught how to use sewing machines and after passing out proficient are given a sewing machine and can start earning money working from home.

The men are taught brick making using a small machine for making concrete blocks and likewise they are given equipment to enable them to start earning a living. Concrete blocks are in great demand for the house building projects and there is a long waiting list of applicants to undertake the course.

Amongst all this there was plenty of time for whale watching all along the coast line of the Indian Ocean. All this was on top of my usual fortnight holiday with Christine and Bethany which this time took us to Halkidinki a lovely seaside spot in Greece. This gave me more sunshine and sand with good food and a first class hotel.

I also managed to go for the usual Mahar Reunion again held at Bedworth in the Midlands where it was good to meet up with old comrades. I also spent a couple of nights in Edinburgh at the invitation of Michael and Mona Shea who have a lovely apartment in Princess Gardens which is right next to the Castle. From the lounge window there is a lovely panoramic view of Princes Street below and views over the Firth of Forth to Fife and the Central Highlands. Michael had been Press Secretary to HM The Queen for many years after spending time in the Diplomatic Service and writing many best-selling novels. I became firm friends with them through cruising together. In between all these activities I gave dozens of talks to local groups, devoted a lot of time to Arthritis Care and Church activities as well as following Newcastle United Football Club at all their home matches and continued to enjoy and excel at my Bowls Club with mote trophies won.

2009 started off in the same fashion of previous years, with a strong desire to get away from the cold dark days of winter. I tried a slightly different approach opting for three shorter holidays taken in the first three months of the year. All were in the Canary Islands where sunshine and warmth was more or less guaranteed. January saw me in Lanzarote, February in Gran Canaria and March in Tenerife. All the hotels were good and the weather lived up to expectations but it was a bit of a bind having to spend so much time flying backwards and forwards all the time. Never the less I enjoyed myself doing a lot of walking and sightseeing and with no meals to prepare and no washing up to be done it was a nice relaxing way to start a new year. Later in the summer Christine, Bethany and I went for a fortnights holiday to Corfu which we enjoyed being at a nice hotel with good food and new territory for us to explore in the nice warm sunshine.

The year would not be the same without a time cruising the oceans, but I had to wait until the end of October for this to happen. The dear old Saga Rose which I had spent a lot of time on was scheduled for her final voyage before being taken out of service and it really was a must for me to be aboard to revive happy memories and to bid farewell in the proper fashion. The farewell voyage was a three week trip around the Mediterranean including a visit to Toulon where she was built. Our first stop was in Vigo the largest town in Galacia and the largest centre for sardine fishing in Europe. It was a bit wet which restricted us but all in all a pleasant place to see.

Next stop was Barcelona in north east Spain in Catalonia. The weather was good and a full day was spent in and around the city looking at the sights. The place is dominated by the spires of Templo Expiatorio de la Sagrada Familia (Church of the Sacred Family), a huge unfinished cathedral notable for its undulating curves the hallmark of its builder Antoni Gaudi. It is a seaside town with lovely beaches and they were still proud to show off the sites of the various Olympic events which were held in the city in 1992. Two days later we docked at Civitavecchia the port for Rome. I spent a full day in Rome seeing all the most famous landmarks and ended up inside The Vatican seeing the Sistine Chapel and St Peters Basilica. I found it very moving being in such spiritual place.

The ship then sailed all round the Italian coastline to reach Venice considered to be one of the most beautiful cities in the world. I joined a group on a panoramic boat trip around the area including visits to a glass factory and lace-making establishments. Afterwards there was plenty time to stroll around Venice and admire the old architecture and famous places.

The Saga Rose was moored all night in Venice. There was a gala dinner in the evening with the main guest being Katherine Jenkins the renowned singer. As luck would have it she dined at the same table as me and I had plenty of time to chat to her. After the meal I asked her if I could have an autograph just to prove to everyone that I wasn't just dreaming the whole event up. Katherine suggested that a photograph would be better of the two of us to which I agreed. I gave my camera to a lady to take the picture of us with or arms round each other's waists. We stood there grinning for ages and the dear lady fumbled away and never took a shot.

Katherine took the camera from her and gave her a quick lesson on how to push a button then we resumed our stance, this time with complete success. I now have a lovely picture of us together with Katherine looking very glamorous in one of her fabulous long gowns and me in my dinner suit along with bow tie. I thanked Katherine for being so kind and she gave me a big kiss on my cheek. How is that for a night out in Venice - unbeatable!

Then it was over the Adriatic for a visit to Dubrovnic where I spent the day meandering around the old city and harbour visiting and remembering places that Pat and I had seen years before when we were in Cavtat. Saga Rose next stopped at Corfu and I spent the time on a panoramic tour. I had been in Corfu for my summer holiday so it all looked very familiar.

The next day for me was a new place being the small fishing village of Katakolon. This small place is just 25 miles away from Olympia the birth place of the Olympic Games which we visited and saw all the old remains of an ancient but prosperous place. This include the site of the first ever games an arena which held over 45000 spectators over 2000 years ago. It is still recognisable as an arena and we were lucky enough to have had Sally Gunnell a gold medallist to show us around the strong sense of history in the air.

The next few days we spent in island hopping in the eastern Mediterranean firstly stopping at Heraklion in Crete then Rhodes and finally at Limassol in Cyprus. All the visits were first class and one does get a liking for the panoramic views in these places and the warm sunshine even though it was November. Our next port broke new and exciting ground for me with a visit to Israel landing at Haifa their largest city which has along and fascinating history. It made the ideal base for firstly a visit to Jerusalem taking in the Mount of Olives, the Garden of Gethsemane, the Church of the Holy Sepulchre and the Wailing Wall. Security was tight with many armed soldiers on the ground.

The following day I visited Nazareth and the Sea of Galilee, the site of the Sermon on the Mount and the baptismal site on the Jordan River. It was terrific seeing all the places which were well known from reading the Bible and it felt as if I was tiptoeing through history.

A couple of days later we docked at Alexandria which is the main Port and second city of Egypt. I chose a visit El Alamein the site of the great victory for the Allies which helped turn the tide of war. Most of my time was spent at the War Grave Cemetery, where over 11,000 soldiers both Allied and Axis are buried. There is a large section devoted to the Indian Army and I paid due respect to the many Indians who gave their lives in that campaign. As usual with the War Grave Commission the place was in perfect condition and very well kept. On we went to Valletta in Malta where we had a Gala Luncheon at La Valletta Hall at the invitation from The Knights of the Order of St John, where a great time was had by all with plenty of ceremony, toasts and flag waving.

In the evening there was a big party in the same place and I was fortunate enough to be on a table hosted by Edwina Curry, the well known political figure. She was a great hostess. We all had a wonderful time and I was on the floor dancing with her till well after midnight.

The visit to the next port of Toulon was very nostalgic as the Saga Rose was built there. Some of the original ship building workers were on board as honoured guests and I think a few tears were shed at the thought that this wonderful ship was on its final voyage. I managed a short visit ashore for a bit of wine tasting and looking at the local beauty spots. Then we went on to Alicante the popular Spanish resort where I took a trip to along the coast to Calpe, a nice spot that I had never been to before.

Two days later we were back in the Atlantic for a visit to Casablanca. It has miles and miles of sandy beaches and along its shores we visited the mighty Hassan 11 Mosque which can and often does have 25,000 worshippers in attendance and room for thousands of others in an overflow area. Our last port was La Carunna in north-west Spain, a city with the name "The Golden City" which has the longest promenade in Europe where you can see the Tower of Hercules which is the oldest working lighthouse. We tied up in Southampton on 6th December after a good celebration and send off of the great old liner.

Apart from holidays it was a busy old year with all my regular activities and a few other jaunts as well. Most memorable was a visit to St Andrews University for the graduation of Anu Choudry who was awarded a Doctor of Letters Degree following her course at St Andrews and also at Bergamo in Italy. I could not have picked a better day weather-wise as the sun shone us all day long. It was great with tea on the lawn with everyone in their finery and really enjoying the day. Well done Anu, as all your hard work paid off.

Some days later Ashok and <sup>Chhanda</sup> spent a day with me on their way back to London. It rained all day which spoilt our plans a little but we did manage a nice lunch at the very upmarket Jesmond Dene Hotel. I had two further contrasting visits to Scotland attending the wedding of Kevin Adie in Aberdeen and then sadly the funeral of Michael Shea in Edinburgh. Michael was a lovely fellow and it was so sad that he passed on at a relatively early age.

I also managed to attend the Mahar Reunion held once again at Bedworth. I was extremely busy with talks every other week to local clubs and also kept active with my good friends at Blue Flames in the summer and St Andrews Church all the year round at bowls, I was still pretty good with a couple of trophies to prove it. Alas the football team I supported did not have a good season and were relegated from the Premier league. A month in the summer was also disrupted when I had two bedrooms refitted with new cupboards and had a lot of redecoration done throughout the house. The year ended with the big wide world still deep in financial chaos but it was good to see Barack Obama being in charge of the USA

The urge to go to warmer places was still with me at the start of 2010. I followed the same pattern as the previous year and took three holidays all lasting a fortnight over the first three months of the year. The venues were slightly changed going to Gran Canaria in January then revisiting my old haunt of Fuengerola on the Costa del Sol in February and ending up in Lanzeroti in March. I was happy and content with these trips away but I was beginning to find the flying a bit of a bind. The need to travel was still strong and my next adventure came in May when I changed tack a little and opted for a three week tour of the National Parks of the USA. organised by Titan holidays.

It was a well organised tour using top hotels and a super tour bus and visited so many famous places. A group of 30 of us flew out from Heathrow to Denver which was our starting point. It is a lovely spot at quite high altitude just on the fringe of the mighty Rocky Mountains and we were given plenty of time to explore the place before setting off the next morning via Estes Park to Cheyenne the capital of Wyoming which was named after the Indian people who inhabited the area. Next day we went on to Rapid City for a two night stay in South Dakota which is the gateway to the Black Hills via Fort Laramie. This was an old army post kept in its original state and full of historical interest.

The next day was spent touring to Mount Rushmore to see the carvings of the famous American presidents on the granite cliffs. The weather on this day was not kind to us with lots of thunder and lightning with plenty of rain. We also saw the Crazy Horse Mountain Memorial which is the biggest carving in the world at 563 feet high and 641 feet long. The next day we were back in Wyoming to stay at Sheridan taking a trip along the way to Devils Tower well known as the site of the spaceship landing in the film Close Encounters of the Third Kind. At the end of the first week we went to Yellowstone National Park visiting Cody a quaint old cowboy town on the way. The main attraction in the Park was a visit to Old Faithful a famous roaring geyser which shoots thousands of gallons of scalding water into the air at regular intervals.

We then went on to Jackson Hole a lovely little holiday town in a secluded valley in the Grand Teton National Park for a two nights stay. It is a popular tourist destination with some good skiing slopes there for use in the winter. The tour then took us down into Salt Lake City in Utah, which is the headquarters of the Mormon Church. We went to their main building and listened to a concert given by their famous choir. Next day we made our way down south to Moab and on the way experiences the incredible beauty of Canyonlands National Park. The Green and the Colorado rivers have sliced their way through the park forming diverse sections of huge red rock pinnacles and towering spires to create a most rugged landscape. The day ended in the

Arches National Park which has over 1700 natural stone arches. This was followed with a two nights stay in Bryce which let us have a day each in Bryce National Park and Zion National Park. The tour then took us south into Arizona past the big Canyon Dam and Lake Powell to the famous Grand Canyon for a two night stay. It is an inspiring place on a huge scale with the Colorado River looking like a small silver streak way down at the bottom of the canyon.

To conclude the tour we made our way over some very arid land to Scottsdale. We went through Navajo Indian country and spent some time in Sedona and Montezuma Castle. That should have been the end of the tour as we were scheduled to fly home from Phoenix the next day. All our plans had to be changed because of a volcanic eruption in Iceland that raised a dust cloud which prevented any flying over the North Atlantic. This proved a bit of a bonus because we were taken to Palm Springs for a two night stay in a very nice hotel which was very relaxing. We then had to get to Los Angeles for our flight home. On the way to the airport we saw mile after mile of wind turbines and solar panels in California where it was certainly hot and windy enough to be profitable. I had been a good trip although rather exhausting with many early starts and thousands of miles travelled. I am pleased I did the trip when I was able to cope with the exertion. I must have been a little bit fitter then and I suppose the message is do it when you can.

It was not long to wait then until July where Christine, Bethany and I spent another lovely fortnight in the sunshine of Tenerife with plenty of trips out to see the sights. I also scanned through the ocean cruise holidays on offer and came to the conclusion that there was nothing for me there this year. My mind turned to river cruising and I thought I would give it a chance and booked with Titan to go on a week-long river cruise on the Rhine. I picked a cruise in starting in August from Amsterdam to Nurnberg using the Rhine and the Main and a few canals as well.

Being on a small boat and travelling at walking pace was a big change from ocean cruising but I thoroughly enjoyed it. The cabin on such a small ship was quite spacious and well appointed as were the public rooms. The food, wine and service were top class and it was non-stop beautiful scenery for all the way along the waterways. I was picked up by car from home to the airport and flew into Amsterdam in less than two hours and was on the ship in no time at all.

We set out along the canals of Holland with plenty of time to explore some windmills and admire the flower fields. We were soon into Germany going south down the Rhine for a stop in the middle of Cologne with plenty of time to see the many sights and have a good look at the huge Cathedral. The river traffic was very dense with pleasure craft and strings of barges going in both directions. It certainly is a working river whilst still passing through great countryside. We had a stop at Koblenz a lovely old city at the confluence of the rivers Rhine and Main.

We docked also at Rudesheim which is well known as being the centre for riesling wine making for a little wine tasting and a visit to the very interesting Siegfried Music Museum. We then passed through the Lorelei Gorge with its 400 feet high cliffs and passed the rock where Lorelei a mystical water nymph is reputed to have drawn many sailors to their deaths by sitting on the rock and singing sweet songs. There was no sign of her on this trip however. The next couple of days saw us in Mainz, Miltenberg, Wurtsburg and Bamberg all old old historical cities with much to admire in them. We finished off at Nurnberg and flew home from Munich. I thought it was an exceptionally good and well organised trip and I appreciated the slow pace of the journey and the opportunity to really see the passing countryside

My normal day to day activities continued unabated with numerous talks, meetings at the Church and Arthritis Care as well as visits to the Mahar Reunion in Bedworth once again, and a trip to Edinburgh to see Mona Shea. I had all the physical effort I needed playing bowls both outside and indoors and still supporting Newcastle United who glory be had been promoted back to the top division

After a year away from ocean cruising, the start of 2011 saw me back into my old established routine of being on a Saga liner exploring the world. This time it was a journey I had longed to go on up the mighty River Amazon. In the middle of January I flew down to Gatwick for an overnight stay and then next day was on a flight to Bridgetown in Barbados. I found this a long and tedious flight on it was a great relief to land and within a couple of hours get on board the Saga Pearl 11. A nice meal and a good night's sleep set me up well for the three and a half week cruise which set off the next day.

The weather of course was perfect in the West Indies and the cold winter weather I had left was just but a memory. We arrived at Port of Spain the capital of Trinidad and Tobago. The city is the home of the Carnival and steel band and is an astonishing melting-pot for peoples and cultures from around the world. It wasn't the carnival season so I missed out on that but I like steel bands and heard a few of those playing during my short stay on the island.

Then it was three days of ocean cruising to reach Belem in Brazil which is just south of the equator and some 90 miles from the open sea in the Amazon estuary. It was founded by the Portuguese many years ago and is a very important trading centre. It has a lot of old Portuguese architecture including a massive fortress which is in good condition still. I was very hot place and a lot of sit downs and drinks was the order of the day.

The ship then made its way to the mouth of the Curua Una River which is a tributary to the Amazon where it anchored for a few hours to let us get onto smaller craft to explore some of the villages on its banks. I got ashore at a small place called Pacoval, originally settled by native Indians and escaped slaves. We had a great welcome from the local population especially the children who gave us plenty of entertainment. I thought it would be pretty primitive village and was most surprised when I discovered it had a good electricity supply powered by solar panels. Evereone seemed to have modern television sets and deep freezers and were most self sufficient. Wherever we went in the next couple of weeks the same standard of living applied. I suppose deeper in the jungle it might be different.

During our trip we went through a lake with hundreds of large water lilies which were most impressive. The other great activity of the day was to fish for piranhas the small flesh-eating fish which abound in the waters. They are so easy to catch with a home-made fishing rod with a length of string and a hook baited with a morsel of meat. Hundreds were caught in no time at all and all were barbequed and eaten and proved to be delicious. Next day we reached Santaram which is situated where the Tapajos and Amazon waters meet. The lakes and forests of the area are home to numerous species of birds, particularly the white egret. During the rubber boom of the 1920s, Henry Ford the car manufacture established large rubber plantations in the area to supply his factories.

Further along the river we reached Boca De Valeria set at the confluence of the rivers Rio de Valeria and Amazon. It is a remote jungle village surrounded by the large rain forests and home to no more than 100 people. It is the custom for all the school children to dress up and be photographed along with their pet parakeets and iguanas and to receive presents back from the visitors.

The ship then took us on to Manaus "Paris of the Jungle" as it is nicknamed for an overnight stay and two day visit. This is a major city with approaching two million inhabitants and is the capital of the Brazil's state of Amazonas. Just like any other major city it was plagued by traffic jams which took me completely by surprise being so far from anywhere. The city itself was built from the riches generated by the rubber boom in the 1920s and its wealth is easy to see in the quality of the public buildings and the infrastructure. It has a most beautiful Opera House and I was in for a treat when I paid it a visit. I found that the Brazilian Youth Symphony Orchestra was having a final rehearsal before the evening's concert. Outside it was blisteringly hot and very humid and I sat in air conditioning for over an hour listening to Mahlar's Second Symphony being very well played indeed.

I also spent time up the Rio Negro River transferring to a motorised canoe to view January Lake. I saw the "Meeting of the Waters" where the muddy yellow waters of the Solimoes and the clear dark waters of the Rio Negro meet and continue to flow together without intermingling to form the mighty Amazon. There was plenty of torrential rain to keep us on our toes during the river trips.

We then began our Journey back down the Amazon to the sea stopping for a day in Parintas which is a small city of some 100,000 people located on an island in the heart of the Amazon.

The city is most famous for the Festival do Boi-Bumba a lively and spectacular show. I went to the afternoon presentation with hundreds of performers and dancers and a tremendous rhythmic band playing at full power the whole time. It is a presentation of a local folk tale involving a large man made bull, a medicine man and the inevitable love story. Food and drink was provided and everyone left the show in a positive mood. Next stop was Alter Do Chao a small village situated on the Tapajos River a tributary of the Amazon. It has a sandy beach and clear water and is a popular spot for swimming.

Every child in the village seemed to have a sloth for a pet which was a real eye opener for us. Finally we reached the open sea again at Macapa. The equator runs through the middle of the town and is clearly marked so you can easily move into the north or south hemispheres with just a step in either direction. It is the home of lots of migratory birds which mix with the local flamingos, toucans, ibises and sea and river turtles. I really enjoyed the trip up the Amazon but I found it hard work and I realised that time was catching up on me and that I was not as fit and active as I once was.

In addition I developed a bad cough from somewhere and there was no getting rid of it. The Saga Pearl was again in open sea and making towards Devil's Island just off the coast of French Guiana. This was a notorious French Penal Colony which was finally closed in 1946 and is now open for tourists. We had a brief stop at the island which does not take long to walk around. All the prison buildings are well maintained amidst all the dense vegetation. I did not look a bad spot but I am sure most of the ex prisoners would hardly agree with that view. We then called in at Paramaribo the capital of Surinam the Dutch controlled territory situated on the Surinam River. It is known as the "Wooden City of South America" with a lot of UNESCO World heritage sites and well worth a visit. Our penultimate destination was Georgetown in Guyana situated on the Demerara River estuary. I paid a visit to a lovely nature reserve with more than 350 species of birds to be seen in some beautiful country side. The cruise ended next day at Port of Spain in Trinidad from where I flew back home.

Christine, Bethany and I went for our summer holiday to Ibiza. It was my first visit there but for Christine it was home from home as she had worked there for a couple of seasons as a holiday rep. It is a popular spot and I enjoyed a nice holiday. My next trip of the year was a two week visit to India in December. My original invitation was from the Mahar Regiment who were celebrating their 70<sup>th</sup> Anniversary at their headquarters in Saugor. My close friend Col. Ashok Choudry however invited me to stay in Pondicherry with him for ten days before I was due in Saugor.

I flew out to Chennai and was picked up there and taken by car to Pondicherry. It is a lovely seaside town overlooking the Indian Ocean a hundred miles or so south of Chennai which for many years was In a French Enclave in India. The influence of French culture was still evident with many roads name as Rue de la????, and the police officers still wearing kepis as head gear. There was not room for me to sleep at the Choudrey's house and I was booked into the Park Guest House which was part of the Ashram. It was lovely quiet spot overlooking the sea and I had a big room with a balcony and shower room overlooking the garden and sea. The Choudry family took me out for many meals in hotels and also at home and always came over to me with breakfast and supper, so I was very well looked after.

Ashok had arranges a programme of visits that kept me busy all the time I was there. The Sri Aurobindo Ashram played a big part of the Choudry family life style and I fully engaged with them as they showed me all the activities of the Ashram community. There were many thousands in the Ashram family and they were engaged in all manner of communal activity and were the most friendly and generous folk that one could meet. They occupied a lot of buildings in Pondicherry and I was invited into them all including the holiest of their shrines as well as the School, dining rooms, workshops and library. They were supported by many very well educated people and were a very strong influence in the locality.

I paid a number of visits to Auroville a new city just outside Pondicherry dedicated to the ideal of human unity based on the vision of Sri Aurobindo and The Mother. In 1966 UNESCO passed an unanimous resolution commending it as a project of importance to the future of humanity. At the centre of the township lies the Peace Area comprising the Matrimandir and its gardens. I spent some time in the Inner Chamber of Peace in absolute total silence and it certainly does have a calming effect being there.

Whilst at Auroville I met with Lt General AK Chatterjee of the Sikh Light Infantry (SLI) and he passed on to me a present to give to the former UK officers of the Regiment on my return home. This I managed to do and subsequently have become an honorary member of the SLI Association and attend their annual dinner. I spent some time at the Ashram School and attended the open evening when there was a drama presentation and also on a subsequent evening when their sports day was held. This was the school that Anu attended and the quality of education on offer is superb as proved by the academic success of Anu.

One highlight of my visit was an invitation as a special guest to the Armed Forces Flag Day celebrations where I was introduced to Dr Iqbal Singh the Lt Governor, the Chief Secretary and other dignitaries at the Governors residence. I had a glorious day out with the family on a car journey that took us to Mahalabarapuram with its temples and monuments dating from the 7th century and still in good condition. The holiday was most enjoyable and educational and I had a great time. Then it was off to Chennai for a flight to Bhopal where I was picked up by the Indian Army and taken to Saugor. I again was the sole British Representative and they treated me with much kindness and respect. As usual the parades and other organised events were superb and I still extol the progress to greatness of the Regiment.

It was a tiring few days and I can remember being plagued by the cough I picked up on my trip up the Amazon. The journey back to Bhopal at the end of the Reunion was memorable. An Indian Brigadier and myself left Saugor at about midnight to catch an early morning flight to New Delhi. We made good progress and arrived at the Airport a little too early and found it locked and closed. The Brigadier knew his way around Bhopal and took us to an Ordnance Depot in town reaching there at about 0430am. The poor sepoy on guard at the barrier was in a state of shock when we demanded entry but the guard commander soon had his men out for inspection and the camp sprung into life to give us a warm welcome. All the officers attended to meet us and food, drink and a shower were on hand in no time at all. What a great welcome and just proves the camaraderie that exists in the army.

A day and night was spent in New Delhi and then home to England just in time for Christmas. In between all these trips life rolled on in its predictable way. My life style did not seem to change year after year. I was always at Church on a Sunday morning and came home and prepared a Sunday lunch for Christine and Bethany who always came around.

In the summer time I always played bowls on Monday afternoon, Wednesday afternoon and Saturday morning in the summer time up at Blue Flames Club in Benton. In wintertime it was always indoor bowls at the Parks in North Shields. Gail always came on a Wednesday morning to clean the house. Thursday evening all the year round was indoor carpet bowling at the Church. The Arthritis Care meeting was always the second Friday evening in the month with an evening Committee meeting in-between. Saturday afternoon was always watching football during the season or gardening in the summer months. Talks and other meetings were also regular features in the diary. Friday morning was always shopping morning with Christine and the washing machine used every Monday and Friday. There was never a dull moment in my life.

For some time the Arthritis Care Meeting had been the cause of worry because of lack of finances. Our expenditure was always rising and our income remained static. Frantic efforts were made to get donations and grants to prolong its existence, but it was of great sadness when all efforts to raise our income failed and we had to close the Newcastle Branch of Arthritis Care. I must also be getting near my sell-by-date as I had to have an eye operation on my right eye as my sight failed me. The operation was a total success and I was in and out of the hospital within half a day. A big improvement on the original operation on my left eye some years before.

2012 started differently to the previous few years in that no holidays had been booked. In 2011 I had two strenuous trips away to the Amazon and India which I had found hard going and the urge to travel seemed to have passed. I suppose this was natural enough as I was approaching my 86th birthday and I was slowing down. It did not worry me as I had a host of activities that occupied my time and there was never a chance of a dull moment.

Brigadier Nickam, one of my Indian Army friends, was in England and I spent a day in his company and we went together and saw some of the sights of London including a ride on the London Eye. In a couple of weeks I was at Wembley supporting York City in their bid to get back their Football League status. They beat Luton Town 2 -1 much to the joy of the York supporters and it turned into a great day out. I also had a day out to Peebles with my Norgas Vets friends from the bowling club.

Christine, Bethany and I ventured to new territory on our summer holiday break, flying into Faro and spending a fortnight in the Algarve. It was extremely hot and we were faced with lots of forest fires. We went on a trip one day along the river and all day the planes were landing in the river to pick up water to drop on the flames. Very exciting!

I had an invitation from the 3$^{rd}$ Battalion of the Mahar Regiment who were based in Ranchi to attend their 70th raising day celebrations at the start of November. This was a not-to-be-missed occasion which I accepted. I attended as the only remaining British Officer of the Battalion and the longest serving member present at the celebration. It was a long trip to New Delhi and on to Ranchi but I was given a most warm welcome when I arrived. My old friend Col Ashok Choudry who had commanded the Battalion on active service on the Siachen Glazier in the high mountains of the Himalayas was also present so I was very well looked after.

It was a most intense three days and nights of activity with formal parades, lots of entertainment and late nights. All the officers of the Battalion were first class and it was in the good hands of Col. Chackravaty who spared no effort in including me in every aspect of the Reunion. I came home with loads of mementoes including a Naga Battle scarf which I treasure still. Then it was a long return journey via New Delhi back home.

Whilst I was there I was dogged by the cough which I had picked up in the Amazon and certainly wasn't 100% fit when I arrived home. By this time it was getting near to Christmas and over the holiday period I was a bit under the weather. By the time Christmas Eve was on us I felt very down. This was picked up by Christine who late on in the evening took me to the emergency medical centre to see a doctor. He told Christine to take me straight to the hospital and I was admitted late in the evening. I was still in clothes and visited the bathroom and there realised that all was not well with me. I managed to stagger back to my bed and ring the red emergency button. Within ten seconds I was surrounded by several doctors and nurses who were injecting me with needles and giving me oxygen to help me to breathe. I was a funny blue colour and really felt quite ill.

I woke up in the morning of Christmas day to be told I had suffered a pulmonary embolism but everything was now stable. There was a Christmas card and present on my locker and I felt much better. I reckon I was a lucky guy, being in hospital when all this happened and so much medical support given to me instantly. I do not think I would have survived in other circumstances. So it was a funny ending to the year and I consider myself lucky to have made it with my Guardian Angel working overtime.

I started 2013 just out of hospital and feeling rather more vulnerable health-wise than I had been previously. Was this a warning to me to take things a little easier and spend less time away from home? Perhaps it was just as well that no holidays had been booked and that I had time to reflect on what kind of lifestyle I should now have. Tests had revealed that I had several mini strokes over the last few years and this was a surprise to me.

The medical people put me on a course of warfarin to thin my blood to prevent a reoccurrence and monitored my progress over the first part of the year. All went to plan and I certainly felt fit enough in myself which was most reassuring. After six months of treatment I got a clean bill of health but was advised to take two tablets (Vista Statin and Clopidogral) each evening for the rest of my days which was no great hardship for me. The hospital doctor that signed me off put me through a whole series of tests on various machines which I passed easily and I remember the last test was a high speed walk around the hospital corridors following the specialist who was more out of breath than me at the end of it. This was most reassuring and I could really put the whole episode behind me.

I was able to get away to Majorca with Christine and Bethany for a nice summer holiday. We stayed in the east of the island near the caves of Drach with lovely weather and good trips around and I arrived home feeling 100% fit after it. I had quite a few days away from home on trips in this country but missed my worldwide jaunts and felt envious when Christine went to Egypt and Bethany managed to get to New York on a school trip. I had to make do with a trip to Scarborough with the Norgas Vets. I also paid a day visit to Edinburgh to see Hugh Mackay who was the SLI representative in the UK to pass on the gift I received from the General I had met some time ago in India. We immediately formed a good friendship and I became an honorary member of the SU Association and later that year was invited down to London to attend their Annual Reunion lunch.

One sad event in the year was the funeral of Keith Gascoigne who was a close friend from my Mahar days. He was a real stalwart and his passing really signalled the end to our traditional reunions of the Regiment in the UK. I also managed to get away to Edinburgh for a bowls tour with the H&SS Bowling Club near the end of the season staying two nights at a good hotel in the centre of the city and playing three good games with a clubs in Rosyth and Edinburgh. Whilst there I found the opportunity to meet up for half a day with Mona Shea my cruising friend. By this time I felt fit and well and the events at the start of the year were dimming in my memory and were no more influencing my decisions.

In all it had been a good year where I continued all my weekly activities with renewed vigour. I was always surrounded by great friends and family so really had no difficulty in pursuing all my old regular activities. I managed to give seven talks in the year, audited the accounts of three organisations and took part in half a dozen Church services.

On the entertainment side I remember seeing two shows one being the popular Pirates of Penzance at the Theatre Royal and the Central Newcastle High School production of Grease with Bethany taking a part in it. Getting that little bit older I was beginning to find driving my car a little bit of a chore. I finally gave up driving in the dark and my day time journeys were just local. 500 miles a year was now my norm but I decided to keep the car just for the sheer convenience, mainly for visits to Church and Blue Flames bowling green.

2014 had now been reached and I was beginning to realise that age was creeping up on me and that I didn't have the mobility, speed and stamina to which I was used. I always used to walk up to the local shops at four lane ends with no problem at all but now it seemed more attractive to me just to jump on the bus to get there. Perhaps it was a good thing that I had no strenuous holidays booked for the coming few months and that I learned to adapt to the new physical constraints. My legs were not as good as they were and left knee was giving me a few aches and I didn't trust it not to let me down at times. I suppose I had to reconcile myself to the fact that I was 88 years old in April and that I should get used to it.

My hearing was also become poor and it was so bad that I had to invest in some pricy hearing aids to give me some help. These gadgets certainly improved things but were no means perfect as they picked up and enhanced all the extraneous noises and drowned out ordinary conversation. They also whistled a lot when using the telephone which was most off-putting but all in all they improved my lot in life. Not with-standing all these ailments I thought myself much fitter than most people of my age and I didn't let it deter me from getting on with my varied activities during the year. I could still hold my own against most people on the bowling green and was still being picked for the teams playing in the leagues. My mind and memory were still as agile as ever and I was still happy to be asked to speak to various meetings on a big range of subjects at a number of venues. My biggest problem was getting to and from the places I was invited to as my driving was limited, but Christine was a great help in giving me lifts.

Christine, Bethany and I went to Tenerife for our two weeks in sun during the summer which was first class. Apart from this I also had time away on a bowling club trip to Edinburgh at the end of the season and again had the opportunity to meet up with

Mona Shea during our stay. I had a second day visit to Edinburgh to visit Hugh Mackay who was hosting a lunch for some old Indian Army officers. I also managed a day trip to Harrogate with the Norgas Vets which turned out to be a most interesting day as we were following the route of the first stage of the Tour de France cycle race through the Yorkshire dales on the day before it took place. All the route was decorated by flags and bunting and lots of cycle related exhibitions. I also had a good Saturday in London attending the SLI annual lunch gathering and meeting up with many like-minded friends. Several times during the year Christine invited me to see films at Silverlink which was a new experience for me as I hadn't been to the pictures for many a long year. Also at this time Christine was a member of a steel band group at the Sage in Gateshead and I went a number of times to hear her play. I think I even bought her a set of steel pans as a birthday present for some practice at home. I love the sound of the steel bands.

At home I embarked on the renovation of the en-suite shower room, the main bathroom and the hall toilet. It upset the house for two or three weeks but it was a job well done to have them all modernised and away from the decor that was dated back nearly thirty years which was looking rather jaded.

One big event of the year was that Andrew moved to the USA to work. he lives in Bristol on Rhode Island, which is rather a nice place and he and Geri seem to enjoy it.

Another year passed and I was soon celebrating my 89th birthday. I have read many times that the majority of people of my age living alone suffer from depression and in many cases can go for days without meeting and speaking to people. I must be a lucky guy as my life is far removed from that kind of existence. My days are still crowded with activity and I have to keep everything logged in my diary to avoid double booking events of forgetting about them. I am surrounded by a large number of very good friends who I meet at varying events and they always keep an eye out for me if I am in need of help. All that coupled with a good family and nice neighbours means that every day is still a treat. Many times I relish a slack day just to get up-to-date with all the chores that need to be done. I still always do the crossword and the Sudoku puzzles on a daily basis and feel very aggrieved if I fail to finish them correctly. It is good to keep the brain active and to this end I still relish giving talks to all manner of groups mostly lasting around an hour a time off the cuff with no notes to refer to at all. Physically I am still OK with most things but I realise I am much slower which irks me somewhat.

Playing bowls a couple of times a week throughout the year is a nice gentle exercise and working in the garden in the better weather certainly helps tone up the muscles. My biggest defects are loss of hearing and poor eyesight. My expensive hearing aids are great for listening to radio or TV and listening to one to one conversation's but are hopeless when there is a lot of background noise to contend with.

2015 turned out to be a year packed with interesting activities as usual to enhance my busy life style. For our summer holidays Christine, Bethany and I went to Tenerife once again. This year however we went slightly more upmarket and booked in at the Melia Sensatori hotel in Guia de Isora. It was a beautiful place, well worth the extra cost with far superior accommodation, food and attention. The weather as usual was superb. I had a Bali bed for my own use outside my room, which was ideal for an afternoon siesta in the fresh air. It boasted several swimming pools including the biggest pool in the Canary Islands. The entertainment was also first class in the evening.

I had a number of trips during the year which included a three day bowling tour of the Lake District based in the Skiddaw Hotel in Keswick, a day's outing with the N.Gas Vets to the Lake District, a visit to Edinburgh to see my good friend Mona Shea, a trip down to London to attend the annual lunch of the SLI and a day's visit to Holy Island with some of my Church friends.

I had two visitors to look after during the year. Firstly, Hugh Mackay from Edinburgh came to see me for a day. He always wanted to have a look around St James's Park, the home of Newcastle United Football Club, so we took the opportunity to spend most of the day on a tour of the ground. Our visit coincided with the appointment of Steve Mcclaren as the new manager of the club and he was there with TV cameras everywhere recording him. We were the only other visitors that day which made it most awkward as they didn't want our paths to cross so it was rather an unusual type of visit for us. They treated us well however and we certainly saw the place in spic and span condition and we were both very impressed with the behind the scenes facilities.

Secondly I had a three day visit from Capt. Aravindhan Rajendran of The Mahar Regiment who was on a visit to the UK. I had met him just recently during my visit to the Third Battalion at Ranchi. He was on secondment to the Indian Army Special Forces (SAS) and was spending some leave across here. He is a very fit, well educated, articulate and gregarious lad who lives a dangerous life when on duty and likes to enjoy himself on his times off. He loved speaking to strangers and could easily make friends with anyone. I took him along for a game of bowls and he was very good at it on his first attempt. He had a passion for food of all kinds and his camera was always in use recording his progress during his stay. Christine also kindly helped me by giving us a tour of the local sights in her car. He had all his belongings in a big rucksack which was so heavy I could not lift it, but which he carried as if it was nothing. During his visits we talked on his mobile with about 20 Indian Army Officers for a couple of minutes apiece exchanging greetings. The Third Battalion were stationed right on the border with the Chinese so it all seemed so surreal.

For my birthday present Christine bought me an hour's practice on an aircraft flight simulater which was great fun. I managed to land a light aircraft at Newcastle Airport and had a very hairy journey around Las Vegas at low level which ended a few times in disaster. I had two triumphs landing a Boeing 757 at Heathrow from about 20 miles out at 10000 feet. Also I did a blind landing on a Cessna light plane bringing it from over St Mary's Island near Whitley Bay to land at Newcastle in thick fog using instruments only. I wasn't much good at breaking once I landed as I always seemed to veer off the runway. It was great fun however.

I helped Christine get a new automatic car as she was finding changing gear on her manual one increasingly difficult. She always gave me a lot of lifts so it was the least I could do for her. Bethany also had an extra holiday going with the School to

Kenya for a couple of weeks taking in some safaris to see the great landscape as well as helping out at some schools in the areas they passed through. All very worthwhile.

On the entertainment side I went to the cinema at least seven times with Christine which must be somewhat of a record for me. I also saw my old friend Katherine Jenkins singing at the Sage in Gateshead, went to a production of Oklahoma at the Theatre Royal and went to another concert at the Sage to hear Christine play her pans.

On the downside I decided to give up my season ticket for NUFC at the end of the 2014/2015 season. I was finding that getting up and down on the many steps in the ground without hand rails to hold onto getting more hazardous. I feel better safe than sorry but I do miss the matches, meeting many friends and the atmosphere in the ground on Match days every other week in the season.

*YPM reunion in York*

*Good friends at St Andrew's Church, Benton*

*Wedding day for Sarah Chrystie*

*Wedding day for Robert Chrystie*

*Charity work in Ho Chi Min City, Vietnam*

*A spot of lecturing on a Saga cruise*

*With Katherine Jenkins in Venice*

*Happy days cruising*

*With Mona Shea in the Pacific*

*Enjoyable meal and company*

*Intrepid explorer on Half Moon Island*

*Falklands War Memorial*

*Chilean weather station at Waterboat Point*

*Magnificent Rio*

*Jacobs Ladder, St Helena*

*Birthday celebrations at sea*

*Top bidder for Saga charity gets his picture*

*Grand Canyon USA*

*With the Choudry family*

*With the Choudry family*

*Anu graduates at St Andrew's M.Lit*

*Anu graduates at St Andrew's M.Lit*

*Receiving presentation at Saugor*

*Chatting about old times with Lieut.General Nanda*

*Paying my respects to the fallen at Saugor*

*Chief of Army staff presenting colours in Saugor*

नये वर्ष के लिए शुभकामनाएं

A Happy New Year

Raj Bhavan
Imphal
Manipur
795001

General & Mrs. K. V. Krishna Rao

*New Year greeting from the Governor*

*With Lieut.General Chatterjee – Sikh Light Infantry*

*Receiving trophy from the Governor of Pondicherry*

*Celebrating with General Sundarji*

*Wreath laying with 3Mahar in Ranchi*

*Ranchi with 3Mahar*

*General Krishna Rao – Chief of Army Staff*

*More UK reunions*

*More UK reunions*

*Graduation Day for James*

*Masters degree graduation for James*

*Graduation day for Alex*

*Holiday in Majorca with young Bethany*

*Young Bethany*

*Relaxing and enjoying life*

*Relaxing and enjoying life*

*Relaxing and enjoying life*

*Champion bowling team*

*Near Bristol, Rhode Island*

# CHAPTER 8

## GETTING OLDER
## AND SETTLING DOWN

2016 was always going to be an auspicious year in my life. On 27th April I would be 90 years old and population records show that over 99% of the male population of the UK never reach this milestone. It was decided that I would hold a big party to celebrate and the first months of the year were spent in much preparation for the great event.

Before it happened Christine and I decided to have a two night break in Paris. I had never in my life been to Paris and it was something I always wanted to do. It was easy to get there with a direct flight from Newcastle to Charles De Gaulle airport in Paris. We booked into a small hotel in the Trocadero area of the City which was very central and very near the Eiffel Tower. We also had the advantage of a metro station just adjacent to the hotel and we made a lot of use of the underground to get around. We soon got used to the many steps and narrow tunnels in the system which worked very well for us. It was a joy to go up the Eiffel Tower and see the great views from the top, which was something I had wanted to do for ages. There were so many things we could have done but time was against us but we managed to tick a few things off our list.

We had a nice boat trip up the Seine as far as Notre-Dame Cathedral passing well known sight-seeing places on our journey and certainly getting good views of the many wonderful bridges on the river. We also had a very good bus tour where we saw the Louvre and its glass pyramid, the Place de la Concorde, the Champs de Elysees up-to the Arc de Triomphe and back with views of many Palaces and famous buildings. We saw the Paris Story presentation and visited a chocolate museum and also the main Lindz chocolate shop.

The weather was not very kind for us as it rained and drizzled the whole time and there was no sunshine at all so it was chilly. This was not quite as I had envisaged Paris in the springtime. We managed to find a great restaurant near our hotel where we were well satisfied with good food and service. We were hampered by a rail strike on our way back to the airport but arrive home on time, a little bit weary but well satisfied with the trip. There is plenty to do on any return trip to Paris so I live in hope of seeing some sunshine there still.

The next big event was my 90th Birthday Party and I have to thank Christine for all the arranging and planning of the event. I sent out invitations to 30 family members for a dinner and overnight stay at the Marriot Gosforth Park Hotel and all went like clockwork and everyone had a great time. It was a nice place with good food and a well stocked bar and top class rooms for our overnight stay. I had to get up and speak for a short time at the end of the meal but it is hard to cover 90 years of life in half an hour. Many of the guests said I should write a book about my life and that coupled with the same views that my old friend Ashok Choudry had been giving me for some years, finally convinced me to start doing just that. Ashok had already agreed to edit and publish a book in India so I had plenty of incentive to start.

Another very big event in the year was a visit to India at the invitation of the Mahar Regiment to celebrate their 75th Raising Day and Platinum Anniversary. I used Emirate Airways for the first time flying to New Delhi via Dubai as a business class passenger and was well pleased with the experience. One advantage was that the flight set-off from Newcastle and they provided a car and driver for the journey to the airport.

I was met at New Delhi Airport and given a warm reception by the 20th Battalion of Mahar Regiment who were stationed in New Delhi on Presidential duties. I arrived shortly after Mrs Teresa May, the British Prime Minister, who was on an official visit to India and they gave me an equally good welcome. I was whisked out of the airport and transported to my hotel in fine style. I don't think the hotel anticipated such a plethora of army personnel delivering me to their doorstep and being told that I was a VIP who had to be given the best of treatment until I was picked up next day to continue my journey.

New Delhi was very misty and murky with smog formed from crop burning and the many fires and firework smoke associated with Diwali and many restrictions were in force. Next day I did a long 10 hour train journey to Saugor arriving late at night but being given a very warm reception by my old friends at the Regimental Centre. As usual I was given good accommodation with lots of help, which enhanced my experience.

The Centre was in good shape with lots of new facilities having been built since my previous visit five years ago. The next three days were full of intense and spectacular events which I entered into with gusto. The warmer weather and the sheer joy of being present at such a great event seemed to improve my mobility and stamina no end. The first evening I attended the final of the hockey competition which was a well fought out and spirited contest. The highlight was the next day with the arrival of the COAS General Dalbir Singh to present the Presidents Colours to the 20th and 21st Battalions of the Regiment as part of the formal parade to celebrate the Jubilee.

The whole event was superb as usual and just helps to enhance my pride for the Regiment and reminds me of the privilege of being an accepted member of the Mahar fraternity. After the parade the COAS spent some time speaking with people and I shook hands with him and exchanged greetings. Thereafter it was a non-top series of activities such as sports, motor cycle and parachuting displays, Sainik Bhoj, Sainik Samellan, Unit socials, JCO's receptions etc. Amongst all these the simple wreath laying ceremony at the War Memorial stands out as a memorable moment.

A formal dinner and speeches concluded the celebrations on the third evening. I presented the Regiment with a solid sterling silver Quaich suitably inscribed for the event and they assured me it would be put to good use rather than gather dust in a trophy cabinet.

A very large birthday cake had been made and 21 Battalion Cos plus Col Kit Bakshi and myself armed with swords made the first cut of the cake in unison to the cheers of all present. To close the evening I was on the dance floor until after midnight. So many wives and daughters of the officers were wanting to dance with me that I had to ration my time to a couple of minutes a time. It was very informal as for most of the time pairs were in groups of a couple of dozen dancers all holding hands and every one having a happy time.

The whole reunion was an unqualified success celebrated with great pomp and panache. I am so lucky to be part of all this. Then it was fond farewells and back to the UK via New Delhi. On the flight home I was listening to the results of the USA Presidential Elections which were very surprising with a victory for Donald Trump. What is the world coming to? Special thanks to Major Manoj and Havildar Anshuk Sharma for smoothing my path all the way.

In between times I managed to get away on holiday to The Sensatori Hotel in Tenerife for a couple of weeks with Christine and Bethany. It was expensive but worth the extra for the facilities provided and proved just as good as the previous year when we first went there. I also paid a return visit to the Lake District with my Bowling Club and was blessed with three days of fine sunny weather for the games. The whole weekend was just relaxation and fun. What would I do without my regular games of bowls each week and meeting my many friends. I also spent a great day out to Holy Island with my friends from Church to enjoy the peace and tranquillity. My regular visits to Edinburgh to catch up with Mona Shea and London for the SU Lunch were also most enjoyable. I also kept in contact with my old Arthritis Care friends who meet regularly at Christa Clemmetsons house in Gosforth.

My speaking engagements were not as numerous as in the past being limited to just five in the year. I still enjoy speaking to groups but getting to and from the venues is not so enjoyable these days.

It was a good year for Bethany as she passed her A level exams and went off to Keele University. Christine had to go into hospital for a small operation on her right thumb which put her out of action for a couple of months with the worst part being she could not drive her car. I also had to pay a number of visits to the Walk In Centre at Byker as I gashed my leg on a garden frame and it took several weeks and a lot of treatment to put it right. Thanks to Christine for all the lifts to the place and being my medical advisor.

I wondered what 2017 had in store for me as I was getting on to 91 and certainly not as agile as I used to be. I keep reasonably fit, but I realise I am no longer a good walker and things I could achieve a couple of years ago are now not possible. My eyesight in my left eye is pretty poor and thank goodness my right eye can take the strain. My hearing gets worse and even with expensive hearing aids in use I have great difficulty in hearing clearly which I find a great disadvantage.

Thank goodness my brain is still functioning well and I have a strong desire to keep up all the regular activities that make my life so happy and content. I am still trying hard to keep up with modern technology and am becoming more proficient in my use of my Apple iPad and my classy Sony Android phone. Compared to the youngsters I am still a dinosaur in these things but it does not worry me in the least. Christine gives me an awful lot of help when things go wrong but I admit I am pretty useless at remembering passwords and the like.

The year soon found me following all my normal pursuits, with bowling on a Monday afternoon and Thursday evening, a few talks to various clubs on some evenings, lots of Church related activities and monthly meeting with my NORGAS and Arthritis Care friends.

The first big adventure of the year was a cruise with Saga on their liner Sapphire at the end of May for three weeks. This was a special cruise to mark the 20th anniversary of Saga cruising and was a most enjoyable time spent in the western Mediterranean where the sun shone brightly and warmly every single day. We sailed from Dover and I had a long journey down there by a chauffeur driven car from Newcastle which went very well apart for the last ten miles to Dover where we were held up for a couple of hours by road-works.

The cruise started off with a great firework display in Dover harbour just as we set sale. I had a nice single, outside cabin to myself and met up with several friends from previous cruises. As usual the life on board was full and varied and now with a much smaller appetite I could not do true justice to the wonderful food and drink which was on offer. I was lucky enough on two of the formal dinner nights to be invited onto the top tables by my old friends Horst Pint, the Director of Hotels and Len Bilston, the Chief Engineer.

There were a lot of interesting speakers on board and I renewed my acquaintance with Edwina Currie and also met Simon Weston for the first time - a remarkable soldier from the Falkland War and we got on well with each other.

The liner called in at Lisbon in Portugal and although I had been there a number of times before, I spent a good half-day on a tram car ride around the city combined with a port wine tasting experience, which was certainly different and ended the day in a nice park on the edge of the Tagus sitting in the sunshine and watching the world go by.

We had a day stop at Malaga, a place I know very well, so I decided on a bus trip to the Guadalhorce Valley to a farm house and vineyard which was a nice leisurely affair with lots of Paella and wine. Then it was on to Marseilles for a first visit there. It is an impressive City dominated by a large port overflowing with visitors and a very interesting spot. The next port of call was Livorno in Tuscany an area which I love. I made a visit to the Torre A Cenaia Estate some miles inland for a gentle drive by horse and cart around the vast estate and as it is in the middle of a wine making area, the inevitable tasting of the many varieties being produced.

Then it was down the west coast of Italy to Civitavecchia, the port for Rome, where I opted for a bus trip to see the main sights of the City. It was again a lovely warm day and it suited me to sit on a bus and see the main sights of Rome. Gone are the days when I could join a walking tour for two or three hours. I was well satisfied to see Circus Maximus, Colosseum, Trevi Fountain, Roman Forum, Spanish Steps etc. Alas there was no time to visit the Vatican City and all its delights but we did manage to have a nice meal with the Vatican in full view.

Then it was back to the ship and over to Corsica, a new stop for me, for a day in Ajaccio. Corsica was an eye opener and I rate it highly. It is a lovely place with magnificent country-side and fabulous beaches and all looking so fresh and clean. I could well spend a couple of weeks in the place to learn a little more about it.

Following that we made our way towards Gibraltar and for half a day hugged the north-west and western coasts of Majorca. I have been to Gibraltar many times so opted for a trip to the Alemeda Gardens and then a cable car ride to the top of the Rock. It was good to watch the antics of the apes at the top. They seem to have the measure of all the tourists. Then we were homeward bound through the Bay of Biscay back to Dover. This had been a great trip which I thoroughly enjoyed and somewhat whetted my appetite for cruising once again. After nearly three weeks of warmth and unbroken sunshine it rained every inch of the way back from Dover to Newcastle.

I had not long to wait for the next big event of the year. Colonel Ashok Choudry and his wife Chhanda) who were on a trip taking in Ireland, the UK and Switzerland) were going to stay a few days with me in Newcastle. I was still busily engaged writing my life story and Ashok had offered to edit and print the book using expertise he had gained in publishing various books on the Mahar Regiment and on our mutual friend General Krishna Rao, so I was in really good hands. A lot of work was still required on my part to finish my story and assemble a large number of photographs to be put in the book. With the assistance of Ashok we managed to abbreviate the last couple of years' experiences and also to get a disk together with all the photographs needed.

It was not all work and we took the opportunity of getting around some of the lovely parts of the country within reasonable travelling distance. The visit did not get off to the best of starts as I stood outside the International arrival gates at Newcastle Airport to greet my guests and became increasingly worried as flights came and went and they still not appear. I got a text message to say they had arrived but they were nowhere to be seen. I had just about given up hope when I wandered to the other end of the Airport to find them at the Domestic arrivals gate. What a sigh of relief! The Airport classes flights from Dublin as Domestic and not International. What a time to learn that lesson.

It was all well after that and we had a great time together. I gave up my bedroom and en-suite for them and moved into another bedroom. I was always a tad worried on how I would cope with the meals and cooking etc but I should not have worried. Ashok and Chhanda took over the kitchen duties in their entirety and looked after me as though I was the guest. So good of them as both are expert cooks and I just so much enjoyed the wide variety of different food they made for me, and no washing-up for me either.

I thought it would be good to book a taxi a number of times to take us to some lovely scenic runs in the surrounding country-side. I managed to get a great taxi driver in Mark Kay who was running a brand new car. We made use of him a number of times and he turned out to be an outstanding courier as he knew the areas we were heading for and he contributed greatly to our enjoyment being most accommodating both with his time and his manner.

One day we decided to go up the Northumbrian coast which is very picturesque. We started off locally at Tynemouth with very little activity on the river but seeing Tynemouth Priory and the great beaches and sea front all the way along to St. Mary's Island and the lighthouse at Whitley Bay. Then it was up to Warkworth Castle where we spent some time going around the well preserved ancient site. Then further along to Amble and Alnmouth with the hope of getting a nice lunch at Seahouses. No such luck as the traffic was thick all the way and there was not one parking space to be had even though we cruised around the harbour car park and several overflow car parks until we gave up in despair. I was really looking forward to having some fish and chips but we had to wait.

We made our way to Bamburgh and managed to get what appeared to be the last parking space available. We managed a lovely lunch in the The Victoria Hotel where the fish and chips were excellent. Bamburgh is a lovely place with its great castle and we enjoyed our stop in the beautiful sunshine there. We then went inland and landed up at Alnwick for a stop and then on to Rothbury. We were hoping to see the great Cragside estate the family home of the late and great Lord Armstrong the well known industrialist and benefactor from Newcastle. It was just on closing time but at least we had half an hour there which gave us a flavour of the place. Then it was home to Newcastle after a pretty good day out.

A couple of days later we travelled over to the Lake District for the day. We aimed for Pooley Bridge at the eastern tip of Lake Ullswater where we had a nice break before joining the ferry which took an hour or so to cover the length of the Lake to Glenridding a small village at the far side. The trip on the lake was a treat with the Cumbrian peaks all around and the country-side majestic all helped by the lovely sunny weather. There was time for more fish and chips at the local hotel before we continued our journey along the side of Lake Windemere. We stopped at Grasmere at Dove Cottage, the home of William Wordsworth the famous poet and although the cottage was closed and we couldn't get in, there was an aura about the place which was quite tangible. Then onwards to Keswick and Lake Derwentwater. Time was now against us and we made our way home by the Military Road to Newcastle which runs alongside Hadrian's Wall with all its old Roman ruins. Again we had a first class time and enjoyable day in beautiful weather.

Two days later we went south towards Yorkshire. After passing Teesside we were in some spectacular country-side going over the North Yorkshire Moors towards Whitby. Whitby is a lovely little seaside town with a great beach and harbour overlooked by the ruins of Whitby Abbey. We made our way to the high point of the Abbey which is remote and open to the elements but had the bad luck of being caught in a thunderstorm with torrential rail which soaked us all to the skin. Poor Mark our driver had to buy a new tee shirt. It was a very informative visit and we soon dried out in a nice place in town where we had our usual fish and chips. Then it was down the coast with a quick visit to Scarborough, a place I have always liked since my childhood. After that it was inland to York where I lived for so long with a quick visit to York University where Ashok's brother attended some years ago. Again time was against us so it was just a fast spin around York to see the Minster and the Walls before heading for home. I felt worn out after 3 days of long car journeys.

As well as visiting my Bowling Club up at Blue Flames one lovely evening, the three of us went for a short walk round or

Church Green Estate. Although we were out for around an hour just walking slowly we did not see another soul on our estate. Nobody on the footpaths or in their gardens even though it was a beautiful evening. Ashok and Chhanda were amazed at this because home in Pondicherry they would have passed a couple of thousand people in that length of time.

A day later I had to leave them alone in my house for the rest of their stay as I was booked to go to Italy on holiday with Christine. My thanks to my neighbours Tom and Claire next door and Thelma opposite my backdoor who provided them with support and friendship in my absence until they flew to Dublin on the next part of their adventure. I am sure we all enjoyed each other's company very much indeed.

I always wanted to visit the Italian Lakes and so far in my life this had eluded me. Christine and I found a flight taking us to Verona which is right on the doorstep for Lake Garda. There was only the two of us for holidays this year as Bethany was in her studies at Keele University, which also allowed us to go earlier and miss school holiday crowds. We picked a swish hotel in Bardolino on the east shore of the lake called the Hotel Cassius Thermae and Spa. It turned out to be a good spot with lovely rooms, good food, nice gardens and good pools and facilities. It was on the edge of the lake with just the lakeside road inbetween us and the water.

For the first couple of days there was thunder and a little rain about, but that soon changed to blue skies and warm sunshine. It was a really restful holiday, although we did have some very busy days out. Twice we went on bus tours northwards into the Italian Tyrol area up past the Dolomites towards the Alps and the borders of Austria and Switzerland. It is one of the richest parts of Italy and sometimes it is difficult to work out if you are in Italy or Austria. Some of the territory was transferred to Italy from Austria after WWl and all signs are in Italian and German. It is beautiful clean unspoiled territory and maintained to the highest standards.

We spent some time in Bolzano a beautiful little town surrounded by peaks of 10,000 feet plus. Just sitting outside at a coffee table taking in the sights and pure air was a joy in itself. The road up to the heights was a series of tight bends at big angles and the bus drivers there deserve medals for bravery. The tortuous roads filled with hundreds of cyclists struggling up impossible slopes looked a nightmare to me.

We got on a cable car at Pordoi which took us up the final slopes to the top. People and cars looked like ants from way up high. There were magnificent views to the Alps from the top where breathing became rather laboured. As well as using cable cars we also had an Alpine railway journey for an hour or so. It stopped at a dozen or so isolated halts where there were hotels and some very expensive looking chalets. You can certainly see why the area is so popular for so many visitors.

Another trip we had was in the direction of Verona on to Mantova another pretty Italian Town surrounded by lots of water and then on to Parco Segurto, a fabulous park with acres of lawns and flowers. Being Italy it almost seemed obligatory to visit the Selva Capezza vineyards near Lugano for a wine tasting session. Lake Garda is a huge lake with steamers going in all directions around it. We did a small trip from Bardolino to Garda for half a day and promised ourselves to use the steamers more often on our next visit. We did spend time just sitting looking at all the activity on the Lake and eating ice-cream which was very relaxing.

The two weeks passed very quickly and we felt there was still a lot to see and admire around the lake. Not to be left out Bethany went on holiday later in the year to Zante with some of her University friends and enjoyed it. In the summertime I spent a lot of time at the bowling green thoroughly enjoying myself and still able to compete with the best of them. The outdoor season ended with a trip to the Lake District where we played 3 local teams with mixed results over three days.

There were some downsides in the year with Christine downcast at the death of her cat Jessie who had been a good companion for 13 years or so. However it did not take her long to get two small kittens, Mistie and Indie, to fill the missing spot. Christine didn't have a good year health-wise, having an operation on her thumb which required her hand to be in plaster for a few weeks. No driving allowed during that time which was a bind. She is still greatly worried by auto immune symptoms which are always with her and the experts seem to be clueless where treatment is involved.

Robert and Debbie paid regular visits to me with Robert always seeming to cook me a good meal which is always much appreciated. Peter my brother-in-law from Grimsby had one or two medical scares but is made of stern stuff and survived hospital visits and operations. Well done Peter and Paggy.

One of the highlights of the year was the wedding of my grandson James McIntosh to Victoria Shepherd-Scott at the lovely venue of Allerton Castle, near Wetherby in Yorkshire, on Saturday 11<sup>th</sup> November.

Christine and myself made a full weekend of it, travelling down from Newcastle and staying for two nights at the Castle Inn, an old coaching station in the village of Spofforth, some 15 minutes drive to the venue. A number of guests were staying there, including Victoria's family and friends and it was a good opportunity to get to know each other. Bethany came up from Keele University for two nights and stayed with us, but Robert and Debbie decided to do the long journey from Shilbottle as a day trip! It was also great to meet up with Andrew and Geri who flew over from the USA for the big event.

For the middle of November the weather was most kind, for although it was cold the sun shone all day which was a big bonus especially with so many photographs being taken of various groups in the magnificent gardens of the Castle. It was a very posh and well managed affair with everything going without a hitch, Victoria looking radiant and James well pleased with himself. They seemed remarkably well matched and I could not have wished for anything better for James.

It was the first wedding I had been at for some years and I must say I enjoyed the company of so many young and vibrant guests who attended. The formal ceremony was followed by a lot of photo-shoots and then we sat down to a sumptuous meal and all the speeches. The evening was taken up with a Disco and this was definitely the time for the youngsters to let off steam and the time for Christine and me to depart back the Castle Inn. James and Victoria subsequently flew off to Dubai and Mauritius for their honeymoon. I can see the McIntosh family line now surviving to the 22$^{nd}$ century.

2018 was here and it promised to be another year of good living and some adventure. One of two things were planned and others were in the pipeline. My first big objective was to progress the publication of my life history with my great friend Ashok Choudry spending a lot of his time assembling all the narrative and pictures and negotiating the whole production with a printing firm in Chennai. This was very difficult to keep track of from the UK and in consequence Ashok had to make many crucial editorial decisions on his own without referring them to me. The deadline had to coincide with a visit by myself to India in January and in the end was very rushed. I was unable to proof read the final submission which would have been the normal procedure if I had been on the spot.

Ashok deserves the highest praise and a medal for his great effort in pushing the whole project forward as it was accomplished to a very high standard and on time. I flew with Emirates from Newcastle to Chennai via Dubai arriving at about 7 am after a fine journey. I was met at the Airport by Ashok and other Mahar soldiers so it was an easy passage out into Chennai. My case was slightly damaged but with swift action by Ashok a new case was provided in double quick time. Arrangements had been made for a visit to Officers Training Academy, which was only a couple of miles from the airport, to relax and have breakfast with Brigadier Reddy, one of the senior officers in charge of the Academy.

It is great to have friends in high places. This set me up well for the long road journey down to Pondicherry. I was again staying at the Ashram Guest House on the sea front and found it still the most peaceful, comfortable and relaxing place for a two week stay. As before the Choudry family plied me with lots of food and refreshment and were the most generous of hosts. A lot of time was spent on the book publication with midnight oil being burned on more than one occasion, but with the end finally achieved with hard copies of the book arriving on time.

There was still lots of time to appreciate the sights of Pondicherry with its wonderful sea front and distinctive French atmosphere. I certainly enjoyed the evening strolls along the front with visits to an Italian ice-cream shop most evenings. I was also very lucky to see a full eclipse of the moon with cloudless skies along with tens of thousands of others on the seafront early one evening.

On one day I had an outstanding visit to the Aravind Eye Hospital in Pondicherry with Ashok who voluntary works there as the Consumer Relations Manager. My eyesight is very poor so any check-up is appreciated. The hospital opened in 2003 and is a model of efficiency and deals with half a million out-patients a year and surgery for 70,000 patients a year. The place was overflowing with people but under the guidance of Ashok I think I got VIP treatment and passed many a long line of patients. I was asked if I would be classed as a private or public case (free treatment) and I opted for the private side. It cost me 100 rupees which is about £1.20 in sterling and covers me for a year. About two-thirds of outpatients go free along with three-quarters of inpatients.

I am used to visiting Newcastle Eye Hospital and the whole procedure I went through was very little different to what I am used to and all along the most modern equipment was used by highly qualified staff. Indeed I had the pleasure of meeting a number of staff who did their training in Newcastle. I finished by meeting the top man of the Hospital namely Dr Venkatesh, a world renowned eye specialist. He had a good look at my eyes and was shocked to see I had a Binkhorst clip in my left eye. Even he had seldom seen one. He took a picture of my eye and said it would be used in his future lectures to his trainees. At least I am some use to medical science.

The Aravind chain now has 15 hospitals in India. The whole operation was founded by a Dr Venkataswamy way back in1976, an eminent eye doctor who had a vision of treating rich and poor alike for the millions of poor sighted Indians. The whole project thrives and is a model of efficiency which deals with the problem on an industrial scale which is the envy of the world. Interestingly Dr Venkataswamy had strong links with Sri Aurobindi in Pondicherry and was one of his followers.

At the end of my visit to India, I was invited to spend a day at the Officers Training Academy which fitted well into my itinerary as I was flying out of Chennai. I had a great day looking around the whole establishment and watching the Officer Cadets going through their paces. What a tough time for them I stood on the saluting base on the parade ground and they all must have wondered who the old codger was who was watching them. Happy Days.

I left behind in India a number of signed copies of the book for the Regiment which I hope will at least be a narrative of a unique time in history signified by Indian Independence. Well done Ashok for your persistence over the years to get me started. Once I reached home plans were made to have another family get-together for a book launch. This we held at the Marriot hotel in Gosforth over a weekend at pretty short notice, which unfortunately meant that not all could attend. Nevertheless it was a happy time had by all and a good ending to the first part of the saga of the book. However. I have begun to think that a UK edition of it would be a good idea. Ashok for the sake of getting the Indian edition published necessarily had to abbreviate a lot of detail in the latter part of the script, which perhaps could be included in a limited UK edition. So it has not yet ended.

The next big adventure of the year was a trip to Rhode Island in the USA to visit Andrew and Geri. They had been living over there for some years since Andrew transferred to the American branch of his company. They loved Rhode Island and made it their real home, and they were happy enough for Robert and myself to stay with them for a couple of weeks starting late in May. Andrew had some leave owing and took the whole time off work to be our guide and driver whilst we were there.

Robert and I flew by Norwegian Air from Edinburgh to Providence and on the way over we had some great views of the south coast of Greenland covered with ice and snow. When we turned south we ran into cloud and saw no more until we started our descent into Providence, which is the capital of Rhode Island. After a remarkably quick exit from the airport we were met by Andrew and taken to Bristol in time for bed.

Wisely they had the foresight to acquire a wheel chair for my use during the holiday which was a great boon for me as my poor walking would have been a real problem getting around. And so started a hectic few days when we spent hours exploring this new countryside in some depth. We soon realised we did not have to go far to see and enjoy great views. Bristol is only a small place of some 22000 people and is a deep water seaport with a lot of boat building and related marine industries. Pilgrims first arrived there in 1620 and like the rest of New England some very old but well maintained touches from the early settlement days still exist.

The weather for us was very kind being mostly hot and dry. We spent hours on walks in local beauty spots such as Colt State Park, Mount Hope Farm and Blithewood mansion and gardens. All beautifully maintained and never far from the waters of Narragansett Bay which was always full of shipping, mostly yachts. We soon started to recognise the big bridges such as The Mount Hope bridge and the Pell bridge which linked the islands in the area.

The biggest place south of Bristol is Newport on Aquidneck Island. It is the sailing capital of the USA having hosted the Americas Cup sailing regatta for many years. It is a summer resort well known for its historic mansions in Bellevue Avenue which were in their heydays at the start of the 20 century. We spent a lot of time in Newport looking at the shipyards and docks and walking down roads full of housing dating way back into the early days of the settlers A drive along the ocean view road at the south tip of the island is a must do also with its opulent houses and great views.

One of the great attractions of Newport are the Mansions. In the early part of the 20th century the very rich would spend a couple of weeks in Newport as part of the social calendar. They vied in building grand mansions just for a holiday home and spared no expense. Sadly the culture changed and the mansions started to fall into disrepair. A trust was formed to protect them and they are now restored to their original beauty and open to the many visitors who flock to see them. I visited The Breakers, The Elms and The Marble House and was staggered at the magnificence of the buildings. I suppose for the Vanderbilts, Rockerfellers and Astors and all their money they just vied with each other to build the best even when they only occupied them for two weeks in the season.

We had several day trips out including a short trip which took us into Massachusetts to Cape Cod on a very windy day. The names of the places such as Chatham, Barnstable and Sandwich indicates where the early settlers came from and they have certainly turned it into a beautiful place. Our longest trip was again into Massachusetts going north of Boston to the lovely small town of Rockport on the tip of the Cape Ann peninsula. As well as boasting many fine beaches its beauty attracts many artists and it is a centre for many music festivals. It is close to Manchester and Gloucester, both noted holiday resorts, with fine beaches where we also spent time sightseeing. Nearer home to soon became used to passing over bridges to reach Jamestown a nice island in itself but one which had to be crossed to reach the far side of Narragansett Bay.

On the very south tip of the island we paid a visit to the Beavertail Lighthouse. There are some beautiful places on the west side of the Bay, none more than Wickford, which we visited a number of times. It is a seaside resort with a small harbour full of pleasure boats. Andrew and Geri use it as their base to go kayaking. The majority of the villages historic 18<sup>th</sup> century houses remain intact and are worth a visit for themselves. It also hosts a popular Arts Festival each year.

We also managed to spend a short time in Wakefield having an ice-cream. Near the end of the holiday we paid a visit for a day to some relations on Pats side of the family who lived nearby in Westerly. Robert with his interest in Ancestry, found he had a cousin by the name of Olivier le Bras who lived nearby with his family and Andrew and Geri had made friends with them. Olivier owned a yacht which was moored in nearby Stonington. We spent a nice evening there getting to know each other.

One of the stand out events was a visit to see the Providence Firewater display. This is a cultural show held several times a year to celebrate the community spirit of the State capital. It takes place on a short stretch of the river in the centre of the city starting at dusk and going on until midnight. Up to 100 steel braziers inset in the river are filled with wooden blocks which are set alight by people in barges moving around the area who replenish them when they start to fade. The whole event which is witnessed by tens of thousands spectators along the banks is very festive with non- stop entertainment of music and dance with a lot of participation. We picked a perfect evening with the temperature staying in the upper twenties and not a cloud in the sky

Twice during our stay we had a walk along the path to Warren some 3 miles up from Bristol. This was a converted ex-railway track but now a favourite spot for walkers and cyclists passing through great scenery and full of wild life. There was also a nice coffee shop in Warren for refreshment before the return walk. I much appreciated the wheelchair for these trips as they were well beyond my walking capacity

We met a lot of friendly people from the local Church which I went to twice and also at a Community Aid organisation where Geri volunteered her help. I owe a lot to Andrew and Geri and Jasper the cat for a memorable visit. The only worry was that Andrews future there was in doubt because of hostile take-over bids being aired for the firm he worked for

The next adventure was a revisit for a fortnight to Bardalino on the shores of Lake Garda. We had been so impressed with our visit there the previous year that we wanted a little more of it. The hotel and the weather didn't let us down and we were totally satisfied once again. We again enjoyed trips to the Dolomites and Mantova, but managed to explore new places around the Lake all of which were very impressive. We had a good day also meeting up with and having a meal with Stew Williams and his wife Gillian, Bowling Club friends who were staying nearby.

Mixed with these exciting holidays was the normal daily routine for when I was home. Lots of permanent engagements throughout the year. Bowling at the indoor rink at the Parks Leisure Centre in North Shields every Monday afternoon in the winter months and games on Monday, Wednesday and Saturday during the summer months at the Blue Flames Sports Club in Benton. I still enjoy bowling, aiming at winning matches wherever possible. I have a great bunch of very good friends who give me so much help to keep me going. We had a good tour to play 3 matches in Scotland which was most enjoyable with good weather with generous hosts. I managed to see my good friend Mona Shea during our stay in Edinburgh.

I also continued playing Carpet Bowls at the Church every Thursday evening throughout the year again with the help from more of my good friends. I attended monthly meetings of the Vets Association at Blue Flames, also at Christa Clemettsons house with old Arthritis Care friends and at the house of Andrew and Shirley Thomas for a Church Discussion Group. Having so many friends is a great bonus and a stimulus to carry on as long as possible.

I managed 2 visits to see Newcastle United. The first visit as the result of winning a seat as a raffle prize and the second as a treat from June and Bruce, my good friends from my old days as a season ticket holder. Over the year my walking ability got worse and I went to the Doctor for advice. He thought I had Parkinsons Disease and he referred me to the specialists at The Campus of Ageing and Vitality in Newcastle. The experts there diagnosed me with Vascular Parkinsonism, apparently resulting from a couple of minor strokes in the past of which I was unaware at the time. No real cure for this but I had to go back for re-examination in July 2019. As mine was an interesting case I was asked to be a guinea pig for three first year medical students to study, to which I agreed and had several meetings with them at home. I hope it advances medical science.

In November it was a treat to attend the wedding of Alex my grandson to Gemma. It was held in Scarborough at a Barn which was different. I contributed at the ceremony with a reading which seemed to go down well. Christine, Bethany and myself booked into a boarding house nearby for two nights over the weekend. Alex and Gemma seem to be a happy match who I am sure will get on well

On a sad note my good neighbour Thelma died after a short illness just before Christmas. We were good friends for over 30 years and it was not a nice way to end the year. The year ended with a short stay in Tenerife where they certainly know how to celebrate the start of a new year

Another year passed and now in 2019, life continued at a pace. I was home from a good holiday in Tenerife and back into the normal daily routine which in the early months of the year was very restricted.

The cold dark and wet weather meant not much outdoor activity. The normal routine was going to Church on a Sunday morning where I meet up so many like minded friends and always come home revived and feeling on top of the world. Christine usually comes to join me for lunch which I have in the oven cooking whilst I am out. I still find it easy enough to prepare a whole range of good Sunday meals which keeps us well fed and happy.

I always look forward to Monday because it is bowls afternoon. In the winter I play at The Parks Sports Centre in North Shields with a close-knit group of great friends. It is hard work for me now as my walking is very substandard but I get an amazing amount of help from my friends which helps keep me going. The more exercise I get the better for me, and I still retain a very competitive spirit and win as many matches as I loose. I am lucky to get a lift door to door from my good friend John each week.

Tuesday is a bit of a rest day when I have time to get up to date with any thing that needs to be done. Wednesday is Cleaning day. Gail my cleaner comes in the morning and keeps the house up to scratch. She has been cleaning for me since before Pat died so really knows her way around the place and keeps everything in tip top condition. Lucky me, as without her help I would be lost. The big event of Thursday is the Carpet Bowls Club at the Church in the evening. Once again, I am treated so well by the other players and never have to bend down to pick up bowls which is a great help to me. I also get house to house transport by my good friends Alan and Sheila. Friday is always washing machine day and drying and ironing.

Saturday I look on as Sports Day with so many big matches to be viewed on TV. So that is my typical week in the winter months. In addition to this I have other activities on a less frequent basis. I have regular meetings with my friends in The Norgas Vets at the Blue Fames Sports Club, a house meeting with my friend Christa who invites a few others also from the now disbanded Arthritis Care Club, and a monthly meeting with some Church friends at Andrew and Shirleys house. How lucky I am to have so many good friends. I seem to be in reasonable health and still sleep like a top.

My first big adventure in 2019 was a trip to France with Robert. He is an expert on Ancestry and his work has uncovered the fact that I had four uncles who died fighting in France during WWl. I previously knew of my Uncle James who was my Mothers younger twin brother who died in 1917. The other three unknown to me were George and James Riddell and George Johnson. We decided to find the graves of each of them and pay our respects.

We set off on Sunday the 19$^{th}$ of May with a train down to London and an overnight stay at the Premier Inn at Kings Cross. Next morning we caught the Eurostar train from St Pancras to Lille via the Channel Tunnel - a new experience for me. Robert had worked out a fine itinerary, travelling by hire car with four overnight stops in the battle fields area where the graves were located. Robert had a good idea of where we were going and with the help of sat nav in the car we succeeded in finding all four graves; not an easy objective because of the large number of war grave sites, some in very remote spots.

We found the Riddell brothers graves fairly close together in the Arras Road Cemetery and the Canadian Infantry Memorial. We stayed overnight in Arras and next day had a long journey to the south passing through some very nice countryside including the Champagne wine growing area and many famous spots where many WWl were fought. We found the grave of James Johnson in St lmogenes Churchyard near the river Marne. Just a small village with very few people about but dominated by the Church.

There was a separate section of the garden devoted to the war graves of a couple of dozen soldiers both French and British. They were in immaculate order courtesy of the War Grave Commission and local inhabitants. We paid our respects, saluting and leaving a cross on the grave before we left. We were the first to visit the grave, and this being over 100 years later, we were very satisfied with our visit.

The next day we drove northwards again through Rheims and Cambrai for an overnight stay in Rancourt. Next day we found the last grave of George Johnson in the Flatiron Copse Cemetery, Marnetz near Vimy Ridge before making our way back to Lille to drop off the car and booking in for an overnight stay in Lille.

We travelled back home on Friday with courtesy of the Eurostar and were soon back in Newcastle. It was a most enjoyable trip around an area of France I had always wanted to see. The weather was dry and warm which was a bonus for us.

With the lighter evenings and warmer weather, I started another season of outdoor bowling at Blue Flames. At 93 years of age I still enjoyed playing but I got a lot of help from my good friends who make easy for me. I am still competitive and managed to win the first cup of the season - the Ernie Hankin Doubles Cup playing with my good friend Stew Williams. He is a County player so he takes much of the credit for the success.

The garden also takes up a lot of my time. I enjoy pottering around in the sunshine keeping the place tidy. I am a slow mover and jobs take a long time, especially as I love sitting in the garden as well. A gardener cuts my grass every two weeks and Jimmy the tree man looks after the trimming of all the bushes and trees, both jobs which are beyond me now.

At the beginning of June, Christine and I flew out to Naples en-route to Sorrento for a two week stay. The arrival at Naples Airport was chaotic with priority given to hundreds of passengers catching a cruise liner at Naples. We felt rather neglected although we had asked for special help. It was a good hours taxi ride to the Blue Atlantic Palace, our Sensitori destination. It was a nice place where we were able to relax in the non-stop sunshine. The food and drink were good and there were plenty spots for sitting in the shade for reading and snoozing. Lunch was always al-fresco in the upper garden where you could always see plenty of tame rabbits running around. The views over the Naples Bay with Vesuvius in the background. We managed a full day trip down the Amalfi coastline with its magnificent views with lots of villages just hanging on the coastline. We would have enjoyed it more if the bus had been better.

Space was cramped and I think it was built for dwarfs. We had another enjoyable trip in a land train for half a day. Up into the hills and at times above the clouds at times with plenty of fresh air and good views around every corner. We had a taxi trip into Sorrento itself for a relaxing morning. The ice creams were very good. The trip home was the same experience as coming as we were mixed up with hordes from the cruise on their return journey. We resolved never to fly out Naples again on cruise days.

No sooner was I back than I found myself packing again to go on a round Britain Cruise. This had the advantage of starting and finishing at Newcastle which was a bonus. The ship was the Magellan, a quite modern liner with around 500 passengers. I had a nice outside cabin on the port side and I enjoyed myself with good food and entertainment, sunny, dry weather the whole time and lots of interesting places to see.

The first port of call was Dundee so it was a great opportunity to meet Irene my cousin who lives in Broughty Ferry. We had a great day as it not often that we get the chance to meet. We had a nice lunch together but spent most of the time back at her house catching up with a lot of news.

Then it was off northwards again to the Orkney Islands landing at Kirkwall. I spent the day on a bus tour of the island having a look around Kirkwall with its impressive 12th century St Magnus Cathedral. Then, travelling up passed Scapa Flow, the big inland harbour much used by the Royal Navy and is a graveyard for many sunken ships. I visited a number of Neolithic sites set up by the Vikings many centuries ago. I found the Island very windy with few trees and it must be tough living there in the winter. The people were very nice natured and seemed to be happy with life.

The ship then turned south with the next port of call being Tobermory on the Island of Mull. It turned out to be the sunniest and warmest day of the year in Mull so I saw it at its beautiful best. The houses overlooking the harbor with all their different coloured walls were resplendent. I took a bus tour around the Island with all its wild countryside as far as Calgary Bay where there was a gorgeous beach where I could easily have spent a week just relaxing.

Then the ship took us down the islands towards Dublin. I had been to Dublin for a day with my Dad just after the war but I had really forgotten what it was like. I found Dublin to be a very vibrant and beautiful place. A bus trip around the city took us through many fine Georgian Squares and also along the main O,Connell Street and Grafton Street. I saw Croke Park, the big

Rugby ground, and off we went to Phoenix Park. This is a magnificent Park being the largest enclosed recreational area in any European Capital. Lots of grassland, trees and formal gardens and even boasts a Zoo. You could easily spend a full day there and not see half of the facilities on offer.

Later in day I spent an hour on a boat trip up the River Liffey and was surprised at all the new development that was in progress along the river front. There were endless cranes on building sites with new office blocks and apartments springing up all over the place. I saw Dublin in a new light and was impressed.

Our next call should have been the Scilly Isles which was a tender landing but some high winds and choppy water made the Captain decide to give it a miss for safety reasons. This was a disappointment as I had never been there before and I really wanted to experience it. So we passed it by and made our way to the Island of Geurnsey. When we lived in Whitley Bay our neighbours in Garsdale Road were Peter and Alison Harris. They moved to the Channel Islands over 40 years ago but I have always kept in touch with them. I let them know that I was docking in St.Peter Port and they were there to meet me on my arrival. We recognised each other straight away and they gave me a tour of the Island in their car. We had a fantastic day in the sunshine and they were able to show me all the places of interest. I stood them a good lunch and we had tea at their house overlooking the beach 50 yards away. It was the highlight of the holiday.

Then the ship made its way to the River Seine for a trip up the river to Rouen. This was a very interesting journey with lots of lovely French countryside to admire and Rouen turned out to be a sizable port some 50 miles inland. It was a Sunday so it was very quiet but with a lot of visitors out sightseeing. It is an ancient city dominated by a very large and well-kept cathedral which was worth a visit. There was time for a couple of hours tour on a road train around the old streets and squares of the city with some good architecture on show.

That was our last port of call before cruising up the east coast of England back to Newcastle. A most enjoyable cruise. It was still summertime with plenty of bowling and gardening to keep me happy. I ended the bowling season going on a tour with the Health and Security Bowling Club to the Lake District, once again staying at the Derwentwater Hotel in Keswick, where we were well looked after as usual.

We had enjoyable games against teams from Keswick, Workington and Cockermouth with reasonable weather adding to the enjoyment. As well as all this there was also time to visit my dear friends in the SLI with a trip to London to attend their Annual Reunion Lunch. My garden looked better at the end of the year than at the beginning. My 2004 car was still running but it passed 17,000 miles near the end of the year. I only do around 10 miles a week so it should last me out. The house was painted outside and some indoor repair was also completed.

My WW2 Battalion of 3MAHAR were celebrating their 75th Raising Day from October 31st to 2nd November 2019 and I was invited to attend. Many people advised me not to travel such a long way on my own but it was an opportunity not to be missed by me.

I flew alone to India with an Emirates flight from Newcastle to Chennai on 26th October without any problems, arriving at 8am. I was given a warm welcome by Mahar soldiers from the nearby Officers Training Academy and my Host for the stay Col. Ashok Choudry. No problems at all with customs or visas and I was soon on my way to Pondicherry, a 3 hours drive to the south for the first part of my stay.

Col.Ashok Choudry retired some 20 years ago but was formerly CO of 3MAHAR when they battled on the Siachen Glacier. He was adjutant at the OTA in Chennai for some time and also acted a ADC to Gen.Krishna Rao when he was COAS. He has been a close friend of mine for many years and along with Chhanda, his wife, helping, I was in safe hands. They live in an upstairs apartment in Pondicherry with a lot of stairs to climb so they thought it wise to book me into a ground floor room at the Aurobindi Ashram Guest House situated on the sea front at Pondicherry. This was a wise choice as it was an idyllic spot, very secluded and quiet, with a beautiful garden where residents meditated and did yoga, all with a backdrop of the beach and

Indian Ocean. Ideal for relaxing in the 30 degree sunshine prior to the busy schedule for the Re-union.

Pondicherry is a nice seaside town still retaining much of its French heritage and is a pleasant place which many holiday makers visit. My time there coincided with Diwali so there was a lot of activity to help pass the time.

The Re-union was at Jaipur where 3MAHAR are part of the Battleaxe Division. They moved into a new Military Cantonment just 6 previously and there was still much work to be done to finish before everything is fully complete. The work already done is top quality. The Choudry family and myself flew from Chennai to Jaipur on 30 October, a day early, so that I would have time for sightseeing before the formalities started. This was my first visit to Jaipur so I had some catching up to do.

We were met at the Airport by the present CO. Col. Prashant Kackar and a whole bevy of Officers JCOs and ORs. It became very clear from that moment on that I had some kind of VIP status. Life is full of many surprises. I was the oldest person on the guest list, the only person from the UK and the only one with WW2 experience, but as Lieutenant very junior indeed.

My first surprise was to be housed in the Brigade Guest Room usually reserved for officers of General Rank. I had access to a drinks cabinet with a dozen or so full bottles of assorted spirits at my disposal. Alas there wasn't time to do it full justice. I had 3 batmen to give me 24 hours assistance which they did with a smile. I wish I could have taken them home with me. A car and driver were always at my disposal, with a back-up truck with a couple of armed guards keeping a discrete distance whenever I was away from the Cantonment. Wherever I went in the next few days I was supported by Col.Choudry and an old friend of mine, Maj Aravindhan, who was D.Co. Commander who stuck to me like glue. The Battalion even imported a cook from another Battalion who was an expert in western cooking who did my every bidding at each meal most excellently.

I was given two trips into Jaipur which is a very big city with the old part being the main tourist attraction with its trademark pink buildings. I am now fully acquainted with its many forts, palaces and museums, although I got some funny looks from the many tourists because of the strong army presence around me.

The first official event I attended was termed a Home coming dinner hosted by the second in command and his wife. There must have been a couple of hundred guests and we dined under the stars on around 25 well set tables each with 8 places, where old friends greeted each other with many a good bear hug.

Day 2 started early with a visit to the Mandir for a united service. The composition of 3Mahar is roughly 45% Buddhist, 45% Hindu, 5% Sikh and 5% Christian. All the Officers seemed to be in the covered part of the Mandir with everyone else outside in rows, with the women separated from the men. All sat crossed legged on the floor apart from a few oldies who had chairs. The service was hard to follow and I really did not understand all the chanting and so forth which lasted half an hour or so. A collection was taken and at the end everyone got a small gift. Everyone went away seemingly happy and content and how they managed that puzzles me.

Then it was on to the opening of a new Administration Block which was inaugurated by the widow of a highly decorated hero of the Battalion. This was followed by an Officers Conclave where the CO and the Colonel of the Regiment gave presentations on past achievements and future prospects followed by a lively discussion on a whole range of current issues.

Thankfully every afternoon was free and there was opportunity to have a siesta to recharge the batteries. The evening event was a Sainik Samman Bhoj where a couple of thousand must have attended. This was an evening of rich entertainment, with Indian traditional dancing, performances by both the Pipe and Brass Bands. Then a big screen showing of a film made of the Battalions exploits over the years. All followed by a Bara Khana to end the day.

Day 3 was a busy time full of surprises. It started with a wreath laying ceremony at the war memorial. Large numbers of wreathes were laid by ex Cos of the Battalion, numerous Brigadiers and Maj Generals. I laid the penultimate wreath followed by The Colonel of the Regiment. Then it was on to a special SAINIK SAMMALON with about 600 serving soldiers and many veterans attending. The top table on the stage in front just had three people - the CO, the Colonel of the Regiment and myself. I felt quite honoured to be invited to speak and managed about 10 minutes talking about past achievements, future prospects and finished with a raised fist shouting the battle cry MAHAR KIJIE 3 times with enthusiastic responses from all present. Very satisfying I can assure you.

After that official photographs were taken to add to the thousands that had been taken over the last day or so. Then it was off to the JCOs Mess for a Sardar Lunch. The evening events were full of suprises. Firstly the newly built Officers Mess had to be officially opened. To my great shock they had chosen me to inaugurate it. The naming plaque was covered with a curtain and it was my privilege to pull the card and reveal all on the Board. My name is there now for all time showing 'Inaugurated on 2nd November 2019 by Lieut Bruce CS McIntosh (retd).' It is known as the Kalidar Mess - the name of a battle where the Battalion earned Battle and Theatre Awards. Incidentally 6SLI have the same award as they were side by side with 3MAHAR in the battle

Then onto the unveiling of the Jubilee Trophy, another cord pulling event for me. Then a final surprise I was given the sword to make the first cut on the celebration cake. I then had to feed cake to the CO and The Colonel of the Regiment and their wives and they all fed me a piece in return. What a lucky lad I am to have been chosen to do all this.

Then formal presents were exchanged. I gave the Battalion a presentation copy of a SGIAN DHUB in a nice case. It was a nice hallmarked sterling silver model latticed with stone plaited effect handle. In the corner of the Mess they have a display cabinet full of things I have given over the years and I am sure the dagger will end up there as well. In return I received a Silver Presentation Plate from the Colonel of the Regiment and numerous other mementos from the Battalion including a cap with 2 lines of scrambled egg on it to show my apparent seniority. Then the final dinner and another late night.

The following day was back to Pondicherry following a Brunch at the CO's house. It was just an incredible unbelievable few days for me. I spent a further three days in Pondicherry winding down in the Ashram and then home. Not without drama mind you.

The flight to Dubai was running late and resulted in a missed connection and a delay of a day. Emirates put me up in a plush 5 star hotel at no cost. I was able to get a guided tour for 3 hours around Dubai which is a lovely rich and clean city with many eye-catching buildings. Then back late to Newcastle with the drama not over as my luggage ended up in Birmingham.

All arrived safely, so ending a fortnight of incredible hospitality in India and honour bestowed on me well beyond anything that I ever anticipated.

There was not much left of 2019 after my visit to India. It has been a turbulent year politically in the country with the seemingly endless Brexit debate going on daily. The country seemed split evenly between Leavers and Remainers. Parliament was deadlocked and this was only broken by a General Election. Boris Johnson replaced Teresa May as Prime Minister and the December Election gave him the mandate to leave Europe on 31st December 2020. This was hard to take as I have always been a pro-European and still feel there was too much chicanery from the Leave side. I still think their aim is a no-trade deal by the end of 2020 which in my mind will be a disaster.

All in all 2019 had been a very busy year and my journeys continued to the end as I flew out to Tenerife the day after Boxing Day for a week in the sunshine. Christine and Bethany were already out there so I was in good company to celebrate the beginning of a new decade.

Now at the start of a new decade I wonder what this has in store for us all. After seeing in the New Year in Tenerife I flew home to a very cold Newcastle, with months more of cold dark days ahead. I was soon into the old routine of mostly staying indoors but with regular trips out to Church, the Parks Sports Centre to play indoor bowls and monthly meetings with my friends from NORGAS Bowls at Blue Flames and with a few from my old Arthritis Care group thanks to the hospitality of Christa. Add in a few trips with Christine to my hairdressers and chiropodist and my life was busy enough for me. Add on to that periodic visits from the rest of the family gave me the opportunity to visit lots of local hostelries to enjoy some nice meals.

Early in the year plans were already in place for various holiday jaunts later in the year. Christine and I booked for a fortnight in Sorrento in early June. We had enjoyed our trip there last year and decided it was good enough for a further try. Alex and Gemma invited me to stay with them for a few days in Yorkshire when the warmer weather came in May. I was also signed up with the British Legion to join a small group they were taking to Kohima to remember VJ75 in August. I also had a weekend away booked with the Bowls Club for a tour of SW Scotland early in September. So much to look forward to.

Early in February I a great overnight stay in York. York City Football Club held a gala dinner on the Friday night to celebrate the closure of their ground at Bootham Crescent before moving to a new stadium. I was present at the very first match played at Bootham Crescent way back in 1932. As it turned out I was the only one present at the Dinner who was there at the start, so I received an ovation from the 200 or so guests. I had the pleasure of sitting next to Alf Patrick who at 96 was the oldest person present. He was a centre forward of great distinction in the 1950s for York so many an old tale was told of past glories.

Towards the end of the evening I was approached by a young man who had travelled down from St Boswells in Scotland, He recognised my name that had been announced earlier in the evening. He introduced himself as Andrew Greenfield who turned out to be the son of Douglas Greenfield who had been the best man at my wedding in 1953. Really a chance in a million that we were together at the same function. I had not seen Douglas for years and he lives in York. Quick arrangements were made for a meeting on Saturday morning before I caught my train back to Newcastle. I was staying at the Royal Station Hotel in York so the three of us had a first class breakfast together and in two hours managed to catch up with many years of lost time. Plans were laid for all of us to attend the last game at Bootham Crescent towards the end of April. Altogether a very good visit to York.

It was just at this time that we became familiar with Covid-19, a Corona virus originating in Wuhan. Two Chinese students at York University were the first cases reported in this country. Little did we know of the implications to follow.

Towards the end of February, a mishap occurred with Bethany falling down her stairs at her student house and breaking her right ankle. This was her last year at Keele University and not the best time for it to happen. The best course of action was to get her up to Newcastle as soon as she was released from an overnight stay in hospital. As she was unable to climb stairs it was thought best for her to stay in my Bungalow. All her possessions including her car had to be left down at Keele. She had her operation to reset her ankle in Newcastle and then was convalescing with me. Almost immediately the Covid-19 pandemic was upon us and the new phrases 'Self Isolating' and 'Social Distancing' were the buzzwords and life changed.

Being 93 I was clinically vulnerable and needed shielding. I was in lock down for 3 months and as Bethany was with me it was the same rule for her. Life changed for the worse for everyone, with life as we knew it suspended. Bethany slowly recovered but was locked in with me which I am sure was not the most exciting experience. Christine could not come nearer than 2 metres from us so life was more difficult for us. Shopping became a weekly problem but after a couple of weeks I was able to get on the priority list for home shopping with Sainsburys which worked well and we had to adapt to a new way of living. Fancy having no haircuts for months on end? Just one of the hardships. Alas, my well-planned holiday events were cancelled. By the time July arrived the stringent lockdown rules we were under were being relaxed and it was good to be able to see my family once again. I have been no further than the end of my drive since the end of February and it is a funny feeling when all this seems quite normal. But at 94 I am still in the high-risk category so it will be a slow passage back to the old ways. My family have been lucky that they have all kept clear of Covid-19, which has caused so much distress to so many people

Bethany is still living with me and her bad fortune turns into good fortune for me, because it could have been a very lonely time for me. She has now graduated with a B.Sc degree. It is sad she is going to miss all the graduation day celebrations with her friends at Keele, which will no longer take place.

I certainly miss seeing all my friends and at Church and Bowls, but regular phone calls help a little. I have not been to Church for months and I miss it. However, we have a very talented Minister in Gavin Hume who keeps in touch with a regular Sunday service on the internet: just a short session but with a simple and straightforward message, which I appreciate. He is a top class musician and provides me with the chance to sing along with the hymns. Well done Gavin.

Since the middle of July I have had to visit the Dermatology Department at the RVI a number of times They had to treat a Carcinoma on my left ear which they lasered out and which has healed up nicely. They then found a more serious Melanoma behind my right ear, which requires an operation to remove it and then have some plastic surgery done to repair the damage. Very good of them in these difficult times to treat me so quickly. I have been in the RVI for 3 days for an operation to remove the Melanoma and a lymph node. Thanks to my Consultant Mr. Bashir and all the staff in Ward 47 I am recovering and look forward to better times again.

So, my story comes to an end with what seems all doom and gloom. But I must end on a more positive note:

August 15th was the 75th Anniversary of VJ Day. My trip to Kohima was cancelled of course but the British Legion was still interested in my input to it. My main desire was to ensure that the Indian Army contribution to the victory was not forgotten. More than 2.5 million Indians volunteered to join the Army and the Forgotten 14th Army was mainly Indian with them providing 80% of the manpower. I had to turn down an offer for a place at the celebrations at the National Arboretum, but the British Legion kindly laid a wreath on my behalf recognising the Indian Army casualties. They also facilitated an interview with the History Correspondent of The Times, which resulted in part of my contribution being in the Online version of The Times and on their podcast for the day. I was also interviewed by the Press Association and extracts of the interview appeared on The Mail Online and other outlets. So, I did achieve my aim of getting my message across.

One other very bright spot was an e-mail I received from the Indian Army. My Battalion 3MAHAR had issued a SPECIAL ORDER OF THE DAY. It was all about me and the special relationship that still exists after 75 years. It was very complimentary about me and a very unique gesture illustrating the comradeship between us. I was very chuffed with this. I must have got something right. I have moved from being a naïve young lad living in a council house in York to being an iconic doyen of a Regiment in the Indian Army. I am not as clever as all that of course. It really must be that Guardian Angel of mine.

It was very complimentary about me and a very unique gesture, illustrating the comradeship between us. I was very chuffed with this. I must have got something right.

I have moved from being a very naive young lad living in a council house in York to being an iconic doyen of a Regiment in the Indian Army. I am not as clever as all that. It must be that Guardian Angel of mine.

*Mahar Sainik, Sammelan Jaipur, 2019*

*Mahar veterans with the Colonel of the Regiment*

*Grand opening of new Officer's Mess, Jaipur*

283

*Mahar wreath laying, Jaipur*

*Wedding of James and Victoria*

*Wedding of Alex and Gemma*

*Reunion with Douglas Greenfield, York 2020*

# CHAPTER 9

## LAST THOUGHTS AND THANKS

I have finished writing a long account of my life story and it was a task which was not easy. Memory is a funny thing and what I have written I believe to be accurate. Some memories are vivid and unforgettable even from a long time ago, whilst others are sketchy and I must admit my mind cannot recall all the many things which I should be able to remember. However it was the best I could manage and it will have to do.

I have certainly lived in momentous times. My Mother and Father were both born in the late 1890s when the world was totally different. At that time the world population was around 1.5 billion people and now it stands at 7.5 billion's. They grew up when the horse and cart was the main mode of transport with a slow pace of life and no great sophistication. No cars or aeroplanes, no radio or TV, no telephones or electronics. The UK was the centre of an Empire which covered half the world, with Queen Victoria still on the throne. It was a devoutly Christian country and Sunday was a special day for rest and worship.

The early part of the 1900s was dominated by WW1 and the country suffered much distress which saw it impoverished in many ways and passed it's zenith. I was born in 1926 and my early life was predicated by the aftermath of the war, when a hard time was endured by many in the lower classes.

The General Strike of 1926 brought the country to a standstill. The Class System was still rigid in the country with very little chance of movement up the scale. I was lucky to be born into a very loving and close knit family way down the social scale, but with culture closely linked to Scotland and its strong Presbyterian ethics. From my very early days I knew the difference of right from wrong, good from evil and knew I had a soul and spirit within me.

I always believed I had a Guardian Angel assigned to me and when I look back on the major decisions and events of my life I cannot help but think that it is true. It is either that or else I must be extremely lucky. I think my life can be roughly divided into a number of ages.

1 to 10 years old - I lived a simple life in a loving and caring family and I don't think I had a care in the world. Getting on towards ten years old it began to dawn on me that I had far more brains than my school friends. Physically also, I was far fitter and could beat my friends in any kind of sports which we played.

11 to 17 years old - winning a scholarship to a Grammar School was a big breakthrough for me. It operated under the banner of The Church of England, the established Church of the UK. It gave me an excellent classical education as well as great doses of Church of England theology and practice. It certainly moved me up the entrenched Class System to the middle class level and my aspirations grew. An equally good result was gained from the Youth Club I attended. It was led by an inspirational man who gave me a vision of what practical Christian conduct was really all about. I can remember reading the psalm which says "When I look at the sky, which you have made, at the moon and stars, which you set in their places - what is man that you think of him; mere man that you care for him." Then standing on a clear starry night and looking at the heavens in wonderment of the vastness of space and time and trying to work out where it all starts and ends and what it all means. The answer is way beyond my comprehension but I am always left with the certainty that there must be a mighty creator somewhere which is reinforced when one also looks in the opposite way through a microscope at life so small that it is invisible to the eye. At this early age the philosophy and psyche of my life was being set. Life is full of choices but I would always go for the graces of love, joy, peace, patience, kindness, goodness, faithfulness, gentleness and self control over the vices of lust, gluttony, greed, sloth, wrath, envy and pride. Love your neighbour as you love yourself is a command which I try to follow, even though at times it is very hard. It has served me well and produces good dividends.

18 to 22 years - war time dangers and experiences. This is where I got my first experiences of leadership. I remember the wise advice of the sergeant in charge of the first unit I was posted

to: 'Don't end up at the end of the column kicking stones, rather be at the front end leading men.' It did not take me long to work that one out as I was clearly fitter both mentally and physically and was ready for the task. I remember at school being taught about the Greek Wars and the General who said "In any battle for each 100 men you have, 90 of them do not want to be there, 9 of them are warriors who will carry the 90 with them and the 100th will be the leader who is responsible for them all." An awesome task but not without honour. With my strong Christian ethic I suppose I could have backed off from conflict, but duty, in a just cause for your country, won hands down for me. Joining the Indian Army was a revelation for me and volunteering for the Mahar Regiment was a life-changing experience

23 to 77 years - the major part of my life, which was shared with Pat. Could I have wished for anything more? I doubt it. My Guardian Angel must have been working overtime to give me so many years of joy and happiness. Pat was a kindred soul, with similar ideas to mine and without her I would have been lost. We both had a love for the environment and the beauty of nature around us, in plants and animals and all things good. We raised a lovely little family and prospered as the years went along. I so much enjoyed my working life and was rewarded by achieving major breakthroughs in efficiency and performance which at times seemed beyond our reach. I also revelled in my voluntary work for the Church I attended, as did Pat in no small measure. Pat was crippled by a serious illness which defied all the efforts of skilled medical staff to control. Of all people why Pat, who was the kindest, most generous spirited and talented person you could meet? I have no answer to that but heaven is a richer place.

78 to 90 years - This was a period of adventures all over the earth, with so much charitable work in far off countries which was a joy. This is also when I made firm friends with Lords and Ladies, famous politicians, entertainers, sportsmen and many others throughout the world. No class barriers now for me. I also indulged in many sporting activities and speaking engagements and generally had a fine time.

90 years plus - Slowing down and feeling a little older, with hearing difficulties, poor eyesight, poor balance, but still looking after myself reasonably well supported by family and friends. I

am still capable, sometimes with assistance, of doing most things. No problems with memory and still immensely happy. I have few regrets after 90 odd years. But why oh! why could I never master playing a musical instrument or learn to speak fluently in more than one language? Whatever mistakes I made were not catastrophic and I always learned from them so I am reasonably content. If I had my time over again I could not wish for much better in this troubled world.

My life would have been different if I had not received help and guidance from many people. I was always willing to listen to sound advice and to act on it.

My family:
    I have always had loving family around me and my character and psyche are all bound up with how I was treated in my early formative years. Was all this by chance? I often wonder what my life would have been like if I had been born at a different time or in a different place. What if I had been born in, say, China, India, Africa or the Middle East? Would I have been a Buddhist, Hindu, Moslem or Jew? Would I still have been the same me or would I have turned out a totally different character? I just rejoice that I had the good fortune to be born on 27th April 1926 into the McIntosh family. That, I am sure, was my destiny and I hope I lived up to expectations.

Teachers:
    I have a high regard for the teaching profession. I always searched after knowledge and had the good fortune to be taught by so many fine teachers. They helped form my character and gave me a love for information which has stayed with me a lifetime. I still love books and now also the internet. It is all really down to the spark given me by teachers long ago.

Stanley Oglesby:
    He was a charismatic man who did more than any to give me a strong faith. Although Church life was deeply ingrained in me with my Presbyterian upbringing and Church of England education, he opened my eyes to something beyond the rigidity

of the formal Churches to a personal belief that an individual was capable of changing things for the better, by always being loving and tolerant to all people at all times. Love your neighbour as you love yourself has been a driving force for me all my life. Hard at times but wise advice.

The 3rd Btn The Mahar Regiment:
The relatively short time I spent with the Battalion was a life changing experience. I joined as a boy and ended up a man. For the first time in my life I had significant responsibilities and duties and was able to display leadership. My sincere thanks go to all the magnificent Officers and men who were with me at the time. We worked as a team and achieved far more than was expected of us. I made lifelong friends and I am still as proud as ever to be part of the Mahar fraternity. What I learned of life in that short period of time I was able to apply throughout my working career much to my advantage.

The Chairman and Chief Officers of The North Eastern Electricity Board:
I spent more than forty years working in progressively senior roles in this organisation. I helped transform it from the pen and paper operation that it was in its early years to a highly sophisticated computer and electronic operation that was always at the cutting-edge of technology. Thank you for having faith in me in the great leap in faith which was required. Success or disaster were both on the cards and we took some brave decisions. Thank you for the substantial pension you still pay me after 30 years of retirement.

Patricia McIntosh:
I was married to Pat for over 50 years. She was a beautiful, loving and generous-hearted person who was my soul mate for so long and gave me unqualified support. She excelled in whatever she put her hand to. She was a loving, kind mother who adored her children and house. She was a top-class biology teacher who lectured other teachers on the arts of teaching the subject to young children. I cannot find words to do justice to the achievements of the love of my life.

My present family and friends:

Life could have been bleak after the death of Pat. With the help of those around me I embarked on a new life of world adventure, sporting activities and charitable work. Grateful thanks to all who love me and give me so much help.

# SPECIAL ORDER OF THE DAY
## BY COL. PRASHANT KACKER, COMMANDING OFFICER

With immense pride and happiness, Kalidhar Battalion celebrated its Platinum Jubilee from 30 October 2019 to 02 November 2019 in Niwaru Military Station, Jaipur. This momentous occasion was graced by 1965 war heroes, Ex-servicemen, Veer Naaris and other family members of deceased Ex-servicemen, serving JCOs and OR whose strength was approximately 700. Among the Ex-servicemen was British Indian Army Officer of Pre-Independence era- Lt Bruce McIntosh.

Lt Bruce McIntosh was born near York (UK) on 2 April 1926. He volunteered to join the British Indian Army during WW II. He graduated from the Officers Training School Bangalore, in 1945, and was commissioned to 3 MAHAR in 1946. Post joining the Battalion at Fort Sandeman (NWFP) he was into active operational service in a hostile area among the savage tribals of NWFP. In October, the Bn converted to a special MMG Unit, and later moved to Kirkee, Poona. After rigorous training in crowd control procedures, the Bn moved to North India during partition and played a sterling role with exemplary conduct saving many Hindu and Muslim lives. In his Autobiography, he recalls, "Maj Krishna Rao was immense - He was OC A Coy, acted as 2IC and sometimes even officiated as CO". He prophetically adds, "Even in those early days, one could tell, he was destined for higher things. What a privilege to serve such a person and be accepted as a friend!"

Lt. Bruce, and three others bid adieu to return home after the war in 1948. After release, he was with banking for a while and then was selected for the North Eastern Electricity Board (UK). Courses in Accountancy, Management, and operations, helped him to reach the zenith over forty years of service. He had the distinction of setting up the first seven ton Main Frame Computer at Newcastle, train and evolve computer programming, set up the first automatic signal exchange and later toured the world seven times including the Antarctic. A man of vast philanthropy, compassion and generosity, he was Chairman of Arthritic Care, Saga Charitable Trust, Secretary British Mahar Officers Association and donated a substantial amount to the Reg! and Bn for the welfare of Families.

Lt Bruce McIntosh is an iconic doyen of the Mahar Regiment and 3 Mahar in particular, in heart and soul- ever ready to break into signature Jaikaras of "3 Mahar ki Jai!...... Mahar ki Jai!...." anywhere and everywhere and sometimes even at most

293

unexpected public places. He has always maintained that the 3 Mahar association was his "Ace" and singularly paved his immense progress throughout life. He has been in regular touch with the Bn and Regt almost all his life, attending reunions of the Bn including those at Ranchi and of the Regt Platinum Jubilee in 2016, at Saugor. And thus, defying all odds and vehement pleas of his own family, he was there with the Bn for the most auspicious Platinum Jubilee Celebrations from 29[1] October to 2nd November. 2019 - upright, ever-alert, and soaking in every moment of every event with indescribable nostalgia, camaraderie, hearty laughter, pride and joy. His was a unique, historic and monumental presence that lent the rarest of rare otherworld impact on the entire occasion and celebrations. In a most befitting gesture, he was given the honour to address the Sainik Sammelan. dedicate the Officers Mess building, unveil the PJ Trophy at the Officers Mess and JCO's Mess. Ever magnanimous and thoughtful, he had a special Scottish traditional dagger "SGIANDUBH", sterling silver gift, for the Bn and PJ Souvenir Ball Pens for all and sundry!

On behalf of All Veterans, All Ranks, All Families and myself, I consider that we were most blessed and fortunate that such a Founding Father and highly realised great soul was amongst us. We are and shall always remain infinitely indebted. We humbly assure him that the Bn shall continue to strive and excel in all spheres, attain great heights and touch the skies. We wish him good health, peace and a happy long life. God Bless.

Printed in Great Britain
by Amazon

28688206R00169